Editor
Heather Douglas

Contributing Editor—Canada
Jennifer Dorval

Illustrator
Clint McKnight

Cover Artist
Brenda DiAntonis

Managing Editor
Ina Massler Levin, M.A.

Creative Director
Karen J. Goldfluss, M.S. Ed.

Art Production Manager
Kevin Barnes

Art Coordinator
Renée Christine Yates

Imaging
Craig Gunnell
Nathan P. Rivera

Publisher
Mary D. Smith, M.S. Ed.

SIXTH GRADE SKILLS
Canada Edition
5 cm
10 cm
V = 785 cm3
Haiku
In the fall, leaves drop
gracefully-they flutter down
a sea of color

Author

Teacher Created Resources Staff

Teacher Created Resources, Inc.
6421 Industry Way
Westminster, CA 92683
www.teachercreated.com
ISBN: 978-1-4206-2746-6

Teacher Created Resources

Table of Contents

Introduction

The wealth of knowledge a person gains throughout his or her lifetime is impossible to measure, and it will certainly vary from person to person. However, regardless of the scope of knowledge, the foundation for all learning remains a constant. All that we know and think throughout our lifetimes is based upon fundamentals, and these fundamentals are the basic skills upon which all learning develops. *Mastering Sixth Grade Skills* is a book that reinforces a variety of sixth grade basic skills.

- **Writing**
- **Reading**
- **Science**
- **Grammar**
- **Math**

This book was written with the wide range of student skills and ability levels of sixth grade students in mind. Both teachers and parents can benefit from the variety of pages provided in this book. Parents can use the book to provide an introduction to new material or to reinforce material already familiar to their children. Similarly, teachers can select pages that provide additional practice for concepts taught in the classroom. When tied to what is being covered in class, pages from this book make great homework reinforcement. The worksheets provided in this book are ideal for use at home as well as in the classroom.

Research shows us that skill mastery comes with exposure and drill. To be internalized, concepts must be reviewed until they become second nature. Parents may certainly foster the classroom experience by exposing their children to the necessary skills whenever possible, and teachers will find that these pages perfectly complement their classroom needs. An answer key, beginning on page 168, provides teachers, parents, and children with a quick method of checking responses to completed worksheets.

Basic skills are utilized every day in untold ways. Make the practice of them part of your children's or students' routines. Such work done now will benefit them in countless ways throughout their lives.

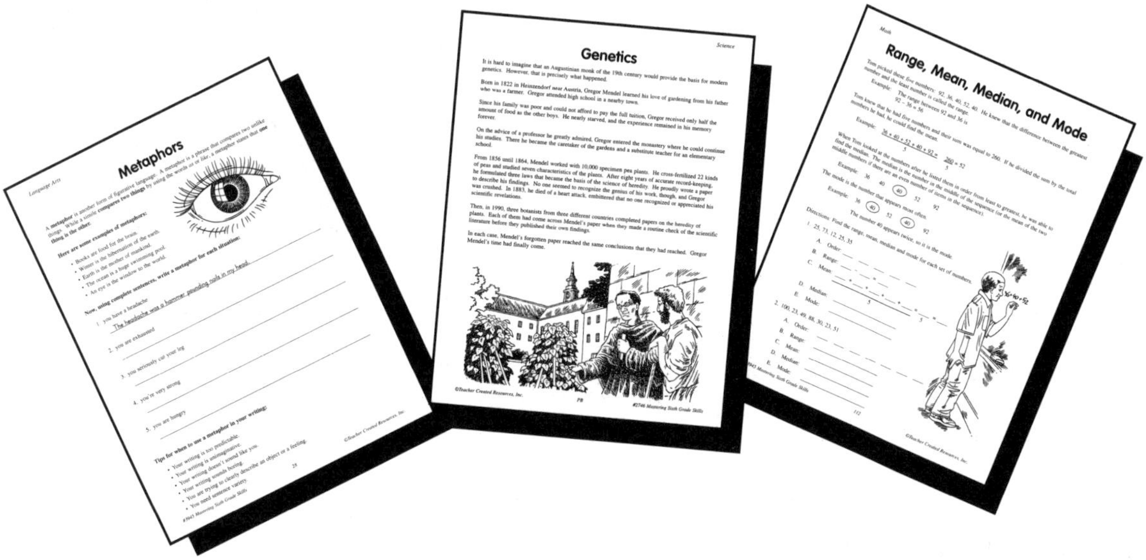

Capitalization

Capitalization Rules

- Capitalize names of people, places, nationalities, and religions: Pierre Trudeau, Newfoundland, Italian, Protestant.
- Capitalize dates, historical events, periods, and special events: World War II, Renaissance, Boston Tea Party, Easter, Saturday, May.
- Capitalize titles for people (mayor, doctor, president) only when they are followed by a name (Doctor Stockton, the doctor).
- Capitalize family titles only when used as names: Ask Mom. Ask your mom. I like Uncle Bob. I like my uncle, Bob.
- Do not capitalize school classes unless a specific title is given, or the subject is a language: history, History 1A, English, Spanish, geometry.
- Do not capitalize directions (south, east, etc.) except when they refer to a specific region: (the South). I live north of the capital. We moved to the East Coast.
- Do not capitalize seasons of the year: winter, spring, summer, fall.

Directions: Mark A if the underlined word is correct as it is, and mark B if it is incorrect.

_____________ 1. My <u>Aunt</u> is named Terry.

_____________ 2. I like <u>Aunt</u> Terry.

_____________ 3. Sit by your <u>Cousin,</u> Tommy.

_____________ 4. I don't want to sit by <u>Cousin</u> Tommy.

_____________ 5. I come from the <u>west</u>.

_____________ 6. I live <u>west</u> of the river.

_____________ 7. I like <u>spanish</u> class.

_____________ 8. I like <u>math</u> class.

_____________ 9. My favorite season is <u>Fall</u>.

_____________10. Is the <u>Mayor</u> in?

_____________11. Yes, <u>Mayor</u> Ruiz is in.

_____________12. Stephen Harper is Cananda's 22nd Prime <u>Minister</u>.

_____________13. <u>President</u> Kennedy lived in the White House.

_____________14. My mother is <u>christian</u>.

_____________15. I like <u>History</u> 101.

Using End Punctuation

Period: Use a period at the end of a statement.

Exclamation Point: Use an exclamation point to express excitement or emphasis for an important point. Exclamation points should be used sparingly.

Question Mark: Use a question mark at the end of a question.

Directions: Put the correct end mark at the end of each of the following sentences.

1. The sun set on the horizon   Wasn't the sight astonishing

2. When the snowflakes stop falling, we will go to the store

3. Where did you get that beautiful, blue ribbon

4. Hurrah We can finally go swimming in the ocean since the storm has abated

5. When will the sound of cracking thunder stop frightening me

6. The daffodils are blooming all over the hillside, creating a waving carpet of yellow

7. The gazelles ran smoothly and silently in the distance

8. When will the moon escape from behind the clouds

9. Wow I am impressed with the colorful vibrancy of fall

10. How often will you be able to come over to my house this summer

11. Although I like the refreshing coolness of snow cones, I usually don't like ice cream

12. Why is the wind picking up speed Will there be a hurricane

13. The puppy quickly scurried under the bushes, hoping that no one had noticed him

14. I will be glad when this project is over and I feel a sense of accomplishment

Punctuating and Capitalizing Quotes

A direct quotation always begins with a capital letter regardless of where the quotation appears in the sentence. However, punctuating direct quotations varies, depending on their placement.

Speaker Before: When the name of the person doing the speaking comes before the direct quote, the direct quote is preceded by a comma. The quote is punctuated like a regular sentence and enclosed by quotation marks.

> Ann said, *"I hope you find what you are looking for."*
> Mrs. Paul asked, *"Do you know the capital of Peru?"*
> Tamara exclaimed, *"Let me go!"*

Speaker After: When the name of the person doing the speaking comes after the direct quote, the punctuation is varied. If the direct quote is a question or exclamation, then the ending punctuation should be added. If, however, the sentence is a statement or request, then a comma is used in place of a period. In all cases, a period is placed at the end of the entire sentence.

> *"I hope you find what you are looking for,"* said Ann.
> *"Do you know the capital of Peru?"* asked Mrs. Paul.
> *"Let me go!"* exclaimed Tamara.

Directions: Write the following sentences, adding punctuation marks where needed. Capitalize the first word of the direct quote.

1. Michael shouted let's get busy with the paint
2. Those who deny freedom to others deserve it not for themselves stated Abraham Lincoln
3. Has anyone in this group ever climbed Mount Everest asked the mountain guide
4. Mr. Cummings said please watch your step through the pond
5. Donna and Chandra complained we don't want to do the dishes
6. Help cried the frightened girl as she grasped the end of the rope
7. What is the time difference between Winnipeg and Toronto he asked the flight attendant

Commas

Directions: Use **commas** to separate items in certain conventional, or customary, situations.

Dates	The Town Book Fair begins on Monday, September 25. Our Constitution Act was signed on March 29, 1867.
Addresses	The Calgary Stampede is held each spring in Calgary, Alberta. The address you requested is 453 Bear St., Edmonton, AB T2Y 6A7.
Friendly Letter Salutation and Closing	Dear Grandma Martha, Sincerely yours,

Directions: Read the following letter and envelope. Insert commas where needed.

Tuesday March 16 1999

Dear Aunt Judy

I want to thank you for the lovely new dress you sent to me for my birthday. I'm sorry you were unable to attend my party on Saturday March 13. We had lots of fun. I plan to come visit you in Victoria, B.C. this summer. Mother wants you to check your calendar for July. She has booked me on a flight to arrive Wednesday July 27 in the evening. Please write or call to let us know if that date is all right. I can't wait to see you!

Yours truly

Kara

Kara James
7008 Milton Road
Calgary AB
T2A 807

Mrs. Judy Kimball
1454 Dresser Road
Victoria B.C.
V0Y 8M2

Showing Possession

Using **apostrophes** to show possession is often confusing for students. Yet, there are only a few basic rules.

To form a possessive for a singular noun, add an apostrophe and an s.

the student's records   Mrs. Smith's red car   the dress's collar

Exception: Sometimes a proper name ending in **s** would be too difficult to pronounce with an added apostrophe and an **s**. Therefore, you must use your judgment.

Mr. Jones' backyard   Hercules' victories   Los Angeles' population

To form the possessive for a plural noun, add an apostrophe.

ballplayers' team   citizens' vote   many flowers' stems

Exception: If the plural does not end in an **s**, add both the apostrophe and an **s**.

mice's cheese   women's locker room   children's books

Common mistakes: You do not use an apostrophe to make a noun plural. You do not use an apostrophe with possessive personal pronouns like the following: yours, ours, theirs, its, hers, or his.

Directions: Show possession in the following examples. Check to see if the noun is singular or plural before adding an apostrophe and an **s**. The first one has been done for you.

1. the food belonging to our dog ____our dog's food____
2. careers belonging to women ____________
3. comments made by my friend ____________
4. some toys that belong to my baby ____________
5. the horn that is attached to it ____________
6. tickets that belong to the passengers ____________
7. some clothes for the children ____________
8. a store owned by Chris ____________
9. a paintbrush belonging to an artist ____________
10. invitations sent by the hostess ____________

Possessives Practice

Directions: To complete each sentence, form the possessive of the noun in parentheses. If the noun is singular, keep it singular. If it is plural, keep it plural.

1. The ________________________ lounge is upstairs. (teachers)
2. Our ________________________ motto is "*A Mari usque ad Mare*." (country)
3. The ________________________ department is on the third floor. (children)
4. ________________________ friends are coming to dinner. (Ross)
5. Where's the ________________________ room? (men)
6. All the ________________________ leaders were there. (cities)
7. All the ________________________ dishes are empty. (dogs)
8. ________________________ dish is full. (Argus)
9. That's ________________________ van. (Karla)
10. The ________________________ practice ends at 3:00. (girls)

Directions: Mark **A** if the underlined word is correct, and mark **B** if it is incorrect.

_____ 1. That's the <u>ladies'</u> room.

_____ 2. I have five <u>cat's</u>.

_____ 3. That <u>babies'</u> mother is Marion.

_____ 4. Our <u>team's</u> mascot is the wolverine.

_____ 5. The <u>mens</u> locker room is closed.

_____ 6. I like old <u>cars</u>.

_____ 7. <u>Chris'</u> mother is bringing lunch.

_____ 8. That <u>ladie's</u> purse is huge.

_____ 9. Your <u>binder's</u> pocket is ripped.

_____ 10. My <u>baby's</u> room is too hot.

Quotation Marks

To add interest to a passage with many direct quotations, such as a passage containing dialogue between characters, a writer may choose to vary the placement of the speaker's name. The speaker's name can come before the direct quotation, after the direct quotation, or within the direct quotation.

Speaker within: When the name of the speaker comes within (or interrupts) the direct quotation, the second part of the quotation begins with a lowercase letter. Commas are used to separate the quote from the rest of the sentence.

"What are some of the animals," asked Mr. Petok, *"that scientists discovered in the Amazon rain forest?"*

"Finish the dishes and complete your homework," said Mother firmly, turning to look me in the eyes, *"before you even think of watching television."*

Directions: Read each direct quote. Create an appropriate speaker for each quote and place the name or description of the speaker in the location identified. Punctuate the sentence properly. The first one has been done for you.

1. The Egyptian form of heaven was known as the Field of Reeds. (speaker within)
   "The Egyptian form of heaven," said the museum curator, "was known as the Field of Reeds."
2. Don't throw that ball in here! (speaker before)
   ____
3. Have you ever been on a roller coaster? (speaker after)
   ____
4. Emperor Qin had over 4,000 statues of soldiers buried in his tomb. (speaker within)
   ____
5. Plant cell mitosis is a rather simple yet mystifying process. (speaker within)
   ____
6. Do you know if Charlie is coming with us? (speaker before)
   ____
7. Please hide me from the sheriff! (speaker after)
   ____
8. Are you certain that he is the new president? (speaker within)
   ____

Semicolons

A **semicolon** looks and acts like a period and comma combined. It separates complete independent clauses like a period, while also separating items within a sentence like a comma. Use a semicolon instead of a period only when the ideas in the independent clauses are closely related.

I called Jessica. She will arrive in thirty minutes.	(two independent clauses separated by a period)
I called Jessica, and she will arrive in thirty minutes.	(compound sentence using a comma and a conjunction—and, but, or, for, yet)
I called Jessica; she will arrive in thirty minutes.	(two independent clauses joined by a semicolon)

Note: Don't use too many semicolons. When editing your work, decide if it is better to make a compound sentence with a comma and a conjunction, two complete sentences, or a sentence with several commas rather than use a semicolon.

Grammatically Correct: In the deserts of northern Africa, the sun beats down all day practically every day of the year; the plants there, some of which are found nowhere else in the world, are tough, thick, and drought-resistant.

Better: In the deserts of northern Africa, the sun beats down all day, practically every day of the year. The plants there, some of which are found nowhere else in the world, are tough, thick, and drought-resistant.

Directions: Read the following sentences and add semicolons where needed.

1. On our first trip to California, I wanted to visit the San Diego Zoo my little sister wanted to go to Disneyland.
2. Our parents settled the dispute for us they decided we could go to both places.
3. At the zoo we saw a zebra, elephant, and lion the tigers were not in their display area.
4. Three days later we went to Disneyland it has imaginative rides.
5. We can't wait to vacation in California again there are so many sights to see.

Directions: Choose two sentences from above to rewrite as compound sentences joined by conjunctions and commas.

1. ____

____

2. ____

____

Colons

Colons are used in conventional situations more often than in text. Below are a few cases.

Time	Ratios	Bible Verses	Business Letter Salutations
3:15 P.M.	9:7	John 3:16	Dear Sir:
4:17 A.M.	2:1	Genesis 1:7	To Whom It May Concern:

The most common placement for **colons** in text is before a list of items. If using a **colon** before your list, do not place it directly after a verb or a preposition. A **colon** is most often used with expressions like *as follows* or *the following*.

Correct	On our camping trip we will need to bring sleeping bags, a camping stove, a flashlight, warm clothes, and a week's supply of food.
Incorrect	On our camping trip we will need to bring: sleeping bags, a camping stove, a flashlight, warm clothes, and a week's supply of food.
Correct	On our camping trip we will need to bring the following items: sleeping bags, camping stove, a flashlight, warm clothes, and a week's supply of food.
Correct	This recipe is made from chicken, curry, onions, brown sugar, and sour cream.
Incorrect	This recipe is made from: chicken, curry, onions, brown sugar, and sour cream.
Correct	This recipe includes these ingredients: chicken, curry, onions, brown sugar, and sour cream.

Directions: Read each list of items. Write a sentence with a colon inserted before each list.

1. bait, tackle, net, and hooks ______________________________________

____

2. ham sandwich, grapes, string cheese, orange juice, and a chocolate chip cookie ____________

____

3. protractor, compass, calculator, ruler, and pencils______________________

____

4. basketball, tennis, swimming, and bowling__________________________

____

Nouns

There are two types of **nouns**: common and proper.

- **Common nouns** describe any person, place, or thing.

  Examples: That young man works at two different jobs after school.

  The toy store is a fun and exciting place to work.

- **Proper nouns** describe specific people, places, or things and are capitalized.

  Examples: Toronto offers thousands of job opportunities.

  John Smith can't wait to move there.

Directions: Change the underlined common nouns below into proper nouns and the underlined proper nouns into common nouns. Then rewrite the sentence in the space provided.

1. I've always wanted to see <u>Italy</u>. ______________________________
2. <u>Kathy Petrini</u> owns the <u>restaurant</u> downtown. ______________________________
3. <u>Mr. Minelli</u> drives a red <u>Honda</u>. ______________________________
4. <u>George</u> likes to play <u>badminton</u>. ______________________________
5. <u>Main Street Deli</u> offers free <u>cookies</u> on Fridays. ______________________________
6. <u>My brother</u> watches <u>Bugs Bunny</u> on Saturday mornings. ______________________________

Here are two sub-types of nouns: compound and collective.

- **Compound nouns** are two or more nouns that function as a single unit.

  Example: The <u>commander-in-chief</u> fought in World War II.

- **Collective nouns** name groups of people or things.

  Example: A *crowd* of people poured into the baseball stadium.

Directions: Underline the compound or collective nouns in the sentences below.

1. A happy family went to the beach one sunny Saturday.
2. My sister-in-law is knitting me a sweater for Christmas.
3. We rode the trolley car all the way downtown.
4. Jackson led the herd of cattle into the stable.
5. Our class toured a museum on a field trip.
6. Did you know that the editor-in-chief of the magazine worked in the circus?
7. Rake up that pile of leaves, please.
8. We asked the passers-by if they wanted their cars washed.
9. A flock of Canadian geese flew overhead.
10. The group of carolers sang beautifully.

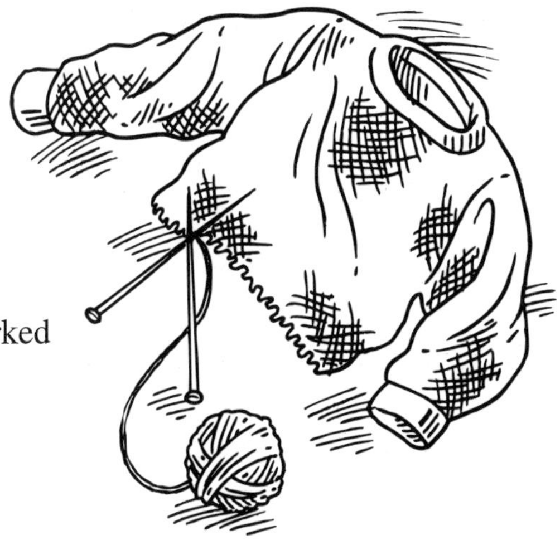

Plural Nouns

Singular nouns refer to one person, place, or thing. Plural nouns refer to more than one person, place, or thing.

1. **Write the plural of the word in parentheses. Hint: Most nouns form the plural by adding *s*. Those that end in *ch*, *sh*, *s*, or *x* add *es*.**

a. There are over seven ____________ in our town. (church)

b. There are lots of ____________ growing in the playground. (tree)

c. The frightened dog hid between the two ____________ . (bush)

d. Jan put all the ____________ on the table. (box)

e. My brother ate three ____________ for lunch. (peach)

f. The six school ____________ were in a line. (bus)

2. **Write the plural of each of the following words. Hint: They are all irregular.**

a. goose ________________ e. tooth ________________

b. man ________________ f. woman ________________

c. foot ________________ g. child ________________

d. louse ________________ h. mouse ________________

3. **Write the plural of the word in parentheses. Hint: Some nouns that end in *o* add *es* to make the plural. Others simply add *s*.**

a. We planted ________________ in the garden. (potato)

b. On our holiday, Kyle took lots of ________________ . (photo)

c. South America has many ________________. (volcano)

d. Hundreds of ________________ were bathing in the river. (hippo)

e. The brave ________________ were all given medals. (hero)

f. I sliced the three ________________ to make a salad. (tomato)

Adjectives

Adjectives are words that describe nouns. They can also describe pronouns because pronouns take the place of nouns. Usually, we find adjectives in front of the nouns they are describing.

That's a blue car.

(*Blue* is an adjective describing the noun *car*.)

She's a nice girl.

(*Nice* is an adjective describing the noun *girl*.)

We also find adjectives in sentences like the ones discussed in the verb section, in which a linking verb is linking the subject of the sentence to a word that describes the subject. The describing word is an adjective since a subject must be a noun or pronoun, and adjectives are the only words that describe nouns or pronouns.

Cindy looks pretty.

(*Pretty* is an adjective describing the noun *Cindy*.)

She is smart.

(*Smart* is an adjective describing the pronoun *she*.)

Directions: Underline the adjective(s) in the following sentences. Beside each sentence, write the adjective(s) plus the noun(s) being described.

1. The big truck hit the little car. ____________________
2. That's a good book. ____________________
3. My cute kitty is washing her sweet face. ____________________
4. Ms. Bronowski is nice. ____________________
5. My dad made a delicious cake. ____________________
6. That's a silly thing to say. ____________________
7. I like chocolate ice cream. ____________________
8. I like the red car better than the blue one. ____________________
9. This book is old. ____________________
10. Here's a shiny new penny! ____________________

Adverbs

Adverbs are words to describe verbs. They also describe adjectives and other adverbs.

- Usually adverbs are describing verbs: We ate fast. *Fast* is an adverb describing the verb *ate*. He speaks quietly. *Quietly* is an adverb describing the verb *speaks*. Note: Adverbs often end in *-ly*.
- Adverbs answer these questions: How? When? Why? How did Bob walk? Bob walked *quickly*. When did Bob walk? Bob walked *yesterday*. Where did Bob walk? Bob walked *upstairs*.
- Some adverbs describe adjectives and other adverbs: He is really nice. *Really* is an adverb describing the adjective *nice*. You read very well. *Very* is an adverb describing the adverb *well*.

Directions: Add adverbs which answer how, where, or when about the verbs in the following sentences. Underline the adverbs you add. Use a different adverb for each sentence.

a. They eat. They eat <u>loudly</u>.

b. She wrote a letter. She <u>quickly</u> wrote a letter.

c. I fell. I fell <u>downstairs</u>.

1. Theresa threw the ball.____________________
2. We read the story. ____________________
3. We flew down the street. ____________________
4. He ate the pizza.____________________
5. Bob hiccupped in class. ____________________
6. The mummy walked. ____________________
7. Students talked. ____________________
8. We watched the news program.____________________
9. The teacher listened. ____________________
10. My friends sat under the tree. ____________________

Directions: Add adverbs to modify the adjectives or other adverbs already in these sentences. Underline the adverbs you add. Do not use the same adverb more than once.

a. John is nice. John is <u>quite</u> nice.

b. You drive fast. You drive <u>too</u> fast.

c. That's not pretty. That's <u>really</u> not pretty.

1. Your cat is cute. ____________________
2. That's a wonderful book.____________________
3. I bought a blue truck.____________________
4. You sing beautifully. ____________________
5. I talk quietly. ____________________

Verbs

Verbs are words that show action or state of being.

- To find the action verb in a sentence, you ask this about the subject: "What is he/she/it doing?"

  Jose is riding the bus.

  What is Jose doing? *Riding.*

- The other kinds of verbs are called *state of being* or *linking verbs*. They don't show action; they link the subject of the sentence to a word that describes the subject or a word that renames the subject.

  Jane is pretty.

  What is Jane doing? She's doing nothing. She just *is*. *Is* is the verb. It links the subject, *Jane*, with a word describing her, *pretty*. The most common linking verbs are forms of the word *be*: *is, are, was, were, am, be, been, being.*

Directions: Underline the verb(s) in each sentence.

1. Ms. Davis talks a lot.
2. She is talkative.
3. I ran into the door.
4. We read *The Golden Rose*.
5. I enjoyed it.
6. I think about *The Golden Rose* all the time.
7. I hope we get other good books this year.
8. I like all kinds of books.
9. I had a root canal yesterday.
10. The dentist was nice.

Directions: Underline the verb in each sentence. If the verb is an action verb, mark **A** after the sentence, and if it is a linking verb, mark **L** at the end of the sentence.

1. Ms. Oudegeest plays with her computer.
2. She also watches TV.
3. She likes *Good Morning Canada*.
4. Max looks mad.
5. He spit at the dog.
6. Spitting is gross.
7. The dog seems mad now.
8. Karla looked out the window.
9. She saw her dad.
10. Her dad is her best friend.
11. Cathy Lew asked for our attention on the intercom.
12. We heard her very well.
13. She sounded funny, though.
14. Cathy Lew is really nice.
15. Students and teachers like her.

Verb Form Practice

Directions: Underline the correct verb form from the choices given.

1. I should have (knew/known) that I could have (froze/frozen) my toes.
2. As soon as Manuel had (chose/chosen) his subject, he (began/begun) his talk.
3. The coat that I had (wore/worn) only once had been (stole/stolen).
4. The dress that I would have (chose/chosen) was (tore/torn).
5. Has the bell (rang/rung), or would I (have/of) heard it here?
6. The man who had (stole/stolen) the money was (knew/known) by the police.
7. You should (have/of) known that the song was (sang/sung) by Marilyn.
8. Has he always (drove/driven) so carelessly, or has he just (began/begun) to do so?
9. She (began/begun) to see that she had (chose/chosen) the wrong topic.
10. Snow (fell/fallen) after the pond had (froze/frozen).
11. Our doorbell is (wore/worn) out because the children have (rang/rung) it too many times.
12. Two cups have (fell/fallen) off the shelf and have (broke/broken).
13. Barbara (sang/sung) the song that was (chose/chosen) by the committee.
14. I would have (brung/brought) my stereo if it hadn't been (stole/stolen).
15. The telephone (rang/rung) just as I (began/begun) to study.

Pronouns

Personal pronouns have two forms: the **subject** and the **object** forms.

Subject I, she, he, they, we

Object me, her, him, them, us

As you can see, the pronouns on the left mean exactly the same thing as the pronouns on the right. For example, *I* and *me* mean the same thing. The difference is that the pronouns on the left are used when they are acting as subjects, and the pronouns on the right are used when acting as objects.

Usually we use the correct form automatically. For example, we wouldn't say, "Me like you." We would say, "I like you." *I* is the subject. Sometimes, though, when another person is added to the sentence, we are unsure. For example, which is correct?

1. Go to the store with Bob and I.

2. Go to the store with Bob and me.

The second sentence is correct. An easy way to test this is to eliminate the other person in the sentence and say the sentence with the pronoun by itself. Here, we would say, "Go to the store with me." We wouldn't say "Go to the store with I." Therefore, me is the correct form of the pronoun for this sentence, even if we add another person.

Directions: Underline the correct pronoun(s) for each sentence.

1. Bob and (I, me) are going.
2. Stand by the captain and (I, me).
3. (We, Us) girls are going to win.
4. Are Sandy and (she, her) going?
5. You and (he, him) make a cute couple.
6. I'm going to the party with Fred and (they, them).
7. If Lucia and (they, them) go, I'm not going.
8. Give the papers to (she, her) and (we, us) before you leave.
9. You can't play with (we, us) boys.
10. If you go with Ranvir and (I, me), we will have more fun.

Directions: Underline the correct pronouns from the choices given in the following sentences.

1. (We, Us) teachers are going on vacation together.
2. You may go with (we, us) teachers.
3. My sister and (I, me) are going to visit Grandma.
4. She can't go with (he, him) and (she, her).
5. They and (we, us) all did well on the project.
6. My father sent Debbie and (I, me) a card.
7. The teacher wrote detentions for (he, him) and (I, me).
8. A package arrived for (we, us) kids.
9. Don't hold this against Nicki and (I, me).
10. The teacher called on (he, him) and (she, her).
11. We are going to have pizza with the boys and (she, her).
12. (He, Him) and (I, me) are going out to dinner.
13. There was a tie between (she, her) and (he, him).
14. (He, Him) and the clerk got into an argument.
15. (They, Them) and the girls are following us.
16. The students and (I, me) are having a good day.
17. (We, Us) and (they, them) are playing the final match.
18. I wrote a letter to (he, him) and (she, her).
19. I like to ride with John and (she, her).
20. The principal was staring at (they, them) and (we, us).

Prepositions, Conjunctions, and Interjections

Prepositions: A preposition is a word or group of words which show how two ideas are related.

Directions: Write a sentence using the preposition listed.

Example: in front of: <u>They put a sign in front of the store</u>.

1. within: ____
2. under: ____
3. in: ____
4. between: ____
5. on behalf of: ____

Conjunctions: A conjunction is a word that connects individual words or groups of words.

Directions: Write a sentence using the conjunction listed.

Example: He will be ready Saturday **or** Sunday.

6. and ____
7. or ____
8. but ____
9. so ____

Interjection: An interjection is a word or phrase used to express strong emotion or surprise.

Directions: Write a sentence using the interjection listed.

Example: **Wow!** Are you really that old?

10. Oh no! ____
11. Wow! ____
12. Yikes! ____
13. No way! ____

Prepositions

Prepositions are words that show a relationship between other words.

To see how prepositions work, look at these two words: **fox log**

Prepositions can show the relationship between the fox and the log:

The fox was *under* the log. The fox was *on* the log.

The fox was *by* the log. The fox was *in* the log.

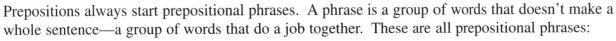

Prepositions always start prepositional phrases. A phrase is a group of words that doesn't make a whole sentence—a group of words that do a job together. These are all prepositional phrases:

under the log, on the log, by the log, in the log

Directions: Under each sentence, copy the prepositional phrase from that sentence. Circle the object of the preposition and underline the preposition.

1. Penguins live at the South Pole.

 ____

2. The students slept during the speech.

 ____

3. The baby was tossed out with the bathwater.

 ____

4. The fish in the pan smelled awful.

 ____

5. The announcer on TV was excited.

 ____

6. I found the keys under the table.

 ____

7. We are going to the movies tomorrow.

 ____

8. The rabbit ran across the road.

 ____

9. Jim put the pizza on the table.

 ____

10. The girls climbed to the top.

 ____

Directions: Rewrite each sentence, adding a prepositional phrase to each.

1. The dog ate his dinner. The dog ate his dinner by the back door.

 ____

2. The boys ran. ______________________

 ____

3. Josh did his work. ______________________

 ____

4. Sally read the book. ______________________

 ____

5. The girls are practicing. ______________________

 ____

Conjunctions

Conjunctions are words that join or connect other words. It's easy to remember the definition if you emphasize it this way: **con**junctions **con**nect words.

Conjunctions are words like *and*, *but*, and *or*. They connect words or groups of words.

I want a car *or* a truck.

I want to eat dinner *and* go to the movies.

I like Bob, *but* my mom doesn't care for him.

And, *but*, and *or* are the most commonly used conjunctions. There are others, though, including *if*, *so*, *although*, *since*, and *because*.

You may go to the party *if* you clean your room.

I like pizza *although* it is fattening.

Since you are late, we will all be late.

Satinder bought a car *because* she saved her money.

Directions: Underline the conjunctions in the following sentences.

1. Tom likes Linda, but she doesn't like him.
2. I will buy chips or salad.
3. My car won't run, so I have to use my mom's car.
4. I will go if my mother gives me permission.
5. I couldn't leave until my brother got home.
6. I'll call José after I eat.
7. I'm going to do my chores, watch television, and eat a banana.
8. *The Simpsons* isn't on since the basketball game went into overtime.
9. Tom's going with us although he doesn't want to go.

Directions: Fill in the blanks with conjunctions.

1. I would like a slice of cheesecake with cherries ____________________ strawberries.
2. We can go to the movies ____________________ go to the park.
3. I like Polly ____________________ she's nice.
4. I will make dinner ____________________ I finish my homework.
5. ____________________ you like chocolate, you will like these cookies.
6. Serena wrote me a letter, ____________________ I haven't seen it.
7. I like Mexican food, ____________________ I don't like beans.
8. I will give you my book ____________________ you keep asking for it.
9. This car has power steering ____________________ air conditioning.
10. You can go, ____________________ the girls can't go.
11. The teacher will take down your name ____________________ give you detention.
12. The best choices would be Anthony, Ricky, ____________________ Danny.
13. Rusty sent me a card, ____________________ it was nice.
14. Louise is nice, ____________________ she is also moody.

Similes

A **simile** is a technique for comparing two things. Similes use the words *like* or *as* to show how the items are alike. Here are some similes.

Her teeth are as white as winter snow.
(Her teeth are white and snow is white.)

The snake was like a garden hose.
(The snake was thin and black and lying in the grass. The garden hose was also thin and black and lying in the grass.)

Explain the comparisons in the following similes:

1. The baby's cheeks are like a rose.

   The baby's cheeks are ____________________ and a rose is ____________________.

2. The full moon is like a cookie.

   The full moon is ____________________ and a cookie is ____________________.

3. The baseball whizzed by like a bullet.

   The baseball is ____________________ and a bullet is ____________________.

4. The coffee is like ink.

   Coffee is ____________________ and ink is ____________________.

Now you try it. Write some similes of your own.

1. The boat is ____

   ____.

2. The cave is ____

   ____.

3. Her hair is ____

   ____.

Read your similes to a friend. See if he or she can explain your comparison.

Metaphors

A **metaphor** is another form of figurative language. A metaphor is a phrase that compares two unlike things. While a simile **compares two things** by using the words *as* or *like*, a metaphor states that **one thing is the other.**

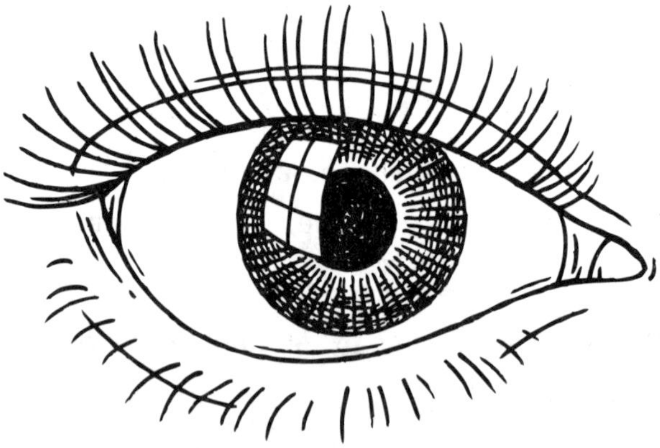

Here are some examples of metaphors:

- Books are food for the brain.
- Winter is the hibernation of the earth.
- Earth is the mother of mankind.
- The ocean is a huge swimming pool.
- An eye is the window to the world.

Now, using complete sentences, write a metaphor for each situation:

1. you have a headache

   The headache was a hammer pounding nails in my head.

2. you are exhausted

   ____

3. you seriously cut your leg

   ____

4. you're very strong

   ____

5. you are hungry

   ____

Tips for when to use a metaphor in your writing:

- Your writing is too predictable.
- Your writing is unimaginative.
- Your writing doesn't sound like you.
- Your writing sounds boring.
- You are trying to clearly describe an object or a feeling.
- You need sentence variety.

More Similies and Metaphors

Metaphorical thinking is not difficult, strange, or out of reach. You probably do it all the time, but you just did not know what it was called. A little boy named Justin used a metaphor one day when he came running into the house yelling, "Dad! Dad! It's raining styrofoam!" He was so happy he ran back outside to dance around in the "styrofoam." Of course, it was not "raining styrofoam." It was hail, but it was like styrofoam. However, Justin's description was more playful and descriptive than to simply say it was hail.

Similes and metaphors are literary devices, or tools, to help a writer be more creative.

A **simile** is a way of comparing two things by using the words *like*, *as*, or *so*. Some examples:

- He's as sharp as a tack.
- An ungrateful child is like a serpent's tooth.
- As sand going through an hourglass, so are the days of our lives.

A **metaphor** compares one thing to another without using words like *as* or *like*. For example:

- She's an accident waiting to happen.
- He's a bear in the morning.

(If you say he looked like a bear in the morning, that would be a simile).

Try writing a simile about life. Begin with, "Life is like . . . "

Here are some examples written by other students:

"Life is like a banana. You start out green and get soft and mushy when you're old. Some people want to be one of the bunch while others want to be top banana. You have to be careful not to slip on the peels."

"Life is like a jigsaw puzzle, but you don't have the picture on the front of the box to know what it's supposed to look like. And you're not sure if you have all the pieces."

Now try completing the following similes (the first one has been completed for you as an example):

An orange is as round and sunny as the sun.

A puppy is as ______________________ as ______________________.

A star is as ______________________ as ______________________.

Ice is as ______________________ as ______________________.

The clouds are as ______________________ as ______________________.

Snow is as ______________________ as ______________________.

And here are some metaphors to complete for practice:

The tree is a giant stalk of broccoli.

The rock is ____.

The rain is ____.

The moon was ____.

The wolf was ____.

The baby is ____.

Idioms

An **idiom** is an expression which means something different from what is actually written. For example, "to put one's foot in one's mouth" is a familiar idiom. It does not literally mean to place one's foot inside of one's mouth. It really means that you have said something you shouldn't have said.

Here are some examples of idioms:

Idioms	Meanings of Idioms
horse of a different color	that's a completely different situation
spill the beans	tell a secret you shouldn't have
to be downhearted	to be sad
a close shave	a close encounter with trouble
for the birds	useless or silly
crocodile tears	fake tears
going to the dogs	falling apart, losing quality
a fork in the road	two different choices or directions
in one ear and out the other	you aren't paying attention
woke up on the wrong side of the bed	having a bad day
zip my lips	you won't share it, keep it confidential
bit off more than you can chew	overwhelmed with what you have to do
costs an arm and a leg	very expensive
keep an eye on	to watch very closely
read my lips	believe what I say
count on me	have confidence in me and what I say
raining cats and dogs	raining heavily outside
step on the gas	pick up the pace, go faster
monkey around	goofing off, fooling around
a broken heart	very sad, let down
stopped dead in my tracks	stopped or ended suddenly

Idioms are used to make a point or show the irony of something. A writer uses idioms to keep their writing interesting and keep the reader interested. Write a paragraph using some of the previous idioms.

____

____

____

____

____

____

____

____

Idiomatic Expressions

An **idiom** is an expression that has a meaning different from the meanings of its separate words. For example, we may say, "Hold your horses," but what we really mean is "Wait, you are being impatient."

A. In your own words, explain the idiomatic expressions below.

1. Are you getting cold feet?

____

2. She blew her stack!

____

3. It is raining cats and dogs.

____

4. He is like a bull in a china shop.

____

5. I'm just as fit as a fiddle.

____

6. He lost his shirt on that deal.

____

7. She's as mad as a wet hen.

____

8. Keep a stiff upper lip.

____

9. It's a one-horse town.

____

10. Don't cry over spilt milk.

____

B. Underline the idioms in each sentence. Then write a word or phrase for the underlined idiom. Make sure that the word or phrase means the same as the idiom.

1. The referee told the crowd to pipe down.

The referee told the crowd to be quiet.

2. At basketball practice, we can't get away with anything!

____

3. When it comes to fighting, my dad puts his foot down.

____

4. I wouldn't turn my nose up at the chance to wrestle him.

____

Alliteration

Alliteration is a poetic technique in which the beginning sound is repeated in words for effect. Tongue twisters often use alliteration to create catchy phrases. Notice the effect of alliteration as you try to say the following tongue twisters:

Six silly sailors swam south.

Bobby bought a bunch of brown bananas.

Alliteration Practice

Underline the alliterative consonants in the following sentences.

Example: <u>S</u>nakes <u>s</u>lither on the <u>s</u>idewalk.

1. The wind whistled through the willows.
2. Magic markers can make masterpieces.
3. Tommy tried to twist, but tumbled.
4. Greg grabbed the garnish gracefully from the bowl.
5. Constance catered to her cat with catnip to keep it from kidnapping canaries.

Use alliteration to finish the lines below.

1. People patiently ________________________________
2. Roger ran ________________________________
3. Six swimmers________________________________
4. Alan always ________________________________
5. Kelly caught________________________________

Now, write five alliterative sentences of your own.

1. ________________________________
2. ________________________________
3. ________________________________
4. ________________________________
5. ________________________________

Personification

Personification is a form of figurative language in which an object, an item, or an animal is given the characteristics of a person. It is personified.

Here are some examples of personification:

- The wind picked up the leaves and scattered them throughout the yard.
- The tree stood firm against the strikes of the blade.
- The rug curls up like it wants to hide.
- The door slammed shut to keep the strong wind from coming inside.
- The sun set slowly over the horizon signaling the time had come.
- The papers raced across the vacant lot.
- The chair tumbled over.
- The tree reached its leafy arms skyward.
- Perspiration rolled down her back.
- The floor groaned as the dancers stomped away.
- The wind whispered through the trees.
- The raindrops danced on the window.
- The book sat on the table.
- The paper flew off the desk.

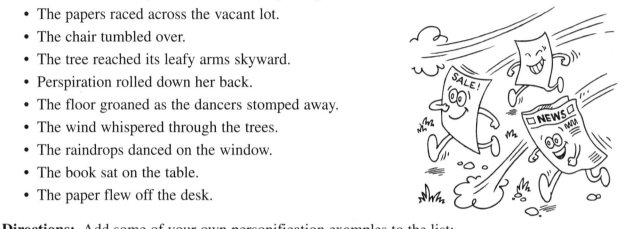

Directions: Add some of your own personification examples to the list:

____
____
____
____
____
____
____
____
____
____
____
____
____

Helpful Tips on Using Figurative Language

If your writing is clear, easy to read, interesting, and if it flows easily, then leave it alone. The only time to use figurative language such as similes, metaphors, and personification is to improve your writing. Adding colorful words and phrases can make your writing better. Be careful not to add too many, just enough to give your writing some pizzazz.

Hyperbole

A **hyperbole** is an exaggeration or an overstatement used for emphasis. A hyperbole is another form of figurative language used to engage the reader.

Here are examples of hyperbole:

- My dad about died when he saw my grades.
- I about had a heart attack when I heard the price of the dress.
- He talked until he was blue in the face.
- She was halfway across the world before she realized she had forgotten her bag.
- I am going to kick that book to Timbuktu.
- The siren was so loud you couldn't hear yourself think.
- Her feet were glued to the ground when she saw the mountain lion.

Directions: Underline the hyperboles in the paragraphs below.

A. It was a rough day at sea. I thought the boat was going to flip right over. The wind came rushing through the sails without a break. The captain almost had a heart attack when he saw the height of the waves. Would we ever see dry land again?

B. The kids were running and screaming around the classroom. You could tell when you walked in there was a substitute that day. It was so loud that you could barely hear yourself think. The substitute was trying to get the attention of the students.

C. This Thanksgiving was wonderful. We had at least fifty people at the feast this year. My mother tried some new recipes and they were all great. I ate so much food I almost burst. I had to take a nap just to be able to walk.

Directions: Write a paragraph below that uses hyperbole.

Directions: Write hyperboles you would like to use in your own writing below.

Vocabulary: Spelling Demons

The following are some of the most commonly misspelled English words.

Word	Syllables	In Context
foreign	for•eign	Do you know how to speak any **foreign** languages?
weird	weird	He had on a very **weird** outfit.
separate	sep•a•rate	Put their gifts in two **separate** bags.
calendar	cal•en•dar	The **calendar** pictured a different dog each month.
a lot	a lot	It took **a lot** of hours to paint the house.
embarrass	em•bar•rass	It will **embarrass** me if I have to get up on stage.
guarantee	guar•an•tee	Did this toaster come with a money-back **guarantee**?
privilege	priv•i•lege	She had the **privilege** of driving her dad's car to school.
rhythm	rhy•thm	The drummer had a natural sense of **rhythm**.
vacuum	vac•uum	Please **vacuum** the living room.
irrelevant	ir•rel•e•vant	Get rid of **irrelevant** information in your essay.
accommodate	ac•com•mo•date	The room can **accommodate** four people.
familiar	fa•mil•iar	Something about that woman is **familiar** to me.
appropriate	ap•pro•pri•ate	Wearing jeans isn't **appropriate** for attending a funeral.

Write the spelling word that begins and ends with same letters as the word given. Some of the spelling words begin and end with the same letters. In that case, an additional line was given.

Example: imminent ____irrelevant____ (*irrelevant* is used again below)

1. four ______________________
2. airplane ______________________
   ____
3. vandalism ______________________
4. shuttle ______________________
5. Internet ______________________
6. gauge ______________________
7. chair ______________________
8. flatten ______________________
9. express ______________________
10. petite ______________________
11. wild ______________________
12. rum ______________________

13. What spelling word in this lesson is actually two small words? ____________________

Vocabulary: Spelling Demons *(cont.)*

Roman Numeral Code

Change the Roman numeral code into spelling words from this lesson. Write each letter beneath the Roman numeral that stands for it.

I = a	II = b	III = c	IV = d	V = e	VI = f	VII = g	VIII = h	IX = i
X = j	XI = k	XII = l	XIII = m	XIV = n	XV = o	XVI = p	XVII = q	XVIII = r
XIX = s	XX = t	XXI = u	XXII = v	XXIII = w	XXIV = x	XXV = y	XXVI = z	

Example: XIX XV XII IV IX V XVIII
s o l d i e r

1. XVIII VIII XXV XX VIII XIII	8. V XIII II I XVIII XVIII I XIX XIX
2. VII XXI I XVIII I XIV XX V V	9. I XII XV XX
3. I XVI XVI XVIII XV XVI XVIII IX I XX V	10. I III III XV XIII XIII XV IV I XX V
4. III I XII V XIV IV I XVIII	11. XVI XVIII IX XXII IX XII V VII V
5. XXII I III XXI XXI XIII	12. VI I XIII IX XII IX I XVIII
6. XXIII V IX XVIII IV	13. VI XV XVIII V IX VII XIV
7. IX XVIII XVIII V XII V XXII I XIV XX	14. XIX V XVI I XVIII I XX V

Synonyms: Similar Meanings

Synonyms are words that have the same or nearly the same meaning. Synonyms are especially important when you decide you need a more exact or a better word to express your meaning when you are writing or reading. At such times, a thesaurus is a helpful reference.

Because a thesaurus entry usually contains several words that are considered synonyms, you also need to use a dictionary to be sure that the word you choose produces the meaning you want. You cannot be sure that every word in the list will work as a substitute for the one you started with.

For example, you may want to describe in a story a character who is stingy, but you want a word that also suggests that the person hides away money. The thesaurus lists several words that could be used in place of *stingy*: *miserly*, *tightfisted*, *penny-pinching*, *cheap*, and *frugal*. One of these is the word you are looking for: *miserly*. When you look it up in the dictionary, you find that it means exactly what you had in mind: being stingy and especially hiding money.

Directions: Use a thesaurus and a dictionary to choose the best synonyms to replace the italicized words in the following sentences. (Remember that one word often leads to another. You may have to go to the next step and look in the dictionary for definitions of one or more unfamiliar words in a definition.)

1. The naturalized citizen, Maria Hernandez, pledged her *allegiance* to the Canadian flag.

   a. feasibility　　b. helpfulness　　c. loyalty

2. Without even a *whimper*, Baby Gerald let a complete stranger give him his bottle.

   a. whoopee　　b. cry　　c. twitch

3. Even the great Inspector Cleverleaux could not *unravel* the mystery.

   a. tighten　　b. calculate　　c. untangle

4. The neighbor's barking German shepherd, Daisy, interrupted my *slumber*.

   a. leisure　　b. relaxation　　c. sleep

5. Because he wanted to *qualify* to go to a top-notch university after he graduated from high school, Terence worked to earn excellent grades in all his classes.

   a. to be eligible　　b. to be barred　　c. to be innovative

6. Mozart wrote *operas* that are performed throughout the world.

   a. violin solos　　b. plays set to music　　c. plays about soaps

Synonyms: Similar Meanings *(cont.)*

7. Only an impolite and insensitive person will *mock* others.

   a. photograph b. ridicule c. impersonate

8. Molly thought she would *keel over* from exhaustion after running the marathon.

   a. collapse b. recover c. become ill

9. My friend Matthew is considered an *ideal* candidate for class president.

   a. indifferent b. poor c. perfect

10. Ontario amethyst and tourmaline from Quebec are both *gems* that Mrs. Trumpet likes.

    a. standouts b. precious stones c. gymnasium

11. It is *essential* that you eat healthful foods if you are going to remain healthy.

    a. extremely b. indicated c. necessary

12. I had to buy a new atlas because the *boundaries* of some countries have changed.

    a. canopies b. campaigns c. borders

13. Mr. Chang, our new neighbor, is an *amateur* photographer.

    a. not professional b. not formal c. not effective

14. One of the events in speech contests in high school and college is *debate*.

    a. night crawlers b. formal argument c. bounty

15. My mother communicated to me an urgent *plea* to clean my room.

    a. pastime b. query c. request

16. It is always a bad idea to try to *deceive* your parents about anything.

    a. annoy b. conceal c. mislead

17. Sometimes it is difficult to decide what would be *suitable* to wear to an event.

    a. appropriate b. considerate c. communicate

Antonyms: Contrasting Meanings

Learning the antonym or the word that means almost the opposite of another word can help you better understand the meaning of that word just as a synonym can. Just as you may find exactly the right synonym in a thesaurus, you may also find an antonym in a thesaurus entry or in a dictionary. There are dictionaries that list both synonyms and antonyms.

Directions: Use a thesaurus and a dictionary to help you choose the sentence that best or most closely expresses the **opposite** meaning of the first sentence in each group. (Remember that one word often leads to another. You may have to go to the next step and look in the dictionary for definitions of one or more unfamiliar words in a definition.)

1. **Pedro Herrera thought the salesman's smile was *artificial*.**
   a. Pedro Herrera thought the smile was confident.
   b. Pedro Herrera thought the smile was sincere.
   c. Pedro Herrera thought the smile was amazing.

2. **The very gracious Lord Hastings *ignored* Louisa's ink-smudged hands when she went through the reception line.**
   a. Lord Hastings noticed Louisa's hands.
   b. Lord Hastings overlooked Louisa's hands.
   c. Lord Hastings admired Louisa's hands.

3. **When visiting the sacred shrine, Murikama behaved very *respectfully*.**
   a. Murikama was reverent at the shrine.
   b. Murikama was alert at the shrine.
   c. Murikama was irreverent at the shrine.

4. **Mayor Burroughs is a *powerful* member of the city council.**
   a. Mayor Burroughs is an insignificant member of the city council.
   b. Mayor Burroughs is a dedicated member of the city council.
   c. Mayor Burroughs is a distinguished member of the city council.

5. **The Smokey Mountains are especially *gorgeous* in both the spring and fall.**
   a. The Smokey Mountains are magnificent in spring and fall.
   b. The Smokey Mountains are ugly in spring and fall.
   c. The Smokey Mountains are amazing in spring and fall.

6. **Bennie *warily* approached the wounded bear.**
   a. Bennie cautiously approached the bear.
   b. Bennie recklessly approached the bear.
   c. Bennie unexpectedly approached the bear.

Antonyms: Contrasting Meanings *(cont.)*

7. **The candidate *brooded* about the mistake he had made.**
   a. The candidate worried about the mistake.
   b. The candidate took advantage of the mistake.
   c. The candidate was untroubled by the mistake.

8. **Gracie was called a *heroine* after she foiled the robbery.**
   a. Gracie was called a champion after the robbery.
   b. Gracie was called a coward after the robbery.
   c. Gracie was called a cadet after the robbery.

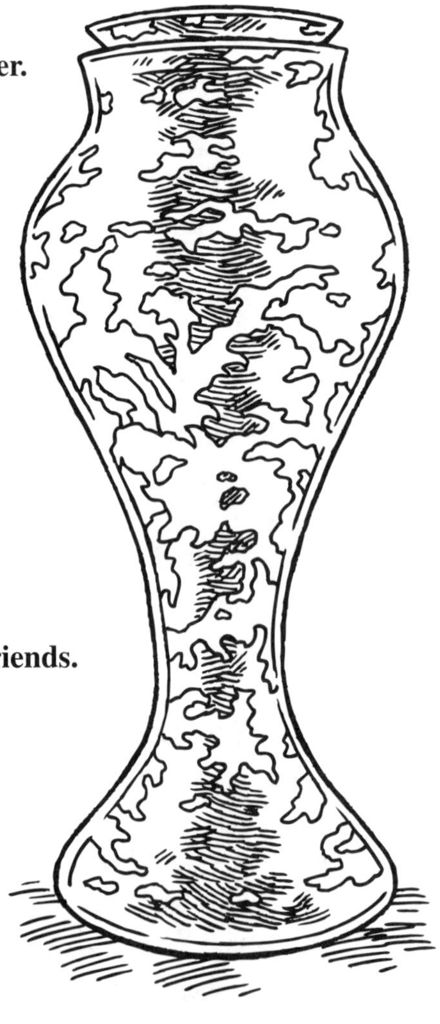

9. **At the flea market, Luke found an *antique* vase for his mother.**
   a. Luke found a very old vase at the flea market.
   b. Luke found a cunning vase at the flea market.
   c. Luke found a new vase at the flea market.

10. **The senator appeared to be a very *dignified* person.**
    a. The senator appeared to be very proper person.
    b. The senator appeared to be a very unseemly person.
    c. The senator appeared to be a very hideous person.

11. **The house the astronomer lives in looks like a *palace* to me.**
    a. The astronomer's house looks like a mansion.
    b. The astronomer's house looks like a hovel.
    c. The astronomer's house looks like a lobby.

12. **Jo Ellen *concealed* the details of her illness from all of her friends.**
    a. Jo Ellen revealed the details of her illness.
    b. Jo Ellen hid the details of her illness.
    c. Jo Ellen criticized the details of her illness.

13. **Romeo decided that he would *forfeit* the race.**
    a. Romeo decided that he would cultivate the race.
    b. Romeo decided that he would give up the race.
    c. Romeo decided that he would participate in the race.

14. **David Day wrote *thorough* biographies of J.R.R. Tolkien.**
    a. Day wrote sketchy biographies of Tolkien.
    b. Day wrote forlorn biographies of Tolkien.
    c. Day wrote comprehensive biographies of Tolkien.

Homophones

Homophones are two or more words that have the same sound but have *different meanings*. These words are problems for many writers, for it is easy to become confused by them.

If certain homophones are a problem for you, you need to find a way to help you remember what each word means. For example, you can remember that *stationery* is writing paper because of the *er* in both *stationery* and *paper*. Try to think of similar ways to distinguish one homophone from another so that you write both words correctly.

Directions: Select the correct homonyms to fill in the blanks in the sentences below.

1. Mrs. Ridley gave her ________________________ for all of us to watch the ______________ of the colorful hot-air balloons as they rose over Edmonton. (*ascent/assent*)

2. The sailors on the *Merry Mermaid* were trying to plot a safe ________________________ (*coarse/course*) through the ______________________. (*straight/strait*)

3. The furniture refinisher did not want to use the _________________ sandpaper. (*coarse/course*)

4. Just as important as remembering to give a _______________________ to someone else is having the ability to accept one gracefully. (*compliment/complement*)

5. Did you remember to ____________________________ the references you used to write your report? (*cite/site*)

6. The climber kept the rope ___________________ as he made his way to the peak. (*taught/taut*)

7. If you look over _____________________, you will see ________________________ house that they have painted red, white, and blue. (*their/there*)

8. Learning your ________________________ will _________________ (lessen/lesson) the chance that you will earn a poor grade.

9. Your ________________________ is required while I open my _______________________. (*presence/presents*)

10. Lucinda ________________________ the test, and that got her _____________ the one thing that she had been dreading the most. (*passed/past*)

Choose the Best Definitions

Directions: For each sentence below and on page 39, choose the definition that matches the way the italicized word is used in the sentence.

1. **Senator Whistler took the *floor* to defend his position on the immigration bill.**
    a. to knock down
    b. upper or uppermost surface
    c. right to address an assembly

2. **Professor Watkins went to Australia to participate in the *dig*.**
    a. an archaeological site
    b. to learn or discover
    c. to break up, turn over, or remove

3. **My vigorous friend Audrey was a *rock* and stayed with me the entire time.**
    a. move back and forth; zigzag
    b. stable, firm, dependable one
    c. naturally formed mineral

4. **Attorney William Joseph's *opposite* in the case was Attorney Justine Modigliani.**
    a. one that is contrary to another
    b. located directly behind or ahead of
    c. sharply contrasting

5. **Catherine Laws, my grade-six teacher, *holds* a degree in music also.**
    a. to restrain; curb
    b. to possess
    c. to regard or consider

6. **When we went sailing Saturday, the seas were very *heavy*.**
    a. weighted down; burdened
    b. of great intensity
    c. violent, rough

7. **The argument between the two wealthy adversaries quickly became *heated*.**
    a. warm a building
    b. degree of warmth or hotness
    c. intense, angry

8. **The nomination committee decided to *block* the investigation of their decisions.**
    a. to impede the passage of
    b. to support or strengthen
    c. to indicate broadly; sketch

Choose the Best Definitions *(cont.)*

9. **The gardener was *broadcasting* grass seed on the football field.**
   a. making known over a wide area
   b. sowing widely, especially by hand
   c. transmitting by air
10. **One *feature* of the agreement was hotly debated in the Senate.**
   a. prominent article in a newspaper
   b. publicize or make outstanding
   c. distinctive quality or element
11. **One requirement of the equestrian class is that you must *groom* your horse.**
   a. to make neat and trim
   b. to clean and brush
   c. to coach or tutor
12. **The official began to *hedge* when he was pressed for details.**
   a. to enclose with hedges
   b. to protect against monetary loss
   c. to purposely make an indefinite statement
13. **The two countries approved a *joint* agreement to regulate trade.**
   a. formed by united action
   b. a place where two or more things are joined together
   c. a cut of meat for roasting
14. **Mahoud stood on the shore and could do nothing as he watched the yacht *keel*.**
   a. to fall as from fainting
   b. to capsize
   c. to lean to one side; tilt
15. **A *local* custom was to meet at the general store to discuss the weekend's events.**
   a. widespread; throughout the country
   b. pertaining to a particular place
   c. making many stops on a route
16. **My parents began teaching us *moral* behavior when my brother and I were quite young.**
   a. concerning the state of mind of a person
   b. established standards of right and wrong
   c. teaching principles by stories or events
17. **The townspeople found the actions of the newcomer *quaint*.**
   a. unfamiliar or unusual
   b. delightfully pretty
   c. a trait or characteristic

Words for Specialized Areas

There are many words for specialized areas of study that end in -**ology**. The suffix -ology means "the science of" or "the study of" something. For example, mineralogy is the study of minerals. Many of these words are used when studying social studies and science.

A. Match the specialized areas with the definitions below.

-ology Words		**Definitions**
1. ________	meteorology	A. study of insects
2. ________	biology	B. study of fruit
3. ________	cytology	C. study of poisons
4. ________	dermatology	D. study of ancestors
5. ________	pomology	E. study of cells
6. ________	genealogy	F. study of life
7. ________	entomology	G. study of weather
8. ________	sociology	H. study of skin
9. ________	toxicology	I. study of society

B. Write the name of the specialist that matches the described field of study. You may use the words listed below to aid you.

1. An ______________________________ studies the eyes.
2. A ______________________________ studies newborn babies.
3. A ______________________________ studies criminal behavior.
4. An ______________________________ studies birds.
5. A ______________________________ studies minerals.
6. A ______________________________ studies the mind.
7. An ______________________________ studies word origins.
8. A ______________________________ studies living tissues.
9. A ______________________________ studies radiation.

mineralogist	etymologist	radiologist	histologist
neonatologist	ornithologist	ophthalmologist	psychologist
criminologist			

Vocabulary Venue

Directions: Using precise vocabulary can clarify your writing. It can be tempting to write the way we and others talk. Rewrite the following paragraphs. Replace the underlined phrases with vivid, precise words.

A. It is very important for everyone to learn how to read. Learning to read can be very difficult. It is like frustrating for some people. Some people don't learn to read because they have learning disabilities. Some people don't think that it is cool to learn to read. Finally, some people are never taught how to read.

B. I am like so excited about going on the trip over spring break. It is like going to be so awesome. My friends all think hanging out at the beach will be cool. We were so looking forward to a week off of school work. The first thing I do when I get to the ocean is jump right in. I don't even care if I have my swim suit on. All I really care about is feeling the breeze on my face and the salt water on my back.

Cause and Effect

Directions: Draw a line to match each cause to its effect. Then create two sentences for each of the first matched pairs. (One sentence should mention the cause first. One sentence should mention the effect first.)

Causes	Effects
• Ruth ate two bags of cotton candy.	• I gave him a round of applause.
• Kevin helped his dad make a cake.	• She got a very bad stomachache.
• Trudy practiced running every morning.	• His dad was proud.
• Zechariah sang a song with his dog.	• She won second place in the marathon race.

1. (Cause mentioned first)

____

____

(Effect mentioned first)

____

____

2. (Cause mentioned first)

____

____

(Effect mentioned first)

____

____

Cause and Effect *(cont.)*

Directions: Now create two sentences for each of the two remaining matched pairs on page 42. (One sentence should mention the cause first. One sentence should mention the effect first.)

3. (Cause mentioned first)

___

___

(Effect mentioned first)

___

___

4. (Cause mentioned first)

___

___

(Effect mentioned first)

___

___

Extra Credit: Compose four original sentences of cause and effect. After writing each one, rewrite it, reversing the order of cause and effect as you did for the previous four sentences.

___

___

___

___

___

___

___

Cause and Effect: Wayne the Victor

I used to miss school a lot. I'd be gone from school one or two days a week, and I really didn't have any excuses. Some days I was just tired or I didn't feel like going to school, so I didn't. Other times, I was mad at my teacher, or I felt like a failure and so I stayed home. When I was missing lots of school I didn't like school. It was hard to get to know people, and my teachers were frustrated with me. I was confused all the time and felt like I didn't belong. I felt like I'd never learn what people wanted me to learn.

Then I realized that I didn't like school because I was gone so much—I didn't give myself a chance to like school. I wasn't giving myself a chance to get to know people or figure out what was going on in my classes. I felt sad and mad inside. I realized I was giving up on myself and failing myself. I decided I was no longer going to give up on myself.

I chose to work on my school attendance first. I decided that no matter what, I was going to go to school every day. I told my brother about my new decision and he said he didn't care. I told my mom about my new decision and she said, "Okay, that's nice, Wayne," but I don't think she really cared either. I started feeling bad inside again because they didn't act proud or anything. So I told myself about my new decision, and then I told myself, "I am proud of you, Wayne! You can do it!" It may sound silly but it did make me feel better! I told myself that no matter how I felt or what my family or teachers thought, I had to make myself go to school every day.

I wrote myself this reminder with big letters on a piece of notebook paper: **Go to school, Wayne! Don't give up on yourself! I am proud of you!** Then I taped it to the wall beside my bed so I'd see it every night and every morning. I made another sign just like it and taped it on the wall in the corner, close to the floor. I decided I would put my book bag in that corner every day when I came home from school and then it'd be easy to find each morning so I could take it to school with me. I had decided that I was going to quit giving up on myself and I was doing things to help myself be a victor.

Cause and Effect: Wayne the Victor *(cont.)*

Directions: Read "Wayne the Victor" carefully. Complete the chart below. The left side of the chart is for "causes." The right side of the chart is for "effects." Make sure that your answers make sense.

Cause	Effect
1. Some days Wayne was tired or just did not feel like going to school.	1. ______________________ ______________________ ______________________
2. ______________________ ______________________ ______________________	2. Wayne did not like school and it was hard to get to know people.
3. Wayne decided he was no longer going to give up on himself.	3. ______________________ ______________________ ______________________
4. ______________________ ______________________ ______________________	4. Wayne started feeling bad inside again.
5. Wayne told himself, "I am proud of you!"	5. ______________________ ______________________ ______________________.

Games with a History

Checkers is one of the most popular board games in the world. The oldest form of the game of checkers began in Egypt in 1400 B.C. and was called alquerque. Checkers is related to another ancient game called draughts. International draughts has a 100-square board. English draughts, also known as checkers in the United States, uses a 64-square board. In 1756, William Payne, an English mathematician, wrote the first book in English about checkers. It is not known when checkers was brought to the United States.

Monopoly® began as a game called The Landlord Game. The Landlord Game was invented in 1903 by a young Quaker woman named Elizabeth Magie. She wanted to teach people about the evils of landlords, who have an unfair advantage over renters. Charles Darrow redesigned The Landlord Game and sold it to Parker Brothers, a popular game manufacturer. According to Parker Brothers, Darrow was the world's first game designer to become a millionaire.

Monopoly® is the best-selling game in the world. Over 200 million copies in 80 countries and in 26 languages have been sold. A Braille edition of Monopoly® was produced in the 1970s. In 1978, a chocolate version of the board game sold for $600. The favorite game piece is the racecar, and the newest game piece is a money sack.

Scrabble® is a very popular game in Canada and the United States. It was invented during the Great Depression by Alfred Butts. He called it Crisscross Words.

Although the first attempts to sell Crisscross Words failed, Butts and his partner did not give up. They eventually trademarked the name Scrabble® in 1948 and produced the game themselves. By the 1950s, it had become so popular that it had to be rationed in the stores because the small factory could not keep up with customer orders. In 1972, the Selchow and Righter Company, a game distributor, bought the trademark rights to Scrabble®. The rest, as they say, is history!

Games with a History *(cont.)*

Directions: After reading the story, answer the questions. Circle the letter before each correct answer.

1. **According to the article, what is the best-selling game in the world?**
   a. draughts
   b. Monopoly®
   c. checkers
   d. Scrabble®

2. **The answer to which of these questions would help you understand the history of games?**
   a. How were games invented?
   b. Why is Monopoly® so popular?
   c. Where was Scrabble® invented?
   d. How many people play checkers?

3. **This passage is arranged by. . .**
   a. newest game to the oldest game.
   b. the history of different games.
   c. the manufacturers of each game.
   d. alphabetical order by inventor.

4. **For this sentence, choose the word that means that Monopoly is a well-liked game.**
   Monopoly® is a very ____________________ game for Parker Brothers, who have sold over 200 million copies of it in 80 countries and 26 languages.
   a. recent
   b. complicated
   c. successful
   d. expensive

5. **Which of these best combines the two sentences into one?**
   Jacks and dominoes were once popular games.
   Electronic games are more popular today.
   a. Jacks and dominoes were popular, and electronic games are more popular.
   b. Once, jacks and dominoes were games, but today they are electronic games.
   c. Jacks and dominoes were once popular; then electronic games.
   d. Jacks and dominoes were once popular games, but electronic games are more popular today.

6. **When Pong® was introduced by Atari in 1977, the machine was big, the animation was slow, and the game was simple. Today, video games are hand held, the action is fast, and the games are complicated. From this information, you can infer that . . .**
   a. some video games seem smarter than humans.
   b. I do not like video games, because I prefer the outdoors.
   c. video games have improved greatly in the last 30 years.
   d. the invention of video games was a good thing.

The History of Pockets

When people put their hands in their pockets, they rarely realize they are using an invention that is only a few hundred years old. For several thousand years, human clothing did not have pockets of any kind. People cut a circle out of cloth or leather and put their money, keys, or other objects in the middle of the circle. Then they gathered up the edges and bunched the circle into a loose bag or purse. They tied a string, usually of leather, around the neck of this purse to keep objects from falling out.

These purses were usually tied onto belts. They dangled by their strings. Thieves would try to cut these strings to steal the purses. Near the end of the 1500s, men began to ask for slits in their trousers exactly where we have side pockets in pants today. A man still tied the strings of his purse to his belt, but then he pushed the purse through the side slit in his trousers. This made it more difficult for a thief to steal the purse.

These purses were also known as pockets even though they were not yet attached to trousers. We don't know who figured out how to sew this pocket into the side seam and make it a permanent part of the trousers. The invention made it easier and quicker to get something from the pocket. No longer did a man have to untie a purse from his belt and then undo the string around it.

Shortly after the pocket became a permanent part of trousers, people began to want pockets in other garments as well. Both women and men asked for them in cloaks and coats. At first, these pockets were attached near the lower hems of long capes and cloaks. A person had to pull up the garment and keep holding it up while reaching into the pocket. This took two hands. Eventually, people asked for pockets at the hip so that it would only take one hand to use the pocket.

Travelers in the days of the first sewn-in pockets had to journey from town to town in horse-drawn carriages. They began to ask for secret pockets so they could hide small valuables from the robbers who often held up coaches. The robbers could not always find a secret pocket sewn inside a piece of clothing. Today, business jackets for both men and women still have these inner pockets to protect valuables.

Modern travelers sometimes still use purses like those of long ago. Today tourists can buy small, flat bags for their passports and money. These are worn around the neck or waist and are kept out of sight, beneath the clothes. Then, even if thieves steal briefcases or women's handbags, tourists will still have the most important papers and emergency money that they kept tucked out of sight.

Three purposes have shaped the history of pockets. The first is safety. To prevent theft, pockets have evolved inside business jackets as secret places for valuables. Pockets also developed because people wanted to reach money, keys, pens, tissues, and other items quickly and easily. The third purpose of pockets was the last one to develop. Only in the last 150 years have people figured out that pockets offer a good way to keep hands warm in cold weather!

The History of Pockets *(cont.)*

Directions: After reading the story, answer the questions. Circle the letter before each correct answer.

1. **What is this passage mostly about?**
   a. how travelers protected valuable papers
   b. how pockets developed over time
   c. how tailors hide pockets in clothing
   d. how people used to carry purses

2. **Which of these statements shows that people use purses today in a way similar to how they were used in the past?**
   a. They are worn around the neck and are sometimes kept out of sight, beneath the clothes.
   b. The robbers could not always find a secret pocket sewn inside a piece of clothing.
   c. Both women and men asked for them in cloaks and coats.
   d. The third purpose of pockets was the last one to develop.

3. **The original pockets were probably sewn near the lower hem of capes and cloaks because . . .**
   a. robbers wouldn't think to look there.
   b. this was where valuables would fit.
   c. hems provide extra fabric needed to make a pocket.
   d. this was a convenient place for people to access.

4. **Why did people start sewing pockets permanently into trousers?**
   a. Permanent pockets allowed people to warm their hands.
   b. The leather used to make purses was hard to find.
   c. This made it easier to get to the pocket without having to unfasten the purse.
   d. It was less expensive to sew the pocket into trousers than to make purses.

5. **Why did people begin putting their small purses in side slits in their trousers?**
   a. This made it harder for the purses to be stolen.
   b. The purses were less likely to be lost.
   c. They didn't like the weight of the purses hanging from their belts.
   d. The purses didn't get in their way.

6. **Pockets kept people's belongings safe. What is another reason people liked pockets?**
   a. They were fashionable.
   b. They could hold more than purses.
   c. They were easy to make.
   d. They were easier to use.

Dinosaurs Roamed the West

More dinosaur remains have been found in the Alberta Badlands than anywhere else on Earth. Alberta has so many remains there, that they have a park named Dinosaur Provincial Park near Brooks, Alberta. There have been over 35 species of dinosaurs found in this area.

The Alberta Badlands is very dry and rocky. It is hard to believe that millions of years ago the ocean was there. The Western Interior Seaway covered much of what is now Alberta, Saskatchewan, and Manitoba. The climate was mild and densely forested with great sequoia-like trees. Large sea creatures lived in the water, and great dinosaurs roamed the earth.

The Albertosaurus was a relative of the Tyrannosaurus; it had a huge head, jagged teeth, and sharp claws on bird-like feet. Albertosaurus was about six meters (6.5 yards) tall and ten meters (11 yards) long and was one of the largest carnivores to have ever lived on land. It had dagger-like teeth and powerful jaws. Like Tyrannosaurus, it possessed tiny forearms and large and well-muscled hind legs.

The Edmontosaurus walked on four legs and ate vegetation; it probably lived in herds. Edmontosaurus, or "Edmonton lizard" takes its name from the Edmonton rock formation. It was one of the largest and last of the duckbilled dinosaurs and weighed 2.7 metric tons
(three tons).

The Edmontonia was about 7 meters (23 feet) long and had hard, bony-plated armor covering. Huge spikes stuck out of its shoulders. It has a wedge-shaped head. It grew to a length of five meters (16 feet) and weighed almost three tons.

Notice that these dinosaurs were named for the area where they were found.

Another important dinosaur discovery was named for Lawrence Lambe. He was a very important Canadian paleontologist. The Lambeosaurus (which means "Lambe's lizard") is on display at the Royal Ontario Museum in Toronto, Ontario. The Lambeosaurus was about 15 meters (49 feet) long and had a large, hollow crest on its head. Scientists believe that the hollow crest allowed the dinosaur to make loud honks and bellows that echoed across the land.

Many other types of dinosaurs have been discovered in this area, and tourists visit the Royal Tyrrell Museum of Paleontology in Drumheller, Alberta, to see the variety of dinosaurs discovered.

Dinosaurs Roamed the West *(cont.)*

Directions: After reading the passage answer the questions. Circle the letter before each correct answer.

1. Where have the most dinosaur remains been found?

a. Alberta
b. Saskatchewan
c. Manitoba
d. Edmonton

2. What was in the Alberta Badlands millions of years ago?

a. a forest
b. an ocean
c. a river
d. a lake

3. The Albertosaurus had . . .

a. lizard-like feet
b. small hind legs
c. tiny forearms
d. weak jaws

4. Which of the following sentences is *true* of the Edmontosaurus?

a. It walked on two legs.
b. It weighed one metric ton.
c. It was one of the last of the duckbilled dinosaurs.
d. It takes its name from the city of Edmonton.

5. The Edmontonia had a __________________-shaped head.

a. round
b. square
c. triangle
d. wedge

6. Scientists believe that the hollow crest of the Lambeosaurus allowed it to . . .

a. make loud growls.
b. make loud honks and bellows.
c. make loud screeching sounds.
d. make deep cooing noises.

7. Would you like to be a paleontologist like Lawrence Lambe? Explain.

____

____

____

Mission to Mars

On July 4, 1997, space exploration took a huge step. On that day, a spacecraft called *Pathfinder* landed on Mars. The National Aeronautics and Space Administration (NASA) sent *Pathfinder* to discover new information about the Red Planet.

The mission was a complete success. After landing, *Pathfinder* sent a small rover, *Sojourner*, onto the planet's surface. *Sojourner* explored more than 250 square meters of Mars. Together, *Pathfinder* and *Sojourner* took more than 16,000 photos of the rocky landscape. Engineers designed *Sojourner* to last for only seven days, but the little vehicle ran twelve times longer! *Pathfinder* surprised scientists, too. It sent back information for almost three months. That was three times longer than it was built to last.

Because *Pathfinder* and *Sojourner* ran for so long, scientists got more information than they ever dreamed of getting. For one thing, they discovered that Mars is very sandy. Pictures of sand dunes around the landing site hint that Mars once had water. Scientists know that water means life. Was there ever life on Mars? We don't know yet.

In addition, the *Pathfinder* mission told scientists that Mars is dusty. Huge "dust devils" on Mars spit enormous amounts of dust into the Martian air. *Pathfinder* also recorded frosty Martian temperatures at 200 degrees below zero Fahrenheit. At that temperature, a glass of water would freeze solid in just a few seconds.

In October, scientists lost *Pathfinder's* signal because the spacecraft's battery had run down. They tried to revive the signal but had no luck. The mission officially ended on November 4.

Scientists hope to use the knowledge from these missions to better understand how life on Earth began. They'll also use it to plan future Mars missions.

Mission to Mars *(cont.)*

Directions: After reading the passage, answer the questions. Circle the letter before each correct answer.

1. **What did NASA do to get information about Mars?**
   a. NASA sent the spacecraft *Sojourner* to Mars.
   b. NASA sent engineers on a three-month space mission.
   c. NASA sent the spacecraft *Pathfinder* to Mars.
   d. NASA sent astronauts to run tests for seven days.
2. **According to the passage, how much longer did the *Sojourner* last than expected?**
   a. Seven days
   b. Twelve times longer
   c. 250 days
   d. Three times longer
3. **What was the main reason NASA considered the *Pathfinder* mission a success?**
   a. Scientists found out that Mars is very cold and dusty.
   b. Scientists got more information than they ever dreamed of getting.
   c. Scientists learned that Mars definitely had water at one time.
   d. Scientists found out that there was once life on Mars.
4. **This article gives you reason to believe that NASA. . .**
   a. thinks missions to Mars cost more than they are worth.
   b. will not send other missions to Mars.
   c. will be sending future missions to Mars.
   d. has all the information it needs about Mars.
5. **You can tell from this passage that . . .**
   a. dust devils on Mars made the photographs hard to see.
   b. Martian temperatures caused *Pathfinder's* battery to fail.
   c. scientists suspect that life on Earth began on Mars.
   d. scientists will look for signs that life existed on Mars.
6. **Based on information in this passage, the reader can conclude that . . .**
   a. *Sojourner* took more photographs than *Pathfinder* did.
   b. scientists will plan a mission to replace the spacecraft's battery.
   c. conditions on Mars are harsher than conditions on Earth.
   d. engineers designed *Sojourner* to last as long as *Pathfinder*.

Danger Is Their Business

Most animals try to play it safe. They know that there is always another animal that would like to have them for dinner—and not as a guest! So animals find ways to stay one step ahead of their enemies. Some animals, like deer, try to outrun danger. Bigger animals, like moose, rely on their great size and strength for protection. Animals like the grouse, a small woodland bird, have special coloring that makes them difficult to see. There is still one more way that animals can protect themselves. Just like in the old saying "fight fire with fire," some animals find protection by walking right into the jaws of danger.

For example, a little bird called a plover makes a living cleaning the mouths of crocodiles. Small, swimming animals called leeches, which look like snakes with suction cups for heads, swim into crocodiles' mouths and attack their gums. Even though crocodiles are very strong creatures, they are helpless against the leeches. So, the crocodiles let the plovers help them. A crocodile that wants to get the leeches out of its mouth climbs onto dry land and opens its jaws wide. A little plover fearlessly hops into the reptile's mouth and eats the leeches. The crocodile needs the leeches removed, so it doesn't attack the little bird, and the plover gets an easy meal.

Other animals find similar ways to use danger to their advantage. An ocean fish called the clown fish lives inside the poisonous branches of a creature called the sea anemone. The sea anemone looks like a small bush, but its branches are really poisonous tentacles. The anemone uses the tentacles as defense and to trap food. The clown fish is immune to the sea anemone's poison, so it makes its home inside the sea anemone's tentacles. This way, the brightly-colored clown fish doesn't have to hide. No matter how hungry the other fish get, they can't touch the clown fish without getting stung by the sea anemone.

Some insects also survive by living in a dangerous place. One species of mosquito actually lives inside a predator's stomach! The pitcher plant is a meat-eating plant. It uses sweet smells to attract insects. The insects land on the plant and slip down its sides into a long tube. The tube leads to a bowl (the pitcher plant's "stomach") full of liquid that kills and digests the insects. Some types of baby mosquitoes, or larvae, are able to swim freely in this liquid without harm. By living in such a dangerous place, these young mosquitoes stay safe from other hungry insects that might otherwise eat them.

These animals all use danger to their advantage. It just goes to show that jumping out of the frying pan and into the fire is sometimes the best way to survive!

Danger Is Their Business *(cont.)*

Directions: After reading the passage, answer the questions. Circle the letter before each correct answer.

1. **The passage is mostly about . . .**
   a. how animals help each other.
   b. using fire to defend yourself against dangerous animals.
   c. why leeches are dangerous.
   d. how some animals survive in dangerous environments.
2. **Insects are probably attracted to the pitcher plant because . . .**
   a. its leaves rustle and sound like other insects.
   b. they know there are mosquitoes inside.
   c. the color of the plant appeals to them.
   d. they are looking for fragrant nectar.
3. **Why can the plover live safely around crocodiles?**
   a. The plover is poisonous to the crocodile.
   b. The crocodile needs the plover to get the leeches out of its mouth.
   c. The crocodile depends on the plover to scare off predators.
   d. The plover hides inside the crocodile's mouth.
4. **The author links "jumping out of the frying pan and into the fire" to. . .**
   a. hitting predators with frying pans.
   b. jumping out of the way of predators.
   c. using danger to avoid dangerous situations.
   d. scaring animals off with fire.
5. **In what way is the crocodile helpless?**
   a. It cannot protect itself from leeches.
   b. It likes to eat small birds.
   c. It cannot resist the taste of leeches.
   d. It is not very strong.
6. **Read the following sentence:**
   The clown fish is immune to the sea anemone's poison.
   What does *immune* to mean?
   a. attracted to
   b. afraid of
   c. unaffected by
   d. unaware of

Diving In

Josh stepped to the edge of the platform. As he looked down, he thought the water seemed as though it was a thousand feet below. This was the third time he had come up here, and for the third time he turned around and walked back to the ladder, afraid to make the dive from the high platform. As he turned, Josh could feel the stares from his classmates, friends, and teachers on the back of his head. He knew what they would say when he got down. They would say he'd better make the dive the next time.

Josh wasn't sure there would even be a next time. He was just too scared to dive from that high platform. It wasn't like it was really that important. This was just an intramural diving team that had been put together by the swimming coach at the junior high school. Josh had made good dives at lower levels, he thought. Mr. Barry, the coach, had even said that if he didn't want to dive from that height, he didn't have to.

He wanted to do it, though. He had wanted to feel like a part of the team ever since that first afternoon when he had seen the other swimmers at practice. He enjoyed the water himself, and he was a good swimmer. When the diving team was started, he leaped at the opportunity to join. When tryouts were posted, his name was the first on the list.

Standing on the ground, Josh stared up at that high-dive platform that now seemed to be so far above him. He looked around the pool at the other swimmers, who were either waiting at the ladder to try their own dives or talking to Mr. Barry about the one they had just completed. Josh was sure that none of them had a problem looking down at the distant water from high on that platform. He figured that since he had never seen anyone else hesitate, only he was afraid.

Suddenly, Mr. Barry began walking toward him. "How are you doing, Josh?" he asked.

"I'm all right, Mr. Barry. I just got a little scared up there, that's all," Josh said.

"Don't worry about it, Josh. You know, when I was young, I got scared up there too," Mr. Barry said.

"So how did you ever get up the nerve to dive from up there, Mr. Barry?" Josh asked.

"I decided that I had to stop thinking about it. And I figured if I could get myself off the board just once, I would be a lot closer to success. So one day I just climbed up the ladder, ran to the end, closed my eyes, and jumped off the board."

Josh suddenly remembered exactly what it was like to be up there, when it seemed like a thousand feet above the water. Then, almost immediately, he thought about the feeling he would get in his stomach when he actually stepped from the platform, and how the water might look, rushing toward him so fast. He thought about how it might feel like he was flying and the way the air would turn silent as he fell.

Josh took a deep breath, turned around, and started walking back to the ladder that led to the high dive platform. He knew it was something he would have to do. Even if it wasn't today, he would do it someday.

Diving In *(cont.)*

Directions: After reading the story, answer the questions. Circle the letter before each correct answer.

1. **The author says that Josh was the first name on the tryout list to show that . . .**
   a. he was very eager to be on the team.
   b. there were few people on the team.
   c. he was scared to dive.
   d. he was in junior high.
2. **Which of these statements is true about the diving team according to the story?**
   a. Diving from the high dive was required.
   b. The coach was an Olympic champion.
   c. The team practiced every afternoon.
   d. It was a junior high intramural team.
3. **What did Josh do before he walked back to the high dive for his next attempt?**
   a. He signed up for tryouts for the diving team.
   b. He watched a teammate dive.
   c. He practiced on a lower diving board.
   d. He spoke with his coach about his fear.

Here is a story about diving. Some words are missing. For Numbers 4 through 6, choose the word that best fills each blank in the paragraph.

Diving is an (4) activity. The sport is a (5) of gymnastic and swimming skills. In the seventeenth century, gymnasts would move their equipment to the beach. The gymnasts would perform their exercises over the water. This (6) activity became the diving that we enjoy today.

4.
   a. enthusiastic
   b. exciting
   c. effective
   d. annoying

5.
   a. definition
   b. combination
   c. congestion
   d. solution

6.
   a. common
   b. reserved
   c. severe
   d. unusual

Letter Club

One day, Tasha got some mail from her friend who recently moved to the other side of the country. Tasha loves getting mail and was very excited. When she opened the envelope, she found a short letter and a list of ten names with addresses. It was an invitation to join a letter-sending club.

Dear Friend:
Welcome to the Letter Club! Copies of this letter have been going around the world for many years now. This letter helps inquisitive people find out about other places. By following the steps below, one young girl got letters from all seven continents—even from Antarctica! Be sure to ask your parents for permission before you join the Letter Club. Then send out your letters today! You, too, can learn about places that interest you and that you want to know more about.

What to do:

1. Look at the list of ten names.
2. Send a postcard or letter to the person whose name is at the top of the list.
3. Remove the name of the person you sent a postcard to from the list.
4. Recopy the remaining nine names and addresses and add your own to the bottom.
5. Send a copy of this letter and the new list to ten people you know, but not to anyone on the list.
6. Start checking your mail for exciting postcards and letters!

How it works:

1. The ten people you send this letter and your list to will send a postcard or letter to the person whose name is first on the list.
2. Then, they will remove that name from the list, add their name to the bottom, and send copies of this letter and their new list to ten people they know.
3. After a while, your name will work its way to the top of the list. When this happens, you will start getting letters from all over world! It usually takes a couple of months before you begin receiving letters.

Because your name will soon appear on so many people's lists, you might receive hundreds of postcards or letters from many different and exciting locations!

Some hints for getting exciting letters:

If you want to get letters from interesting places, try sending this letter and your list to people you know who live far away from you. For example, maybe your grandparents live in another province, or you have a friend who moved out of town. If you try to send this letter and your list as far away as possible, you will be sure to get letters from faraway places, too!

Letter Club *(cont.)*

Directions: After reading the story, answer the questions. Circle the letter before each correct answer.

1. **In order to get letters from all over the world, the passage suggests that Tasha . . .**
    a. write to a young girl who got letters from all seven continents.
    b. send out letters only to people in her hometown.
    c. send letters to ten of her friends.
    d. write a letter back to her friend.
2. **In order to participate in the Letter Club, Tasha should . . .**
    a. find the names of ten people she doesn't know to send letters to.
    b. decide what countries she wants to get mail from.
    c. send a postcard to all the people listed in the letter from her friend.
    d. ask her parents for permission to join the club.
3. **When this letter talks about inquisitive people, it means people who are . . .**
    a. unusual.
    b. curious.
    c. boring.
    d. careful.
4. **According to the letter, copies of the letter . . .**
    a. first came from a girl in Antarctica.
    b. have been going around the world for a long time.
    c. need to go to all seven continents.
    d. should be signed by your parents.
5. **In what way does the welcome letter to the Letter Club try to interest the reader in joining?**
    a. By telling the reader about other countries
    b. By suggesting the reader might get lots of mail
    c. By indicating that the Letter Club is a new idea
    d. By telling the reader letters will start arriving in a few days
6. **As a result of receiving the letter, Tasha will probably . . .**
    a. travel to ten faraway places.
    b. follow the instructions in the letter.
    c. put her name at the top of the list.
    d. return the letter and list to her friend.

School Reporter

Damaras was in the school cafeteria eating lunch when she spied her friend Anna. "Hey, Anna. Guess what? My article is going to be in the next issue of the school newspaper!"
Anna gave her a big smile. "That's so wonderful. I can't wait to read it."
Damaras was a new reporter on the school paper. For her first assignment she had covered the upcoming school play. Damaras had interviewed both the lead actress and the lead actor. She had researched the history of the play, which had been written by a man from London. She had spoken with the director, Mr. Clausen, who was also a social studies teacher, and she had sat in on rehearsals to see what it was like to be in the play.

Another student, Troy, who was sitting at the same cafeteria table, overheard them. He asked, "You wrote a story for the paper?"
Damaras nodded. "It will be printed this Thursday. I think it's going to be the lead story!"
Later that day, as Damaras was waiting for her English class to start, another student, Jeff, turned around in his chair and called over, "Hey, Damaras. I heard you wrote the lead story for the next school paper."
Damaras said, "Yes, I did, but how did you know?"

"Troy told me," Jeff replied.
Their teacher, Mr. Kim, overheard them. He looked at Damaras. "You wrote a lead story? That's wonderful, Damaras."
Then the whole class started talking about it. Some students raised their hands and asked how they could be a part of the school newspaper.

Jeff quizzed Damaras, "Are you going to be a reporter when you grow up? Is that your plan?"
Damaras blushed. She was not used to getting so much attention.
On Thursday, when the paper came out, Damaras ran to find a copy of it as soon as she got to school. She went to the classroom that served as the newspaper office. She picked up a copy and looked at the first page. It was not her article at all! Damaras was disappointed that her story was not on the first page. Then she skimmed the rest of the paper and realized her article was not even in the paper at all!
"Oh no!" Damaras cried in dismay. "Now everybody will think I wasn't telling the truth!"

She put the newspaper in her book bag and walked to her locker. As she walked, she kept wondering why her article was not in the paper. The newspaper was put together by students with the supervision of an English teacher, Mr. Kline. Damaras started thinking that maybe one of the editors had not liked her story. Maybe Mr. Kline had not thought that her story was well written. Damaras saw her friend Anna down the hall and quickly reversed directions. She did not know what to tell Anna or anybody else if they asked why her story was not in the paper. She dreaded her English class because everyone there thought she was going to be published.

There were still ten minutes before school started, so Damaras sought out Mr. Kline in his classroom. He greeted Damaras warmly. "Ah, one of our fine reporters!" Damaras could not smile back. She was thinking she should offer to quit the school paper, because they did not like her work. Finally, she asked, "Why didn't my story make the paper? I worked really hard to research and write it."
Mr. Kline looked surprised. "Of course it made the paper," he said. "We all loved it. We're running it as the lead story of next week's paper."
Damaras looked confused. "Next week's paper? I thought I submitted it for this week's issue."
Mr. Kline then reminded Damaras that production time for the paper made it necessary to submit articles at least one week before the issue in which they were scheduled to appear. Damaras had been so excited to see her story in the paper, she had confused the publishing schedule!
"Oh no!" Damaras laughed, relieved to hear they liked her work. "Now how will I explain that to everybody?"

School Reporter *(cont.)*

Directions: After reading the story, answer the questions. Circle the letter before each correct answer.

1. **What does the phrase "She sat in on rehearsals" mean?**
   a. Damaras sat on the stage during the rehearsals.
   b. Damaras watched the rehearsals for the play.
   c. Damaras wrote about the play rehearsals.
   d. Damaras tried out for the play during rehearsals.

2. **Why did Damaras think that her article would be running in this week's issue of the newspaper?**
   a. She knew that she was the best writer in the school.
   b. The school play was going to be over by next week's issue.
   c. New reporters always wrote an article during their first week.
   d. She submitted the article before this week's issue was published.

3. **Which of these explains what Mr. Kline probably meant when he said upon seeing Damaras, "Ah, one of our fine reporters!"?**
   a. He was complimenting Damaras for writing a good article for the paper.
   b. He was being sarcastic because Damaras had missed the deadline.
   c. He was trying to make Damaras feel good since her article was not in the paper.
   d. He was talking to somebody else who was in the room at the same time.

4. **According to your answer for Number 3, how might Mr. Kline describe Damaras?**
   a. eager
   b. disorganized
   c. conceited
   d. careful

5. **Part of the humor in this story is the fact that the news of Damaras's newspaper article spreads quickly around the school. Choose the action which best demonstrates this event.**
   a. The whole English class talked about being part of the school newspaper.
   b. Damaras interviewed Mr. Clausen, the director of the school play, for her article.
   c. Jeff asked Damaras if she is going to be a newspaper reporter when she grows up.
   d. Jeff heard about Damaras's article from Troy, who overheard Damaras and Anna talking.

6. **Which of these sounds most like something that Damaras would do?**
   a. Damaras takes credit for the school cafeteria article.
   b. Damaras argues with Mr. Kline for not publishing her article.
   c. Damaras does not confuse the deadlines for the newspaper again.
   d. Damaras writes a story without doing research.

Poetry: This is Me!

Phrase poetry can describe an item or person without using complete sentences! Write a phrase poem using the example poem as a guide. End your phrase poem with a word that describes the subject of the poem.

Morgan
Rides a bike
loves spaghetti
chats on the phone
hits the tennis ball
loves babies
Alive!

Subject:

Phrase 1 ______________________________

Phrase 2 ______________________________

Phrase 3 ______________________________

Phrase 4 ______________________________

Phrase 5 ______________________________

One Word: ______________

I Am What I Am

Fill in the blanks below and you will have a poem about the person you know best—you!

I am ______________________________

And ______________________________

But I am not ______________________________

Or ______________________________

I like ______________________________

And ______________________________

But I don't like ______________________________

Or ______________________________

I feel ______________________________

But I don't feel ______________________________

Poetry Patterns

Alphabet

by Jima Dunigan — by ____________________

Carefree	____________________
Dolphins	____________________
Even	____________________
Flip	____________________
Gracefully	____________________

Acrostic

by Jima Dunigan — by ____________________

Fierce	**C** ____________________
Righteous	**O** ____________________
Energetic	**O** ____________________
Dude	**L** ____________________

Concrete

(special shape or design)

by Jima Dunigan — by ____________________

Dizzy LEAVES FALL

to the ground.

Quatrain

(four-line stanza with rhyming lines)

Ghost Town
by Jima Dunigan

Not far west of Wyoming there lies
A little town that men despise.
The streets that once glittered with gold
Now are barren, dusty and cold.

____
by
____
____
____
____

Definition

(not necessary to rhyme, any length)

Friendship	**Homework**	**Caterpillar**	____________________
by Jima Dunigan	by Jima Dunigan	by Jima Dunigan	by
fun	hard	crawly	____________________
laughing	tedious	creepy	____________________
work	boring	leggy	____________________
entertaining	learning	long	____________________
company	mastering	fuzzy	____________________
forever	confidence	frightening	____________________

Poetry Patterns *(cont.)*

Cinquain (five lines)

One-word title	**Blankets** by Jima Dunigan	**Soup** by ________________
Two describing words	Snuggly, soft	________________
Three action words	Heating, comforting, cuddling	________________
Four feeling words	Warming body and soul	________________
One synonym for the title	Comforter	________________

Limerick (five lines)

	Boy from Rome by Jima Dunigan	**Girl from Spain** by ________________
Lines 1, 2, 5 rhyme	There once was a boy from Rome	________________
	Who could not find a home.	________________
Lines 3, 4 rhyme	He searched and he tried	________________
	'Til he found a bride.	________________
	They made a home of their own.	________________

Haiku

(three lines giving a general impression)

	Footprints by Jima Dunigan	____________ by ____________
Line 1—five syllables	See the red berries	____________
Line 2—seven syllables	fallen like little footprints	____________
Line 3—five syllables	on the garden snow.	____________.

5 Ws

	My Dog by Jima Dunigan	**Please Write** by Jima Dunigan	**My Friend** by ____________
Who:	My dog	Teacher	My friend
What:	curls up	says write	____________
When:	every night	each day	____________
Where:	on my bed	in school	____________
Why:	because I let him.	to master the art.	____________

Autobiographical Writing

Write a personal history of your life so far. Use the framework below to help you orginize your information.

My Memories

Hi! My name is ______________________________

I was born in ____

A funny story about me is ____

____

____

When I was a baby, I used to play with ____

____

____

This year, I want to learn how to ____

____

____

Some of my friends are____

____

____

My favorite foods are ____

____

____

My pets are ____

____

____

Some of my talents include ____

____

____

Something that I like about me is____

____

____

Autobiography/Biography Planner

Auto = self *Bio* = life *Graph* = write or draw

Choose a person for whom you wish to write a biography. He or she can be a famous person with materials and research available, or someone you know. It may be you. If you choose to write about yourself, it is an autobiography. Use the chronologically sequenced boxes below to create an autobiography or biography.

1. Birth

Name ______________________________
Boy ______________ Girl ___________
Date of birth ______________________
Length at birth_____________________
Weight at birth _____________________
Place of birth______________________
Mother____________________________
Father ____________________________
Sister _____________________________
Brother ____________________________

2. Firsts

First Word __________________________
First Birthday _______________________
____
____
____
____

3. Relatives

____
____
____
____
____
____
____

4. Preschool Experiences

____
____
____
____
____
____
____

5. Kindergarten

____
____
____
____
____
____
____

6. Grade-One Experiences

____
____
____
____
____
____
____

(For more, continue on the back of this page.)

Example of a Business Letter

Directions: Read the sample business letter below. Use this example to help you write your own letter on the next page.

3122 East Broadway Street
Regina, SK S7X 4Y6
January 11, 2007

Ms. Alice Christfield, Editor
The Town Crier
2119 South Main Street
Regina, SK S7X 4Y6

Dear Ms. Christfield:

I am a student at the Winstone Academy School, and I am concerned about a particular issue in our community. Every time I go to Rockfield Park, the community playground, there is trash all over the grass surrounding the play area. Whenever I go to the park, there are fast-food wrappers, empty soda cans, napkins, and plastic cups scattered on the ground. I would like to appeal to the citizens of our town and ask them to clean up when they leave the park.

There are many reasons to clean our community playground. First, if we don't clean up, we could attract wild animals like foxes and opossums to the playground. This could make the play area unsafe for small children. Second, if we don't clean up, the police or other town officials may come to clean up. This may mean they will need to add personnel to their staff and eventually our taxes will go up. Finally, if we don't clean up, our town will get a reputation as a messy town. When visitors come, they will think that we don't take pride in our community. I don't think we want to send that message.

My request is simple. If you use the community park, clean up your trash. There are trashcans next to the picnic area and next to the play area. If you get to the park and there is trash on the ground, take a few moments with your family to clean it up. We all need to work together on this, so that after awhile the park is always clean and no one will accept trash on the ground.

Ms. Christfield, thank you in advance for printing my message in *The Town Crier*.

Sincerely,

Anna Wintergate

Anna Wintergate

Business Letter Frame

Directions: Use this writing frame to write the rough draft of your business letter. Be certain to include the heading, inside address, greeting, body, closing, and signature.

____

____

____

____

____

____

____

Dear ______________________________:

____

____

____

____

____

____

____

____

____

____

____

____

____

Sincerely,

____

____

Narrative Paragraph

One kind of paragraph is called *narrative*. A narrative paragraph gives the details of an experience or event in story form. It explains what happens in a natural time order. You have probably written a narrative paragraph before, but you just didn't know what to call it. You have definitely spoken a narrative paragraph. On the first day of school, you probably went home and told someone all about it in chronological order. In each of the paragraphs below, choose one of the main ideas in parentheses or use one of your own. Use another piece of paper if you need more room.

The first time I ever (*rode a bike*, *cooked*, *baby-sat)* was a total disaster.

First, ____

____

Next, ____

____

Then, ____

____

Finally, ____

____

I had never been (*more embarrassed, more angry, more excited*) in my life!

____

____

____

____

On (*my first day at school, my last birthday, my last vacation*), I

____

____

____

____

Narrative Writing Questionnaire

Plan a narrative about a personal experience. Answer these questions to help you write a personal narrative.

Event: ____

Where did the event take place?

____

Who was with you?

____

What happened? Describe it in detail.

____

____

____

____

What happened that was exciting, scary, funny, or interesting?

____

____

____

How did the experience end?

____

____

How did you feel at the end?

____

____

____

Story Map

Use this story map to help you plan a narrative story. Follow the arrows to the next step.

Setting (where and when the story takes place)

Characters (people/animals in the story)

Conflict/Problem (What is wrong in the story?)

Action/Events (What happens?)

Resolution (How does the story end?)

Expository Paragraph Model

Automobiles are expensive to own. After buying a car you have to have money for insurance that the law says you must have in case of an accident. Cars, even new ones, need occasional costly repairs. Even if you drive carefully, you will sometimes make mistakes and might get a ticket, which you must pay for or your license will be taken away. Even if you never get in an accident or get a ticket, you have to fill the car with gas, and prices are at an all-time high.

- Why is the topic sentence a good one? ____________________
- Do the supporting sentences explain the controlling idea? ____________________
- Are all the sentences related? ____________________
- Underline your choice of the following for a concluding sentence to this paragraph.
  1. Owning a car will cost the owner plenty of money.
  2. Also, you could get in trouble driving without a license.
  3. Commercials on television tell you that you must have insurance.
- Why didn't you pick either of the other two? ____________________

Directions: Choose one of the following topics and write a clear expository paragraph.

1. fast-food restaurants
2. horror movies
3. any sport

____

____

____

____

____

____

____

Writing Expository Introductory Paragraphs

Below you will find several facts which could be used to open an essay. Your job is to write at least two more sentences for each. *The middle sentence(s) should give some examples* that can be used to support the first sentence. *The last sentence,* we know, *must state an opinion or attitude.* (You can change the sentences below if they do not serve your paragraph well.)

1. All schools can use improvement, and ours is no different.
2. Almost all students look forward to summer vacation.
3. Eating continuously at fast-food restaurants can cause problems.
4. Computer training is important for the future.

Use the space below to write one introductory paragraph.

Mixed-Up Stories

All stories need a *setting, characters, conflict*, and a *resolution*. Select one item from each group to use in a story. You can add other characters, settings, objects, and situations to your story.

A.	B.	C.	D.
a phone call	a playground	a child	a dog
an argument	a circus	a teacher	a jump rope
a letter	a classroom	a nurse	a purse
an accident	a swimming pool	a firefighter	a book

The Five-Paragraph Essay

Beginning: Start with an attention-getting device. The introductory sentence tells the main topic of the essay and names the three sub-topics. TR = use a transitional word. ¶ = indent for a new paragraph.

¶

Middle: Body paragraphs begin with a Who or What sentence. The next two boxes will tell When, Where, How, or Why. The last sentence of each paragraph is an example or incident sentence.

¶ Who or What is the subject?	¶ Who or What is the subject?	¶ Who or What is the subject?
When, Where, How, or Why	When, Where, How, or Why	When, Where, How, or Why
When, Where, How, or Why	When, Where, How, or Why	When, Where, How, or Why
Example or Incident (little story)	Example or Incident (little story)	Example or Incident (little story)

Ending: The conclusion paragraph (1) summarizes, (2) re-states the main topic, or (3) comes to a conclusion based on the evidence presented. The concluding paragraph lets the reader know the essay is finished.

¶

Generic Essay Writing Frame

Introductory Paragraph

(Introduces the topic and sub-topic ideas—minimum 30 words.)

Body

(Body paragraph one gives details about the first sub-topic—minimum 75 words.)

Generic Essay Writing Frame *(cont.)*

Body *(cont.)*

(Body paragraph two gives details about the second sub-topic—minimum 75 words.)

(Body paragraph three gives details about the third sub-topic—minimum 75 words.)

Conclusion

(The conclusion summarizes the ideas of the essay or draws a conclusion point based on the information presented within the essay—minimum 30 words.)

Adding Signed Numbers

Sample

–4 + +5 ——— +1	Step 1: Start at 0. Step 2: Go left 4 spaces for –4. Step 3: From –4, go right 5 spaces. Step 4: Answer = +1

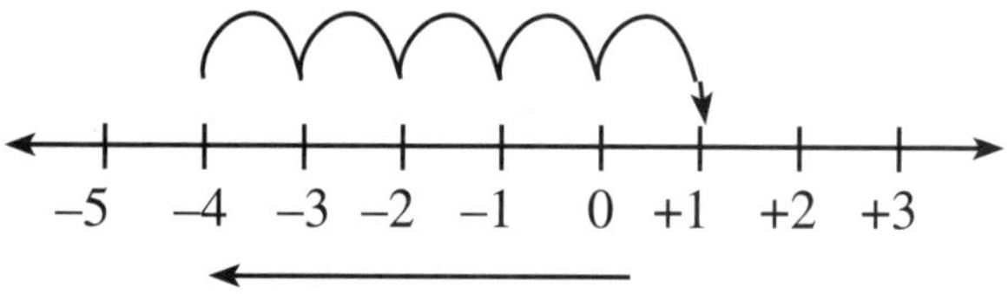

Directions: Use a long strip of paper to make a longer number line to help you. Complete the strip to positive 25 (+25) and to negative 25 (–25). Use your number line to help you solve these addition problems. Remember, always start at zero (0) when adding on the number line.

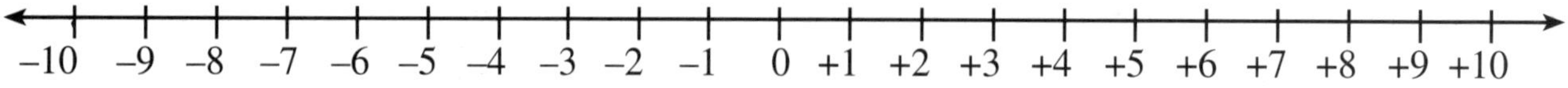

1. –4 + –6 =

2. –6 + –2 =

3. +3 + +4 =

4. –9 + –7 =

5. –12 + –9 =

6. –16 + –8 =

7. –23 + +10 =

8. +24 + –14 =

9. +18 + –16 =

10. –25 + +12 =

11. +13 + –19 =

12. –19 + +17 =

13. +20 + –13 =

14. –7 + –17 =

15. –13 + +9 =

16. –11 + –12 =

17. +15 + +10 =

18. –18 + +15 =

19. –18 + –7 =

20. +5 + –20 =

21. +6 + –27 =

Adding Signed Numbers *(cont.)*

To add numbers with the *same* sign, add the numbers and keep the sign.

$$\begin{array}{r} +23 \\ + \; +14 \\ \hline +37 \end{array} \qquad \begin{array}{r} -40 \\ + \; -15 \\ \hline -55 \end{array}$$

To add numbers with *different* signs, subtract the number with the smaller absolute value from the number with the larger absolute value. Then use the sign of the number with the higher absolute value.

$$\begin{array}{r} +40 \\ + \; -20 \\ \hline +20 \end{array} \qquad \begin{array}{r} -70 \\ + \; +35 \\ \hline -35 \end{array} \qquad \begin{array}{r} +80 \\ + \; -40 \\ \hline +40 \end{array}$$

Directions: Use a number line to help you check your work. The first one is done for you.

1. $\begin{array}{r} +25 \\ + \; -19 \\ \hline +6 \end{array}$

2. $\begin{array}{r} +19 \\ + \; -23 \\ \hline \end{array}$

3. $\begin{array}{r} +23 \\ + \; -7 \\ \hline \end{array}$

4. $\begin{array}{r} -34 \\ + \; -25 \\ \hline \end{array}$

5. $\begin{array}{r} +56 \\ + \; -45 \\ \hline \end{array}$

6. $\begin{array}{r} -67 \\ + \; +54 \\ \hline \end{array}$

7. $\begin{array}{r} -98 \\ + \; +76 \\ \hline \end{array}$

8. $\begin{array}{r} +76 \\ + \; -45 \\ \hline \end{array}$

9. $\begin{array}{r} +76 \\ + \; -99 \\ \hline \end{array}$

10. $\begin{array}{r} -100 \\ + \; +78 \\ \hline \end{array}$

11. $\begin{array}{r} +124 \\ + \; -145 \\ \hline \end{array}$

12. $\begin{array}{r} +200 \\ + \; -234 \\ \hline \end{array}$

13. $\begin{array}{r} -99 \\ + \; -11 \\ \hline \end{array}$

14. $\begin{array}{r} -231 \\ + \; +199 \\ \hline \end{array}$

15. $\begin{array}{r} +145 \\ + \; -201 \\ \hline \end{array}$

16. $\begin{array}{r} -238 \\ + \; +198 \\ \hline \end{array}$

17. $\begin{array}{r} +900 \\ + \; -450 \\ \hline \end{array}$

18. $\begin{array}{r} -456 \\ + \; -123 \\ \hline \end{array}$

19. $\begin{array}{r} +932 \\ + \; -756 \\ \hline \end{array}$

20. $\begin{array}{r} -1000 \\ + \; +999 \\ \hline \end{array}$

21. $\begin{array}{r} +789 \\ + \; -987 \\ \hline \end{array}$

Adding and Subtracting Integers

Directions: Solve each problem. Use the letters next to the problems to solve the riddle at the bottom of the page. Many letters will be used more than once while other letters will not be used at all.

H. 7 + (-5) = ______

Q. -8 + 4 = ______

D. 4 + (-6) = ______

B. -15 + (-3) = ______

F. -28 + 28 = ______

G. |-9| – |2| = ______

O. 6 + -9 = ______

W. -7 + -8 = ______

K. -2 + (-4) = ______

Q. -7 – (-3) = ______

X. -15 + (-6) = ______

S. -19 – (-18) = ______

A. 7 – 16 = ______

V. -2 – (-8) = ______

U. 8 – (-3) = ______

E. -9 + (-7) = ______

Y. -2 + 7 = ______

J. -18 + (-3) = ______

Z. (6 - 2) – (-4) = ______

N. 6 - [2 - (-3)] = ______

M. 6 + [2 - (-4)] = ______

I. 10 + 22 + (-7) + (-30) = ______

P. -31 + 62 + (-9) = ______

T. 9 + 24 + (-5) + (-25) = ______

R. -5 + -6 + -9 = ______

L. |-20| + |-19| - 2 = ______

C. 5 x 3 – (8 – 6) = ______

Riddle: Why did the dentist decide to join the army?

___ ___   ___ ___ ___ ___ ___ ___ ___
2 -16   3 2 -3 11 -11 2 3

___ ___   ___ ___ ___ ___ ___
2 -16   -15 -3 11 -41 -2

___ ___   ___   ___ ___ ___ ___
-18 -16   -9   -11 -3 -3 -2

___ ___ ___ ___ ___
-2 -20 -5 -41 -41

___ ___ ___ ___ ___ ___ ___ ___.
-1 -16 -20 -11 -16 -9 1 3

Evaluations Exponents

Reminder

- To determine the value of a term with an exponent of 2, multiply the base times itself.

  $6^2 = 6 \times 6 = 36$

- To determine the value of a term with an exponent of 3, multiply the base times itself. Multiply that answer times the base again.

  $\mathbf{4^3 = 4 \times 4 \times 4 = 16 \times 4 = 64}$

Directions: Evaluate these expressions by determining the value of the exponents. The first one is done for you.

1. 6^2
   $6 \times 6 = 36$
   36
2. 3^2 ______
3. 5^2 ______
4. 2^2 ______
5. 10^2 ______
6. 11^2 ______
7. 5^3 ______
8. 6^3 ______
9. 9^2 ______
10. 8^3 ______
11. 7^2 ______
12. 10^3 ______
13. 7^3 ______
14. 13^2 ______
15. 2^3 ______
16. 3^4 ______
17. 2^4 ______
18. 9^3 ______
19. 5^3 ______
20. 2^5 ______
21. 14^2 ______
22. 1^3 ______
23. 15^2 ______
24. 20^2 ______
25. 30^2 ______
26. 40^2 ______
27. 50^2 ______

Multiplying with Exponents

A number multiplied by itself can be written as an exponent.

The **exponent** tells how many times to multiply the base number by itself.

5^2 is "5 squared" or "5 to the second power."

$5^2 = 25$

5^3 is "5 cubed" or "5 to the third power."

$5^3 = 5 \times 5 \times 5$

$5 \times 5 = 25$

$25 \times 5 = 125$

$5^3 = 125$

Directions: For each of the terms below, write an equation and solve it. The first one is done for you.

1. 3^2 __3__ x __3__ = __9__

2. 7^2 ______ x ______ = ______

3. 4^2 ______ x ______ = ______

4. 9^2 ______ x ______ = ______

5. 2^2 ______ x ______ = ______

6. 8^2 ______ x ______ = ______

7. 10^2 ______ x ______ = ______

8. 6^2 ______ x ______ = ______

9. 11^2 ______ x ______ = ______

10. 12^2 ______ x ______ = ______

Directions: For each of the terms below, write two equations and solve them. The first one is done for you.

11. 2^3 __2__ x __2__ = __4__

__4__ x __2__ = __8__

2^3 = __8__

12. 3^3 ______ x ______ = ______

______ x ______ = ______

3^3 = ______

13. 5^3 ______ x ______ = ______

______ x ______ = ______

5^3 = ______

14. 7^3 ______ x ______ = ______

______ x ______ = ______

7^3 = ______

15. 4^3 ______ x ______ = ______

______ x ______ = ______

4^3 = ______

16. 6^3 ______ x ______ = ______

______ x ______ = ______

6^3 = ______

17. 10^3 ______ x ______ = ______

______ x ______ = ______

10^3 = ______

18. 9^3 ______ x ______ = ______

______ x ______ = ______

9^3 = ______

19. 11^3 ______ x ______ = ______

______ x ______ = ______

11^3 = ______

20. 12^3 ______ x ______ = ______

______ x ______ = ______

12^3 = ______

Multiplying with Signed Numbers

Directions: Compute the positive and negative values indicated in the problems below.

Reminders

- A negative times a negative is a positive.
- A positive times a negative is a negative.
- A negative divided by a negative is a positive.
- A positive divided by a negative is a negative.
- A negative divided by a positive is a negative.

1. Jill owes $4 to Jennifer, $4 to Michelle, and $4 to Eileen. How much does she owe altogether? ________________

2. Joey owes $5 to 4 different friends. How much money does he owe altogether? ________________

3. What is the product of $^{-}7$ and $^{-}6$? ________________

4. The total bill at a restaurant was $49 to be split evenly among 7 friends. How much money did each friend owe? ________________

5. How much is $^{-}81$ divided by 9? ________________

6. How much is $^{-}100$ divided by $^{-}10$? ________________

7. A group of 18 patrons each owe $15 at a restaurant. What is the total amount owed by all 18 customers? ________________

8. What is the product of $^{-}12$ and $^{-}13$? ________________

9. How much is $^{-}16$ times 4? ________________

10. What is the quotient when $^{-}45$ is divided by $^{-}9$? ________________

11. A group of 15 teenagers owes $75 at a pizza parlor. If they split the bill evenly, how much will each person owe? ________________

12. How much is $^{-}200$ divided by $^{-}10$? ________________

Multiplying by Using the Commutative Property

In multiplication the order of the factors does not affect the answer.

Examples

5 x 8	=	**8 x 5**	**90 x 60**	=	**60 x 90**
↓		↓	↓		↓
5 x 8 = 40	*(or)*	**8 x 5 = 40**	**90 x 60 = 5,400**	*(or)*	**60 x 90 = 5,400**

Remember, a x b = b x a.

Directions: Use the information above to solve these multiplication problems.

1. 9 x 8	**2.** 8 x 9	**3.** 7 x 6	**4.** 6 x 7	**5.** 10 x 8	**6.** 8 x 10
7. 10 x 17	**8.** 17 x 10	**9.** 19 x 10	**10.** 10 x 19	**11.** 20 x 30	**12.** 30 x 20
13. 50 x 40	**14.** 40 x 50	**15.** 80 x 60	**16.** 60 x 80	**17.** 40 x 70	**18.** 70 x 40
19. 90 x 30	**20.** 30 x 90	**21.** 60 x 70	**22.** 70 x 60	**23.** 75 x 55	**24.** 55 x 75
25. 45 x 25	**26.** 25 x 45	**27.** 23 x 67	**28.** 67 x 23	**29.** 42 x 17	**30.** 17 x 42

Multiplying by Using the Associative Property

In multiplication the factors may be grouped in any order. The answer will be the same.

Example

5 x (6 x 7) = (5 x 6) x 7

5 x (6 x 7) = 210 **(or)** **(5 x 6) x 7 = 210**

Remember, a x (b x c) = (a x b) x c.

Directions: Use the information above to help you solve these multiplication problems.

1. 7 x (8 x 9) = ______________

2. (7 x 8) x 9 = ______________

3. 6 x (5 x 10) = ______________

4. (6 x 5) x 10 = ______________

5. (12 x 10) x 5 = ______________

6. 12 x (10 x 5) = ______________

7. (10 x 20) x 30 = ______________

8. 10 x (20 x 30) = ______________

9. 20 x (50 x 80) = ______________

10. (20 x 50) x 80 = ______________

11. (90 x 80) x 25 = ______________

12. 90 x (80 x 25) = ______________

13. 15 x (25 x 10) = ______________

14. (15 x 25) x 10 = ______________

15. (25 x 41) x 12 = ______________

16. 25 x (41 x 12) = ______________

17. (25 x 15) x (44 x 23) = ______________

18. 25 x (15 x 44) x 23 = ______________

19. (44 x 14) x (33 x 13) = ______________

20. 44 x (14 x 33) x 13 = ______________

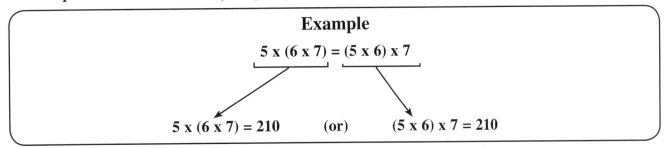

Using Two-Digit Multipliers with Three-Digit Multiplicands

Step by Step

1. Multiply 409 times 8, which equals 3,272.
2. Place an automatic zero (placeholder) in the ones place when multiplying 409 times 3 (tens), which equals 12,270.
3. Add the two partial products (3,272 + 12,270 = 15,542). Don't forget to add a comma every three digits starting from the ones place.

$$\begin{array}{r} \mathbf{409} \\ \underline{\mathbf{x\ \ 38}} \\ \mathbf{3,272} \\ \underline{\mathbf{+\ 12,270}} \\ \mathbf{15,542} \end{array}$$

Directions: Use the information above to help solve the problems on this page. The first one is done for you.

1. $\begin{array}{r} 507 \\ \underline{\text{x } 37} \\ 3,549 \\ \underline{+\ 15,210} \\ 18,759 \end{array}$

2. $\begin{array}{r} 609 \\ \underline{\text{x } 58} \end{array}$

3. $\begin{array}{r} 706 \\ \underline{\text{x } 76} \end{array}$

4. $\begin{array}{r} 108 \\ \underline{\text{x } 25} \end{array}$

5. $\begin{array}{r} 607 \\ \underline{\text{x } 45} \end{array}$

6. $\begin{array}{r} 304 \\ \underline{\text{x } 39} \end{array}$

7. $\begin{array}{r} 107 \\ \underline{\text{x } 98} \end{array}$

8. $\begin{array}{r} 509 \\ \underline{\text{x } 76} \end{array}$

9. $\begin{array}{r} 608 \\ \underline{\text{x } 88} \end{array}$

10. $\begin{array}{r} 706 \\ \underline{\text{x } 99} \end{array}$

11. $\begin{array}{r} 405 \\ \underline{\text{x } 55} \end{array}$

12. $\begin{array}{r} 407 \\ \underline{\text{x } 66} \end{array}$

13. $\begin{array}{r} 231 \\ \underline{\text{x } 78} \end{array}$

14. $\begin{array}{r} 289 \\ \underline{\text{x } 65} \end{array}$

15. $\begin{array}{r} 578 \\ \underline{\text{x } 93} \end{array}$

16. $\begin{array}{r} 374 \\ \underline{\text{x } 69} \end{array}$

Multiplying Decimals

Keys to Multiplying Decimals

- Line up the numbers. You don't need to line up the decimal points, however.
- Multiply the numbers as you would multiply whole numbers.
- Count the number of decimal places in both numbers that are being multiplied. Make sure the decimal places in the product equal the number of decimal places in the problem.

Directions: Multiply to solve each problem.

1. $46.98 x 2

2. $1.49 x 3

3. $21.06 x 5

4. $9.99 x 7

5. $1.57 x 34

6. $105.13 x 4

7. $45.03 x 13

8. $17.10 x 15

9. 0.84 x 3.15

10. 2.08 x 0.9

11. 0.28 x 9.51

12. 0.0076 x 0.30

13. $10.50 x 0.60

14. 47.8 x 0.1

15. 14.2 x 9.7

16. $5.75 x 0.24

17. $5.58 x 1.5

18. 0.14 x 0.87

Using One-Digit Divisors with Two-Digit Dividends

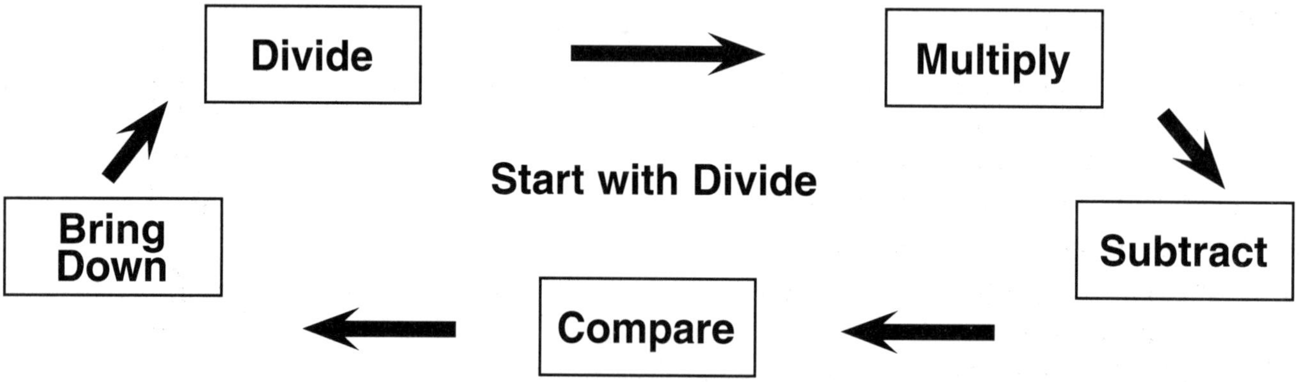

Directions: Solve the division problems below. The first one is done for you.

1. 7)78 = 11 R1
   - 78 − 7 = 0 (bring down 8) → 08
   - 08 − 7 = 1
2. 5)84
3. 2)26
4. 6)67
5. 3)86
6. 4)99
7. 9)81
8. 1)34
9. 6)78
10. 9)96
11. 5)56
12. 4)57
13. 2)33
14. 3)56
15. 8)90
16. 4)67
17. 1)23
18. 7)46
19. 5)44
20. 6)56
21. 9)90
22. 7)35
23. 3)38
24. 4)87
25. 2)47

Dividing with Two-Digit Divisors

Follow these steps when solving long division problems:

Sample

1. Because the first digit (6) in the dividend cannot be divided by 12, divide 66 by 12. The closest multiple of 12 to 66 is 12 x 5 = 60. Place 5 in the quotient.
2. Multiply 12 x 5 and write the number 60 below 66.
3. Subtract 60 from 66. The answer is 6.
4. Because the number 6 is less than the divisor 12, bring down the 0 and divide 60 by 12.
5. Multiply 12 x 5. The answer is 60. Place 5 in the qoutient.
6. Subtract 60 from 60. The final answer is 55.

$$\begin{array}{r} \text{x55} \\ 12\overline{)660} \\ -60\downarrow \\ \hline 60 \\ -60 \\ \hline 0 \end{array}$$

Directions: Use the sample above to help you do these problems. The first one is done for you.

1.

$$\begin{array}{r} \text{x21 R17} \\ 22\overline{)479} \\ -44\downarrow \\ \hline 39 \\ -22 \\ \hline 17 \end{array}$$

2. $31\overline{)975}$

3. $23\overline{)748}$

4. $21\overline{)661}$

5. $33\overline{)497}$

6. $41\overline{)453}$

7. $21\overline{)887}$

8. $33\overline{)715}$

9. $22\overline{)519}$

10. $31\overline{)428}$

11. $24\overline{)534}$

12. $22\overline{)721}$

Dividing and Multiplying

Directions: Write the division problem and solve. Multiply to check the answer. The first one is done for you.

1. 8,400 cookies divided into 40 boxes **Check:** $40\overline{)8400}$ = 210 − 80 40 − 40 00 210 x 40 000 +8,400 8,400	**2.** 41,916 pieces of bubble gum divided into 28 cartons **Check:**	**3.** 33,320 decks of playing cards divided into 136 cases **Check:**
4. 3,600 marbles placed into 90 pouches **Check:**	**5.** 8,928 potato chips placed into 9 gigantic bowls **Check:**	**6.** 28,917 game pieces for 81 board games **Check:**
7. 35,620 paper clips placed into 260 canisters **Check:**	**8.** 180,930 ants in 37 colonies **Check:**	**9.** 8,840 peanuts for 65 elephants **Check:**

Decimals: Multiplication and Division

Sweet Buggy Bites is a company that creates unusual kinds of candy. They make chocolate-covered ants, grasshopper kisses, sweet 'n' sour crickets, beetle bites, and other candy-coated bugs. Use your knowledge of multiplication and division with decimals to compute these answers.

Reminders

- Count all of the places to the right of the decimal in the multiplication problems and have the same number of places to the right of the decimal in the answer.
- If the divisor has a decimal, move it to the right of the divisor and move the decimal in the dividend the same number of places to the right.

Example: 3.1 x 0.4 = 1.24

Example: $.12\overline{)24.36}$ to $12.\overline{)2436.}$ (quotient: 203)

1. A bag of beetle bites weighs 1.47 kg. There are 7 candies in each bag. How much does each bite weigh? ________________
2. A box of chocolate-coated ants weighs 8.35 grams. How much do 12 boxes weigh? __________
3. A bag of sweet 'n' sour crickets weighs 9.81 grams and holds 9 candies. How much does each candy weigh? ________________
4. A large box of grasshopper kisses weighs 18.36 grams. Each candy weighs 1.8 grams. How many candies are in the box? ________________
5. A super-sized bag of beetle bites weighs 2.255 kg. What is the weight of 20 bags? ________________
6. A mini-box of chocolate-covered ants weighs 4.025 grams. Each ant weighs .05 grams. How many chocolate-covered ants are in each box? ________________
7. A large box of sweet 'n' sour crickets weighs 13.467 grams. How much do 72 boxes weigh? ________________
8. A regular box of grasshopper kisses costs $4.83 for 21 candies. What is the cost for each candy? ________________
9. A regular box of sweet 'n' sour crickets costs $9.50 for 25 candied crickets. What is the cost for each cricket? ________________
10. A box of beetle bites weighs 1.095 kg. How much does a carton of 144 boxes weigh? ________

Dividing Decimals

Directions: Solve the division problems. Round to the nearest hundredth.

1. $\frac{.7}{.14} =$

2. $\frac{6}{43.2} =$

3. $\frac{4}{.3704} =$

4. $\frac{3}{.0048} =$

5. $\frac{.8}{60} =$

6. $\frac{9.2}{230} =$

7. $\frac{.8}{27.2} =$

8. $\frac{\$30}{.04} =$

9. $\frac{\$42}{.24} =$

10. $\$65 \div \frac{4}{5} =$

11. $\frac{45.6}{8} =$

12. $\frac{.258}{6} =$

13. $\frac{3.43}{.7} =$

14. $\frac{7.2}{.09} =$

15. $\frac{60}{1.2}$

Directions: Change each decimal to a fraction or a mixed number. Reduce to the lowest terms.

16. .35 =

17. .064 =

18. 3.4 =

19. 3.125 =

20. 18.33 =

21. 4.625 =

22. .0084 =

23. 66.75 =

24. .318 =

25. .0625 =

26. 4.25 =

27. 1.10 =

Directions: Change each fraction to a decimal. Round to the nearest hundredth.

28. $\frac{4}{5} =$

29. $\frac{3}{8} =$

30. $\frac{2}{3} =$

31. $\frac{7}{9} =$

32. $\frac{5}{6} =$

33. $\frac{5}{8} =$

34. $\frac{1}{3} =$

35. $\frac{7}{10} =$

Using Square Roots

The **square root** of a number is another number that multiplied by itself will equal the first number.

The square root of 9 is 3 because 3 x 3 = 9.

This radical symbol $\sqrt{}$ indicates that you need to find the square root.

$$\sqrt{25} = 5 \qquad \sqrt{36} = 6$$

Directions: Use the samples above to help solve these problems. Use a calculator to help you check the answers on the more difficult problems.

1. $\sqrt{4}$ = _______
2. $\sqrt{16}$ = _______
3. $\sqrt{49}$ = _______
4. $\sqrt{81}$ = _______
5. $\sqrt{100}$ = _______
6. $\sqrt{64}$ = _______
7. $\sqrt{121}$ = _______
8. $\sqrt{144}$ = _______
9. $\sqrt{169}$ = _______
10. $\sqrt{225}$ = _______
11. $\sqrt{196}$ = _______
12. $\sqrt{400}$ = _______
13. $\sqrt{900}$ = _______
14. $\sqrt{4{,}900}$ = _______
15. $\sqrt{6{,}400}$ = _______
16. $\sqrt{1{,}600}$ = _______
17. $\sqrt{490{,}000}$ = _______
18. $\sqrt{640{,}000}$ = _______
19. $\sqrt{160{,}000}$ = _______
20. $\sqrt{810{,}000}$ = _______
21. $\sqrt{250{,}000}$ = _______
22. $\sqrt{90{,}000}$ = _______
23. $\sqrt{360{,}000}$ = _______
24. $\sqrt{10{,}000}$ = _______
25. $\sqrt{9{,}000{,}000}$ = _______
26. $\sqrt{81{,}000{,}000}$ = _______
27. $\sqrt{25{,}000{,}000}$ = _______
28. $\sqrt{36{,}000{,}000}$ = _______
29. $\sqrt{49{,}000{,}000}$ = _______
30. $\sqrt{64{,}000{,}000}$ = _______

Calculating Square Roots

A number multiplied by itself is *squared*. Look at the examples below. The number 3 squared is 9. The square root of 9 is 3. The number 4 squared is 16. The square root of 16 is 4.

$3^2 = 3 \times 3 = 9$ $\quad$ $4^2 = 4 \times 4 = 16$

$\sqrt{9} = 3$ $\quad$ $\sqrt{16} = 4$

Directions: Use your knowledge of multiplication facts to calculate the square root of each of the following problems.

1. $\sqrt{16}$ = _____ **2.** $\sqrt{36}$ = _____ **3.** $\sqrt{144}$ = _____ **4.** $\sqrt{25}$ = _____

5. $\sqrt{64}$ = _____ **6.** $\sqrt{81}$ = _____ **7.** $\sqrt{121}$ = _____ **8.** $\sqrt{1}$ = _____

9. $\sqrt{9}$ = _____ **10.** $\sqrt{100}$ = _____ **11.** $\sqrt{49}$ = _____ **12.** $\sqrt{4}$ = _____

You can calculate the square root of some very large numbers using your knowledge of the multiples of 10. For example, the square root of 100 is 10 because 10 times 10 equals 100. The square root of 10,000 is 100 because 100 times 100 equals 10,000. The square root of 1,000,000 is 1,000 because 1,000 times 1,000 equals 1,000,000. The square root of 3,600 is 60 because 60 times 60 equals 3,600.

Directions: Compute the square root of each of the numbers listed here. Look for a pattern. Check your answers with a calculator.

13. $\sqrt{2{,}500}$ = _____ **14.** $\sqrt{3{,}600}$ = _____ **15.** $\sqrt{400}$ = _____

16. $\sqrt{100}$ = _____ **17.** $\sqrt{6{,}400}$ = _____ **18.** $\sqrt{4{,}900}$ = _____

19. $\sqrt{900}$ = _____ **20.** $\sqrt{16{,}900}$ = _____ **21.** $\sqrt{8{,}100}$ = _____

22. $\sqrt{1{,}600}$ = _____ **23.** $\sqrt{14{,}400}$ = _____ **24.** $\sqrt{12{,}100}$ = _____

25. Describe the pattern you discovered.

____

Order of Operations

Reminder

Evaluate expressions in this order: PEMDAS

1. Parentheses: Do these operations first.
2. Exponents: Find these values next.
3. Multiply and Divide: In order from left to right.
4. Add and Subtract: In order from left to right.

Directions: Evaluate these expressions. Be sure to follow the order of operations listed above. The first one is done for you.

1. $4^2 + 9 - (3 \times 5)$
$4^2 + 9 - 15$
$16 + 9 - 15 = 10$
<u>10</u>

2. $6^2 - (9 \times 2) + 12$ ______

3. $10 + (8 \times 3) - 3^2$ ______

4. $(8 \times 8) - 4^3 + 1$ ______

5. $8^2 + (4 \times 5) - 21$ ______

6. $(9 \times 5) - 2^3 + 16$ ______

7. $15 \div 5 + 7 - 2^2$ ______

8. $(9 + 11) - 3^2 + 7$ ______

9. $(6 \times 5) - 14 - 4^2$ ______

10. $12^2 - 9 \times 12 - 4^2$ ______

11. $13^2 - (11 \times 9) + 16$ ______

12. $13 + (6 \times 8) - 5^2$ ______

13. $17 - (9 + 8) + 2^3$ ______

14. $9^2 - (27 + 13) - 6^2$ ______

15. $44 - 7 \times 6 + 4^2$ ______

PEMDAS: Easy Applications

The acronym for this order of operations is PEMDAS.

Parentheses **E**xponents **M**ultiplication **D**ivision **A**ddition **S**ubtraction

A popular expression for remembering this is **P**lease **E**xcuse **M**y **D**ear **A**unt **S**ally.

Directions: Find the numerical value of the following expressions using the correct order of operations.

1. 9 x 5 – 4 + 3 x 4 = _______

2. 12 + 8 x 6 ÷ 2 x 8 = _______

3. 3 + 6 x 8 – 5 x 2 = _______

4. 7 + 8 ÷ 4 + 3 – 2 = _______

5. 22 ÷ 11 + 12 – 3 = _______

6. 9 x 8 – 6 x 3 + 7 = _______

7. 13 + 5 x 6 ÷ 2 + 10 = _______

8. 35 ÷ 7 x 8 + 2 – 4 x 2 = ______

9. (100 ÷ 5) x 5 + 4 – 9 = ______

10. 88 ÷ 11 + 56 ÷ 8 + 12 – 5 = ______

Remember the following facts:

- The fraction bar (—) means division.
- The raised dot (•) means multiplication.
- Numbers written next to parenthesis or parentheses next to each other also require multiplication.

Directions: Find the numerical value of these expressions.

11. $5(8) - \frac{30}{5} + 4 \times 3 =$ _______

12. $(7)(9) + \frac{9}{3} - 20 \times 3 =$ _______

13. $8(9) + 10 \bullet 5 + 8 \bullet 2 =$ _______

14. $3 + 8 \bullet 10 - 13 \times 3 =$ _______

15. $17 + 5 - 6 \bullet 4 + \frac{12}{3} =$ _______

16. $9 + \frac{44}{4} - 8 \times 2 + 20 - 3 =$ _______

PEMDAS: Parentheses and Exponents

Sample

Read the problem.	$3 + (2 \times 4) - 2^2 + 3 = ?$
Do the work in the parentheses first.	$3 + 8 - 22 + 3 = ?$
Get the numerical value of the exponent next.	$3 + 8 - 4 + 3 = ?$
Add and subtract in order from left to right.	$11 - 4 + 3 = ?$
	$7 + 3 = ?$
Record your answer.	$3 + (2 \times 4) - 2^2 + 3 = 10$

Directions: Find the numerical value of each expression.

1. $(2 \times 3) + 3^2 - 5 \times 3 =$ ______

2. $10^2 - (3 \times 30) + 8 =$ ______

3. $4 + (2 \times 10) - 2^2 =$ ______

4. $8 + (5 \times 5) - 3^2 =$ ______

5. $4^2 - 13 + (12 \times 2) =$ ______

6. $7^2 + 3(2 \times 4) - 3 =$ ______

7. $3 + 5^2 - (12 + 3) =$ ______

8. $9 + 4^2 - (5 \times 5) + 2 =$ ______

9. $11 - 2^2 + (3 \times 2) - 4 =$ ______

10. $2(4 \times 5) + 3^2 - 2^2 =$ ______

11. $18 - (3 \times 4) + 5^2 - 2 =$ ______

12. $7(4 \times 2) - 4^2 + (2 \times 9) =$ ______

13. $10^2 - 3 \times 4 + (6 \times 4) - 5 =$ ______

14. $12^2 + 3 - 2(2 \times 4) - 5^2 + 11 =$ ______

15. $(15 + 7) \times 2 \times 3 - 6(4 \times 3) + 12 =$ ______

16. $(12 - 5) + (2 + 13) - 2^2 + 30 =$ ______

Adding and Subtracting Fractions

To add fractions with the same denominator, add the numerators and write the sum over the same denominator. To subtract fractions with the same denominator, subtract the numerators and write the difference over the same denominator. Always write the sum or difference in lowest terms.

1. $\frac{5}{6} - \frac{3}{6} =$ _____
2. $\frac{4}{7} + \frac{2}{7} =$ _____
3. $\frac{7}{12} - \frac{4}{12} =$ _____
4. $\frac{5}{16} + \frac{3}{16} =$ _____

To add or subtract fractions with different denominators, first write equivalent fractions with a common denominator. Then add or subtract. Write the sum or difference in lowest terms.

5. $\frac{3}{5} + \frac{2}{8} =$ _____
6. $\frac{3}{5} + \frac{5}{7} =$ _____
7. $\frac{7}{9} - \frac{1}{2} =$ _____
8. $\frac{4}{5} - \frac{3}{4} =$ _____

To add or subtract mixed numbers, determine if the fractions have to be changed to equivalent fractions. First change the fractions to equivalent fractions and then proceed with the addition or subtraction.

Sometimes the mixed number will have to be renamed. Change the whole number to a fraction equal to one and add it to the fraction portion, resulting in an improper fraction.

Proceed with the addition or subtraction. Write the sum or difference in lowest terms.

Directions: Add or subtract. Then write the answer in lowest terms.

9. $\frac{7}{10} - \frac{5}{10}$ _____
10. $\frac{3}{8} + \frac{5}{12}$ _____
11. $\frac{3}{4} - \frac{1}{5}$ _____
12. $\frac{5}{16} + \frac{3}{8}$ _____

13. $4\,{}^{3}/_{4} + 5\,{}^{5}/_{6}$ = ____________________

14. $9\,{}^{7}/_{8} - 6\,{}^{2}/_{4}$ = ____________________

15. $5\,{}^{2}/_{3} - 2\,{}^{4}/_{9}$ = ____________________

Adding and Subtracting Fractions

Directions: Compute the answers for these problems.

1. $\frac{2}{5} + \frac{1}{4} =$

2. $\frac{1}{4} + \frac{1}{2} =$

3. $\frac{3}{4} + \frac{1}{8} =$

4. $\frac{4}{6} - \frac{1}{2} =$

5. $\frac{7}{9} - \frac{1}{3} =$

6. $\frac{8}{12} + \frac{1}{4} =$

7. $\frac{5}{8} + \frac{1}{4} =$

8. $\frac{4}{5} + \frac{1}{10} =$

9. $\frac{5}{9} + \frac{1}{3} =$

10. $\frac{2}{5} + \frac{1}{3} =$

11. $\frac{11}{20} - \frac{2}{5} =$

12. $\frac{1}{8} + \frac{1}{6} =$

Directions: After adding or subtracting, be sure to simplify (reduce) your answers to these problems, if necessary.

13. $\frac{4}{7} + \frac{2}{3} =$

14. $\frac{5}{6} + \frac{5}{8} =$

15. $\frac{5}{9} + \frac{4}{6} =$

16. $\frac{5}{8} - \frac{5}{12} =$

17. $\frac{7}{9} - \frac{5}{12} =$

18. $\frac{4}{9} - \frac{2}{8} =$

19. $\frac{5}{6} + \frac{4}{7} =$

20. $\frac{4}{12} + \frac{7}{8} =$

21. $\frac{9}{10} - \frac{3}{4} =$

22. $\frac{7}{9} + \frac{3}{6} =$

23. $\frac{5}{10} + \frac{5}{12} =$

24. $\frac{11}{15} + \frac{1}{10} =$

Multiplying Fractions

Sample: $\frac{3}{4} \times \frac{1}{6} = ?$

Step 1 ⟶ Multiply the fractions. $\frac{3}{4} \times \frac{1}{6} = \frac{3}{24}$

Step 2 ⟶ Write the fraction in simplest form by dividing the numerator and denominator by the greatest common factor, which in this case is 3. $\frac{3 \div 3}{24 \div 3} = \frac{1}{8}$

Sample: $\frac{3}{5} \times \frac{10}{24} = \frac{\cancel{3}^{1}}{\cancel{5}_{1}} \times \frac{\cancel{10}^{2}}{\cancel{24}_{8}} = \frac{2}{8} = \frac{1}{4}$

Directions: Compute the answers to these problems. Remember to cancel whenever possible. Reduce answers to simplest terms.

1. $\frac{2}{9} \times \frac{3}{8} =$
2. $\frac{5}{9} \times \frac{6}{8} =$
3. $\frac{1}{4} \times \frac{8}{9} =$
4. $\frac{3}{9} \times \frac{4}{12} =$
5. $\frac{4}{15} \times \frac{10}{16} =$
6. $\frac{6}{8} \times \frac{11}{18} =$
7. $\frac{7}{9} \times \frac{3}{21} =$
8. $\frac{4}{7} \times \frac{21}{28} =$
9. $\frac{5}{12} \times \frac{8}{10} =$
10. $\frac{4}{8} \times \frac{3}{9} =$
11. $\frac{6}{8} \times \frac{9}{12} =$
12. $\frac{9}{21} \times \frac{14}{10} =$
13. $\frac{6}{10} \times \frac{6}{9} =$
14. $\frac{10}{25} \times \frac{4}{6} =$
15. $\frac{8}{12} \times \frac{8}{20} =$

Directions: Compute the products. Cancel as often as possible. The first one is done for you.

16. $\frac{2}{5} \times \frac{5}{9} \times \frac{3}{4} = \frac{\cancel{2}^{1}}{\cancel{5}_{1}} \times \frac{\cancel{5}^{1}}{\cancel{9}_{3}} \times \frac{\cancel{3}^{1}}{\cancel{4}_{2}} = \frac{1}{6}$
17. $\frac{5}{6} \times \frac{3}{7} \times \frac{4}{12} =$
18. $\frac{4}{7} \times \frac{11}{8} \times \frac{21}{5} =$
19. $\frac{2}{3} \times \frac{4}{5} \times \frac{9}{16} =$
20. $\frac{7}{8} \times \frac{6}{21} \times \frac{3}{16} =$
21. $\frac{1}{3} \times \frac{3}{5} \times \frac{5}{2} =$

More Multiplying Fractions

Directions: Multiply the fractions. Remember to write the answer in simplest form when possible.

1. $\frac{1}{2} \times \frac{3}{4} =$

2. $\frac{2}{3} \times \frac{1}{7} =$

3. $\frac{3}{8} \times \frac{3}{5} =$

4. $\frac{1}{5} \times \frac{6}{7} =$

5. $\frac{1}{2} \times \frac{1}{3} =$

6. $\frac{2}{3} \times \frac{1}{4} =$

7. $\frac{1}{3} \times \frac{6}{7} =$

8. $\frac{4}{9} \times \frac{1}{2} =$

9. $\frac{1}{2} \times \frac{1}{2} =$

10. $\frac{1}{2} \times \frac{3}{2} =$

11. $\frac{1}{3} \times \frac{3}{4} =$

12. $\frac{2}{9} \times \frac{3}{4} =$

13. $\frac{3}{8} \times \frac{2}{5} =$

14. $\frac{5}{8} \times \frac{7}{9} =$

15. $\frac{1}{2} \times \frac{1}{2} \times \frac{1}{2} =$

16. $\frac{1}{2} \times \frac{1}{4} \times \frac{4}{5} =$

17. $\frac{1}{2} \times \frac{2}{3} \times \frac{3}{5} =$

18. $\frac{5}{9} \times \frac{3}{7} \times \frac{14}{15} =$

19. $\frac{6}{7} \times \frac{7}{8} \times \frac{4}{5} =$

20. $\frac{11}{15} \times \frac{10}{11} \times \frac{3}{4} =$

21. $\frac{9}{10} \times \frac{1}{4} \times \frac{8}{9} =$

22. $\frac{5}{6} \times \frac{14}{15} \times \frac{2}{21} =$

23. $\frac{20}{21} \times \frac{9}{16} \times \frac{4}{5} =$

24. $\frac{3}{4} \times \frac{5}{7} \times \frac{2}{11} =$

25. $\frac{11}{12} \times \frac{3}{4} =$

26. $\frac{7}{8} \times \frac{2}{14} =$

27. $\frac{4}{15} \times \frac{5}{13} =$

28. $\frac{3}{5} \times \frac{10}{21} =$

29. $\frac{121}{300} \times \frac{10}{11} =$

30. $\frac{125}{470} \times \frac{320}{1{,}000} =$

31. $\frac{289}{1{,}222} \times \frac{2}{17} =$

32. $\frac{14}{525} \times \frac{15}{320} =$

Dividing Fractions

To divide fractions, do the following steps:

1. Get the reciprocal by flipping the divisor upside down.
2. Change the sign to multiplication (x) and cancel where possible.
3. Multiply the numerators and then multiply the denominators.
4. Simplify answers where possible.

$$\frac{3}{4} \div \frac{1}{4} = \frac{3}{4} \times \frac{4}{1} = \frac{3}{\cancel{4}_1} \times \frac{\cancel{4}^1}{1} = \frac{3}{1} = 3$$

Directions: Compute the answers to these problems. The first one is done for you.

1. $\frac{2}{3} \div \frac{1}{3} = \frac{2}{\cancel{3}_1} \times \frac{\cancel{3}^1}{1} = \frac{2}{1} = 2$

2. $\frac{4}{5} \div \frac{2}{5} =$

3. $\frac{2}{5} \div \frac{1}{5} =$

4. $\frac{4}{3} \div \frac{1}{3} =$

5. $\frac{3}{9} \div \frac{1}{9} =$

6. $\frac{4}{6} \div \frac{1}{6} =$

7. $\frac{7}{8} \div \frac{1}{2} =$

8. $\frac{5}{9} \div \frac{2}{3} =$

9. $\frac{7}{12} \div \frac{1}{2} =$

10. $\frac{6}{10} \div \frac{1}{3} =$

11. $\frac{7}{8} \div \frac{1}{4} =$

12. $\frac{6}{9} \div \frac{2}{3} =$

13. $\frac{9}{12} \div \frac{1}{4} =$

14. $\frac{4}{7} \div \frac{1}{14} =$

15. $\frac{2}{9} \div \frac{2}{3} =$

More Dividing Fractions

Directions: Divide the fractions below.

1. $3\frac{2}{3} \div 4\frac{2}{3} =$

2. $4\frac{3}{7} \div 2\frac{4}{7} =$

3. $2\frac{1}{3} \div 3\frac{1}{6} =$

4. $5\frac{6}{7} \div 6\frac{3}{14} =$

5. $3\frac{3}{5} \div 5\frac{4}{5} =$

6. $\frac{5}{6} \div \frac{2}{3} =$

7. $\frac{1}{4} \div \frac{3}{8} =$

8. $\frac{5}{12} \div \frac{2}{24} =$

9. $\frac{3}{10} \div \frac{12}{30} =$

10. $\frac{1}{5} \div \frac{4}{15} =$

11. $\frac{13}{20} \div \frac{3}{10} =$

12. $\frac{2}{7} \div \frac{2}{3} =$

13. $\frac{1}{6} \div \frac{2}{5} =$

14. $\frac{4}{9} \div \frac{1}{2} =$

15. $\frac{8}{9} \div \frac{3}{4} =$

16. $\frac{3}{6} \div 1\frac{2}{3} =$

17. $2\frac{1}{3} \div \frac{3}{4} =$

18. $3\frac{3}{4} \div \frac{3}{5} =$

19. $6\frac{1}{2} \div \frac{2}{3} =$

20. $1\frac{1}{2} \div 6 =$

21. $\frac{5}{7} \div 3\frac{4}{5} =$

22. $\frac{1}{4} \div 3\frac{1}{5} =$

23. $2\frac{3}{8} \div \frac{4}{5} =$

24. $3\frac{3}{4} \div \frac{1}{9} =$

25. $\frac{2}{5} \div 3\frac{8}{9} =$

26. $\frac{3}{8} \div 12 =$

27. $15 \div \frac{1}{10} =$

28. $2\frac{3}{6} \div \frac{1}{3} =$

29. $3\frac{2}{3} \div \frac{9}{10} =$

30. $2\frac{1}{2} \div \frac{1}{4} =$

Fractions and Decimals

A *mixed number* is a fraction greater than 1, written as a whole number and a fraction. A fraction written with the numerator larger than the denominator is called an *improper fraction*. Improper fractions should be changed into proper fractions or mixed fractions. To change an improper fraction into a mixed fraction, divide the numerator by the denominator.

Example: $\frac{16}{5} = 3\frac{1}{5}$ $\quad 5\overline{)16}$ = 3 r1; $16 - 15 = 1$ or $3\frac{1 \text{ (remainder)}}{5 \text{ (divisor)}}$

Directions: Write the fraction as a mixed number or a whole number.

1. $\frac{25}{6} =$ 2. $\frac{13}{4} =$ 3. $\frac{40}{5} =$ 4. $\frac{38}{7} =$ 5. $\frac{27}{9} =$

Directions: Write the mixed number as a fraction.

6. $3\frac{2}{7} =$ 7. $5\frac{3}{5} =$ 8. $7\frac{2}{9} =$ 9. $4\frac{3}{8} =$ 10. $2\frac{9}{10} =$

Directions: Write the quotient as a mixed number. Write the fraction in lowest terms.

11. $5\overline{)11}$ 12. $8\overline{)38}$ 13. $5\overline{)48}$ 14. $8\overline{)74}$

Mixed numbers may be written as decimals. To write a mixed number as a decimal, first write the fraction as a decimal by dividing the numerator by the denominator. Then add the whole number and the decimal.

Example: $2\frac{3}{5}$ $\quad \frac{3}{5} = 5\overline{)3.0}$ = 0.6 $\quad 2 + 0.6 = 2.6$

Directions: Write the fraction or the mixed number as a decimal. Round to the nearest hundredth.

15. $\frac{2}{8}$ $\quad 8\overline{)2.0}$

16. $\frac{3}{4}$ $\quad 4\overline{)3.0}$

17. $6\frac{4}{20}$ $\quad 20\overline{)4.00}$

18. $\frac{1}{2}$

19. $\frac{3}{8}$

20. $\frac{15}{25}$

21. $3\frac{6}{10}$

Converting Fractions to Percents

A fraction is converted to a percentage by dividing the denominator into the numerator.

numerator ⟶ $\frac{1}{4}$ ← denominator $\qquad 4\overline{)1.00}$ = .25 $\qquad \frac{1}{2} \qquad 2\overline{)1.00}$ = .50

Always place a decimal point and two zeros to the right of the numerator in the dividend. This converts the fraction to a decimal which is used to compute the percent.

Directions: Convert the fractions in these problems into decimals. Use the decimals to compute the percentages. The first one is done for you.

1. $\frac{1}{2}$ of 24 = 12

$2\overline{)1.00}$ = .50

$$\begin{array}{r} 24 \\ \times .50 \\ \hline 12.00 \end{array}$$

2. $\frac{3}{4}$ of 32 = ______

3. $\frac{5}{10}$ of 80 = ______

4. $\frac{1}{4}$ of 84 = ______

5. $\frac{3}{10}$ of 105 = ______

6. $\frac{9}{10}$ of 56 = ______

7. $\frac{1}{2}$ of 87 = ______

8. $\frac{3}{5}$ of 204 = ______

9. $\frac{1}{5}$ of 94 = ______

10. $\frac{3}{20}$ of 66 = ______

11. $\frac{7}{20}$ of 52 = ______

12. $\frac{7}{10}$ of 48 = ______

Directions: Some fractions need to be divided to three or more places. Round the answers to two places.

13. $\frac{5}{8}$ of 64 = ______

14. $\frac{7}{8}$ of 88 = ______

15. $\frac{1}{8}$ of 14 = ______

Working with Fractions, Decimals, and Percents

Directions: For problems 1–5, write the fraction as a decimal. For problems 6–10, write the decimal as a fraction. For problems 11–15, write the decimal as a fraction in lowest terms.

1. $\frac{7}{10}$ = ________
2. $\frac{2}{5}$ = ________
3. $\frac{3}{4}$ = ________
4. $\frac{3}{20}$ = ________
5. $1\frac{3}{4}$ = ________
6. 0.26 = ________
7. 0.03 = ________
8. 0.2 = ________
9. 0.78 = ________
10. 0.825 = ________
11. 0.05 = ________
12. 0.02 = ________
13. 0.125 = ________
14. 0.04 = ________
15. 6.9 = ________

Directions: Write each as a decimal and a percent.

	decimal	percent
16. six hundredths	________	________
17. seventy hundredths	________	________
18. 63 per hundred	________	________
19. 3 out of 100	________	________
20. thirty-one hundredths	________	________

Directions: Complete the table.

	percent	fraction	decimal
21.	25%		
22.	2%		
23.	0.5%		
24.	33%		
25.	40%		

Calculating Fractions, Decimals, and Percents

1. Mrs. Anderson's Girl Scout troop has $600 in savings. The girls collected 50% of the money by recycling aluminum cans, 15% of the money came from donations, and 35% of it came from their annual auction. How much money was raised by recycling cans? _______ donations? _______ by having an auction? _______

2. Your purchases total $24.95. If the sales tax rate is 6%, what is the total amount that you must pay? (round up to the nearest penny) _______

3. On Monday, 100 students arrived on two buses. On Tuesday, many students had the flu, and only 75% of Monday's group arrived at school. How many students had the flu? _______

4. Two hundred and fifty people are expected to turn out for the company picnic. Sixty percent of them will be children. How many children are expected to attend? _______

5. Four hundred new homes are being built in the town of Frankfort, and only 5% have swimming pools. How many have swimming pools? _______

6. Marco had 300 trading cards. His friend, Juan, told Marco he will give him 75% more. How many cards is Juan going to give to Marco? _______

7. Johnson's Drugs has penny candy. Ian purchased $0.65 of taffy and $0.20 for root beer barrels. There is a $0.02 sales tax. How much does he pay? _______

8. A round-trip subway train ticket costs $0.55. A 20-trip pass costs $9.50. If you took 20 trips, how much did you save by buying the pass? _______

9. On a cell phone, there is a charge of $0.03 per minute. How many minutes can you talk for $0.78? _______

10. A big shipment of computer parts arrived at Don's Computer World. It weighed 360 pounds. Inside the shipment, each box weighed 1.25 pounds. How many boxes were in the shipment? _______

11. At $0.17 per kilogram, how many kilograms of gumdrops can you buy for $1.02? _______

12. Eli painted $\frac{1}{16}$ of the living room wall and stopped when the phone rang. What percent of the wall did he paint? _______

Range, Mean, Median, and Mode

Tom picked these five numbers: 92, 36, 40, 52, 40. He knew that the difference between the greatest number and the least number is called the range.

Example: The range between 92 and 36 is
92 – 36 = 56

Tom knew that he had five numbers and their sum was equal to 260. If he divided the sum by the total numbers he had, he could find the mean.

Example: $\frac{36 + 40 + 52 + 40 + 92 =}{5}$ $\frac{260}{5} = 52$

When Tom looked at the numbers after he listed them in order from least to greatest, he was able to find the median. The median is the number in the middle of the sequence (or the mean of the two middle numbers if there are an even number of items in the sequence).

Example: 36 40 (40) 52 92

The mode is the number that appears most often.

Example: 36 (40) 52 (40) 92

The number 40 appears twice, so it is the mode.

Directions: Find the range, mean, median, and mode for each set of numbers.

1. 25, 73, 12, 25, 35

A. Order: ____ ____ ____ ____ ____

B. Range: ____ – ____ = ____

C. Mean: $\frac{\_\_\_\_ + \_\_\_\_ + \_\_\_\_ + \_\_\_\_ + \_\_\_\_}{5} = \frac{\_\_\_\_}{5} = \_\_\_\_$

D. Median: ____________________

E. Mode: ____________________

2. 100, 23, 49, 88, 30, 23, 51

A. Order: ____ ____ ____ ____ ____ ____ ____

B. Range: ____________________

C. Mean: ____________________

D. Median: ____________________

E. Mode: ____________________

Range, Mean, Median, and Mode *(cont.)*

3. 18, 36, 24, 18

A. Order: ____________________

B. Range: ____________________

C. Mean: ____________________

D. Median: ____________________

E. Mode: ____________________

4. 22, 70, 22, 84, 36, 42

A. Order: ____________________

B. Range: ____________________

C. Mean: ____________________

D. Median: ____________________

E. Mode: ____________________

5. 170, 200, 305

A. Order: ____________________

B. Range: ____________________

C. Mean: ____________________

D. Median: ____________________

E. Mode: ____________________

6. 45, 66, 89, 69, 77, 22, 66

A. Order: ____________________

B. Range: ____________________

C. Mean: ____________________

D. Median: ____________________

E. Mode: ____________________

Working with Mode, Median, and Mean

It is important to recognize the **measures of central tendency** (*mode*, *median*, or *mean*), which is most representative of a set of data. Sometimes one of the measures is clearly the most useful. Sometimes two or three measures may be equally valuable.

- If all three numbers are identical or very close, you know the data is likely to be statistically valid.

> Daily high temperatures for a week: 79°, 80°, 81°, 78°, 79°, 82°, 77°
> Mode: 79° Median: 79° Mean: 79° (79.4°, rounded off)

- A reading of 79° is clearly representative of this week's high temperatures.

Directions: Find the mode, median, and mean in each set of data. Indicate which measure or measures you think is most representative of the data.

1. Number of dots on selected ladybugs: 15, 0, 7, 9, 13, 2, 13, 15, 16, 13, 9, 13, 0

Mode: ________________ Median: ________________ Mean: ______________

Most representative measure: ____

Reason: ____

2. Number of candy-coated chocolates in small bags: 22, 24, 25, 22, 21, 26, 23, 22, 23, 23, 25, 24

Mode: ________________ Median: ________________ Mean: ______________

Most representative measure: ____

Reason: ____

3. Length of red worms (in centimeters): 10, 8, 6, 5, 12, 8, 7, 9, 11, 8, 6, 9, 10, 8, 8

Mode: ________________ Median: ________________ Mean: ______________

Most representative measure: ____

Reason: ____

4. Number of drops of water that will fit on a penny: 21, 40, 46, 34, 56, 46, 99, 65, 48, 38, 69, 54, 50, 61

Mode: ________________ Median: ________________ Mean: ______________

Most representative measure: ____

Reason: ____

5. Number of drops of water that will fit on a dime: 40, 38, 42, 16, 23, 28, 44, 25, 41, 23, 45, 30, 29, 27

Mode: ________________ Median: ________________ Mean: ______________

Most representative measure: ____

Reason: ____

Outliers

Some sets of data include quantities that affect the mean so that the average seems not to represent the data correctly. These quantities, called **outliers**, usually are very different from the other quantities in the set. They can be much larger or smaller than most of the other numbers.

Look at Justin's reading grades.

When a teacher averages grades, she or he usually finds the mean.

mean grade: 95

Justin's Reading Grades

vocabulary quizzes: 98, 95, 96

comprehension tests: 92, 90, 95

classwork: 98, 95, 95, 96

Find Justin's other average grades. **median grade:** 95 **mode grade:** 95

Grade Scale

100 – 94	A
93 – 85	B
84 – 77	C
76 – 79	D
69 – 0	F

Justin has a high average at this point, as shown by the mean, median, and mode. But what if Justin does poorly on just one vocabulary quiz? Re-average Justin's grades, this time with an additional vocabulary quiz grade of 31.

mean grade: 89 **median grade:** 95 **mode grade:** 95

When the teacher averages Justin's grades, she or he will assign him a B even though he has earned an A on most of his class work. Justin's grades are better represented using the median and mode averages instead of the mean. In this set of data, 31 is an **outlier**.

Directions: Find the mean, median, and mode for each set of data below. Then, decide which number is the outlier for each set of data.

Average Number of Points Scored by the Byrd High School Cardinals Girls Basketball Team

64	62	78	64	70
65	66	64	72	63
74	31	61	75	66

1. mean score ___________
2. median score ___________
3. mode score ___________
4. outlier ___________

Average Number of Points Scored by the Byrd High School Cardinals Boys Basketball Team

73	78	80	76	74
74	48	80	78	74
72	70	74	76	68

5. mean score ___________
6. median score ___________
7. mode score ___________
8. outlier ___________

Finding Median and Mode from Graphs

Directions: Use the graph as your source for data. Then, find the median and mode for each set of data.

Grade-four and -five students read books as part of their reading program. The number of books each class reads in one week was totaled and graphed below.

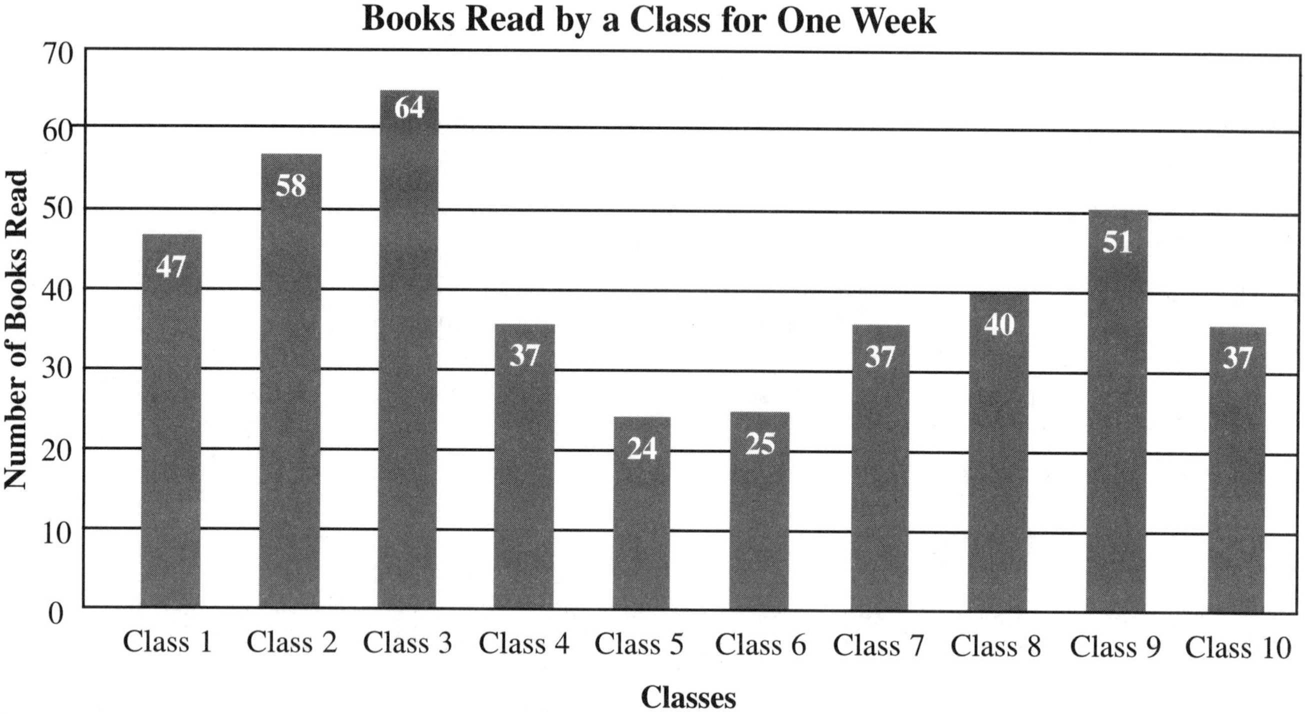

1. What is the mode number of books read by the grade-four and -five classes? _________

2. What is the median number of books read by the grade-four and -five classes? ________

For each book read, students took a test. The results of their tests are seen below as percentages.

Hint: To find the number of tests for each score, multiply the number of tests taken by the percentage.

Scored 100: 30%
Scored 80: 30%
Scored 60: 20%
Scored 40: 10%
Scored 20: 5%
Scored 0: 5%

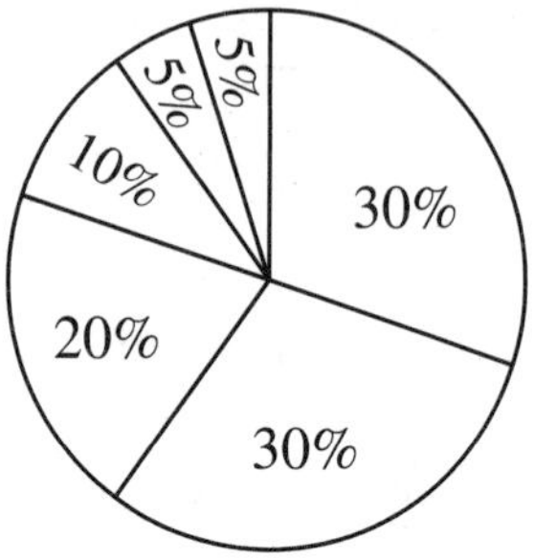

3. What percentage of students score 80 or 100? _________

4. Based on the percentages, if 100 tests were taken, how many students would score 60? ________

5. Based on the percentages, if 500 tests were taken, how many students would score 80 or 100? ________

6. What is the median score? ________

7. What is the mode score? ________

Calculating Median and Mode with Stem-and-Leaf Plots

Stem-and-Leaf Plot
A stem-and-leaf plot may help you organize large sets of data to easily find the median and mode. To make a stem-and-leaf graph, list digits in the tens and higher place values in the stem. List the digits in the ones place value for each data in the leaf. For the number 72, the 7 is the stem and the 2 is the leaf. For the number 690, the 69 is the stem and the 0 is the leaf.

Directions: Use the information above to answer the questions below.

Rhonda's Garden Plan

beans – 12	celery – 16
carrots – 20	cherry tomatoes – 18
lettuce – 18	brussels sprouts – 8
tomatoes – 16	potatoes – 20
cucumbers – 20	leeks – 16
radishes – 30	onions – 20
peas – 20	watermelon – 30

Rhonda is planning her garden. She decides on the numbers of each vegetable shown on the chart. Create a stem-and-leaf plot on another sheet of paper to find the median and mode number of vegetables she plants.

1. Median number of plants _______

2. Mode number of plants __________

A new play runs for two weeks, for a total of 20 performances. The capacity of the theater is 870 patrons. Create a stem-and-leaf plot on another sheet of paper to determine the median and mode number of attendees.

Play Attendance

performance #	1	2	3	4	5	6	7	8	9	10	11	12	13	14	15	16	17	18	19	20
attendance	870	870	851	845	863	831	846	828	799	856	789	779	800	842	863	865	789	850	870	870

3. During how many performances was the theater filled to capacity? __________

4. What was the median number of attendees? __________

5. What was the mode number of attendees? __________

6. If you were the producer of this play, would you extend its performance? Why or why not?

____

____

Look at these stem-and-leaf plots. What is the median? What is the mode?

Stem	Leaf
0	3 4 4 8
1	6 7 7 9
2	0 1 5 8 8
3	2 2 2 2 6
4	3 7

7. Median __________

8. Mode __________

Stem	Leaf
12	0 1 6 7
13	3 4 5 7
14	0 1 1 6

9. Median __________

10. Mode __________

Tables and Plots

This line plot illustrates a survey of hours spent during one week on computer-generated games by 29 sixth-grade students in one classroom. Study the plot and answer the questions below.

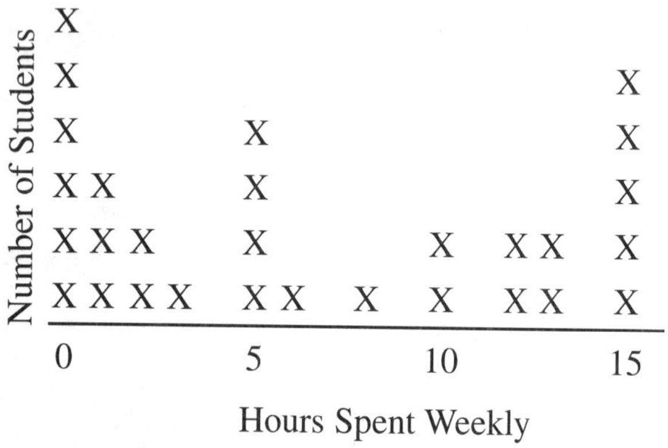

Note: Each X represents one student.

1. How many students did not spend any time playing computer games? __________

2. How many students spent 3 hours a week playing computer games? __________

3. How many students spent 5 hours a week playing computer games? __________

4. How many students spent 15 hours a week playing computer games? __________

5. How many students spent 10 hours a week playing computer games? __________

6. How many students in the class spent 10 hours or more a week on games? ______

7. How many students in the class spent less than 10 hours a week on games? ______

8. How many students spent 13 hours a week on games? __________

This frequency table illustrates a survey of pets owned by grade-six students in one classroom. Study the table, complete the frequency totals, and answer the questions below.

Survey of Pets Owned by Grade-Six Students

Pets	Tally	Frequency
Cat	////////	8
Dog	////////////	
Snake	//	
Bird	///	
Mouse	///	
Hamster	////	
Fish	//////	
Other	///	

9. How many more dogs are owned than cats? __________

10. What is the most frequently-owned pet? __________

11. What is the least frequently-owned pet? __________

12. How many more cats are owned than mice? __________

13. What is the total number of pets owned by these students? __________

14. How many four-legged animals are owned (that aren't in the "other" category)? ______

Double-Bar Graphs

This double-bar graph illustrates a survey of the relative popularity of soccer and football as participant sports for boys in the third through the eighth grades.

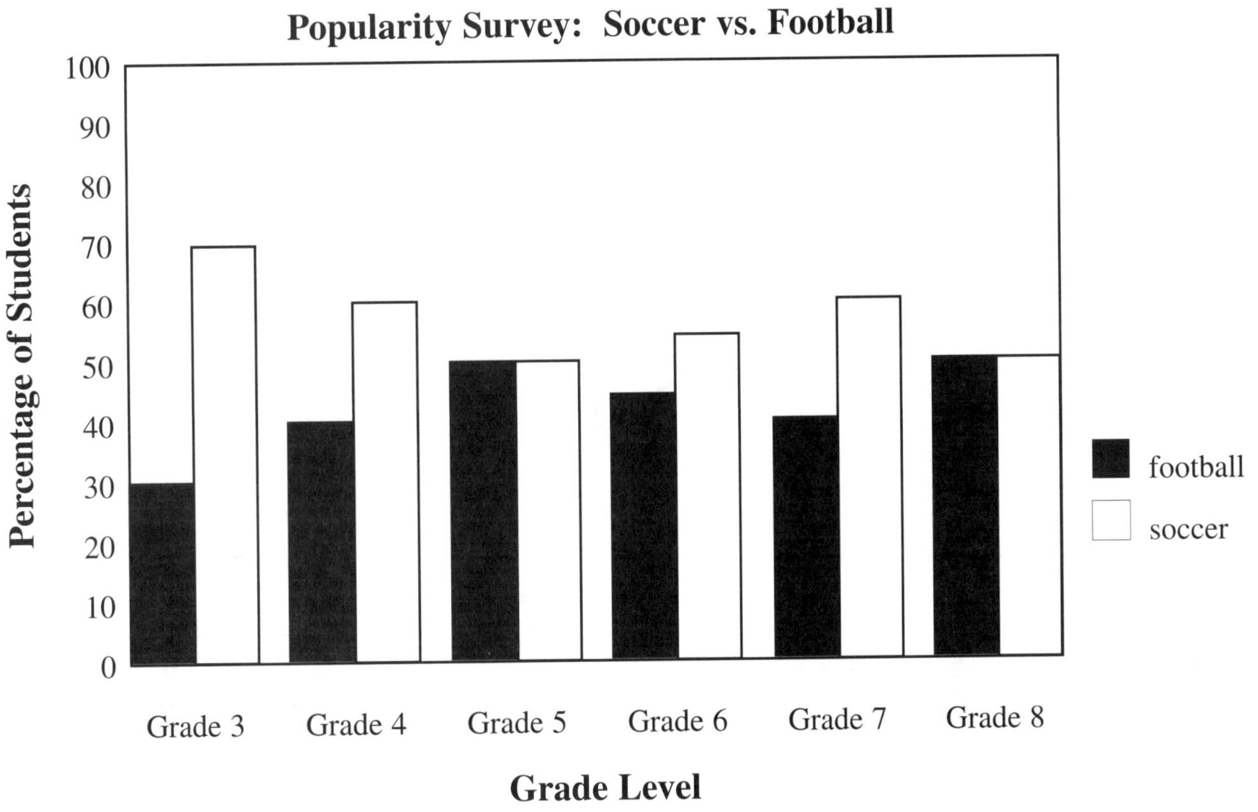

1. What percentage of grade-three boys preferred to play football? ____________________

2. In which two grades do boys like to play soccer and football equally well? _____________

3. What percentage of boys in grade four prefer soccer? ____________________

4. Is there any grade in which more boys prefer football? ____________________

5. What percentage of boys prefer football in grade six? ____________________

6. What percentage of boys prefer football in grade seven? ____________________

Stem-and-Leaf Plot

Directions: Arrange the test scores below in a stem-and-leaf plot from least to greatest. After organizing all of the data in the plot, count the number of leaves per stem. Then look below the chart to find the letter which corresponds to the number of leaves. Find the answer to the following question by writing the correct letter on the appropriate line.

Question: Where do Australian children go to play?____________________________

Test Scores: 96, 81, 79, 79, 100, 100, 93, 87, 62, 67, 91, 80, 91, 83, 47, 98, 93, 88, 88, 70, 75, 63, 63, 100, 57, 58, 96, 74

Stems	Leaves

Number of Leaves	Letter

Letters

A = 6 **D = 8** **G = 11** **K = 3** **U = 2**

B = 5 **E = 9** **H = 12** **O = 1** **T = 4**

C = 7 **F = 10** **I = 13**

Organizing Data

Directions: Arrange the following data (test scores) in the Frequency Table. Notice the frequency for each number, and find its corresponding letter in the Letter Bin. Write the letters in the letter column to find the first part of the answer to the riddle.

Question: Who did the vampire play with when he was younger? ______________________________

Frequency Table

Scores	Tally	Frequency	Letter
65			
68			
69			
78			
79			
85			
87			
88			
89			
90			
95			
97			
98			

Test Scores: 85, 85, 85, 85, 85, 79, 79, 79, 79, 87, 90, 90, 78, 78, 68, 69, 69, 85, 69, 68, 98, 90, 69, 68, 78, 68, 87, 97, 79, 69, 98, 90, 89, 89, 89, 97, 97, 68, 78, 78, 85, 69, 85, 65, 68, 68, 69, 87, 90, 85, 90, 88, 69, 88, 69, 78, 87, 97, 78, 90, 78, 90, 90, 79, 85, 97, 69, 90

Letter Bin

T = 1
S = 2
N = 3
L = 4
K = 5
I = 6
H = 7
G = 8
E = 10
R = 10
C = 0

Using the same data, complete the chart below. Circle the letter that each number group reaches to find the last word of the riddle.

	1	2	3	4	5	6	7	8	9	10	11	12	13	14	15	16	17	18	19	20
60–69				X				J			G			P				D		
70–79			W			A				E				O	C		B			
80–89							Q			Z			F		Y				O	
90–99		M		N					H			L				K	R			

Creating Graphs

1. Create a line graph that shows how many Grand Slam sneakers were sold from week to week.
   - Week 1: 23 pairs
   - Week 2: 19 pairs
   - Week 3: 15 pairs
   - Week 4: 23 pairs

2. On a Monday each of 80 people purchased one item in the store. Create a circle graph that shows the amount of each item that was sold.
   - T-shirts: 20 sold
   - Sneakers: 40 sold
   - Athletic Posters: 10 sold
   - Other Athletic Equipment: 10 sold

Type of Shoe	Sold at Regular Price	Sold at Discount Pirce
Grand Slam	25 pairs	25 pairs
Metro	15 pairs	10 pairs
Neo Running Shoes	20 pairs	25 pairs

3. Use this information to create a double-bar graph inside of the box below. Use a ruler.

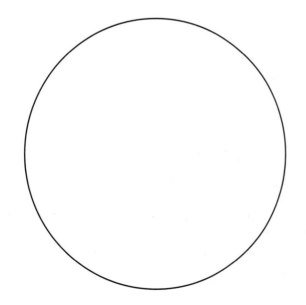

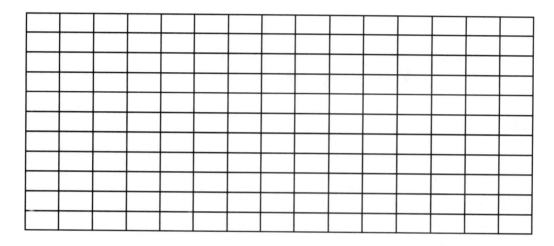

Coordinates (Positive and Negative)

Coordinates must always be plotted using the *x* axis for the first number in a number pair and the *y* axis for the second number of each pair. (*Note:* Always go across before you go up or down.)

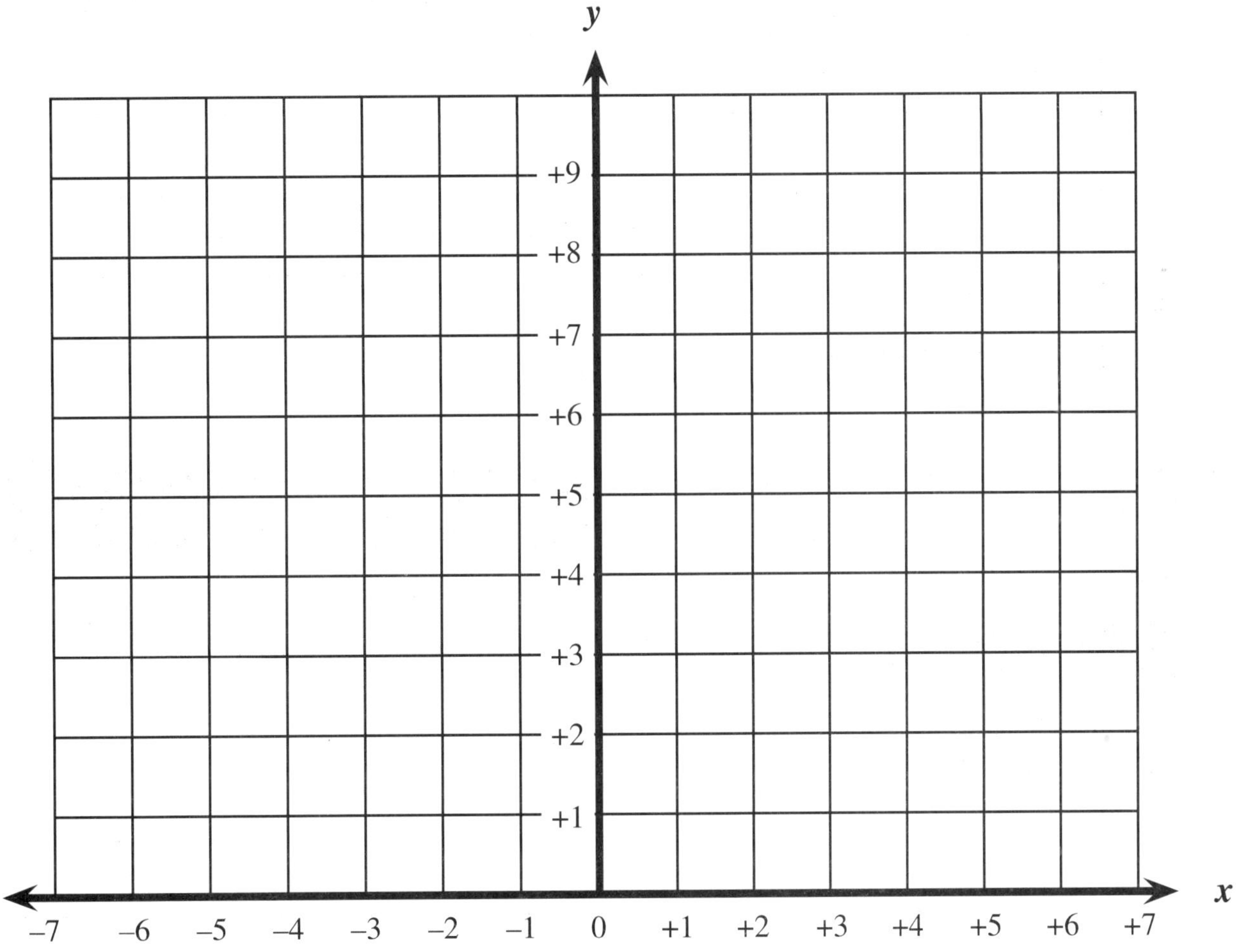

Directions: Graph these coordinate number pairs. Connect each dot with a ruler as you proceed. (**Note:** You will go over some line segments more than once.)

First Shape

A. (+1, +3) B. (+6, +3) C. (+6, +8) D. (+1, +8) E. (+1, +3)
F. (+6, +8) G. (+1, +8) H. (+6, +3)

Second Shape

I. (–2, +2) J. (–6, +2) K. (–7, +5) L. (–6, +8) M. (–2, +8)
N. (–1, +5) O. (–2, +2) P. (–6, +8) Q. (–2, +8) R. (–6, +2)
S. (–7, +5) T. (–1, +5) U. (–4, +5) V. (–4, +8) W. (–4, +2)

Identifying Coordinate Points

Directions: Write the coordinates for each point.

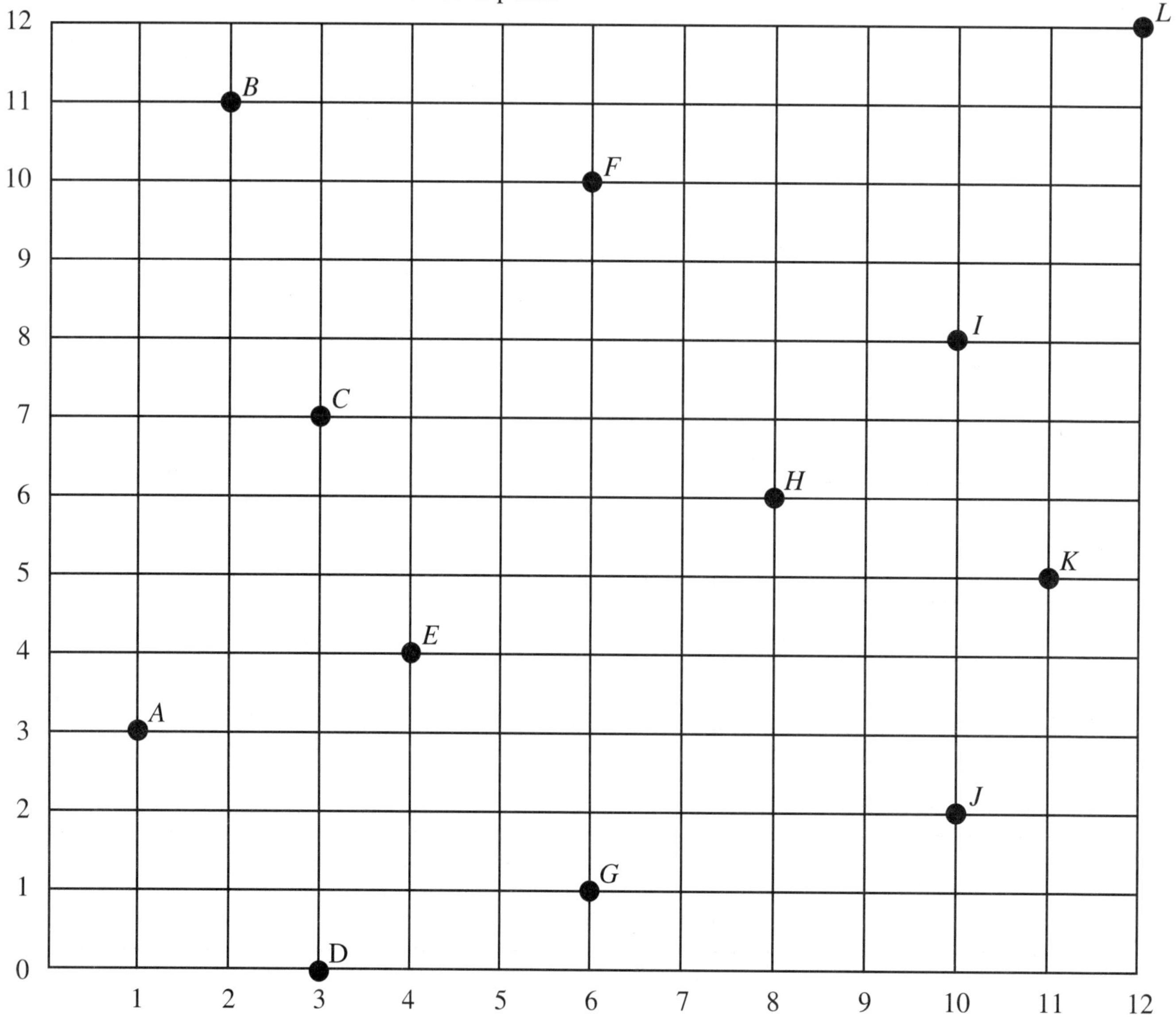

1. *K* = ______	**4.** *L* = ______	**7.** *H* = ______	**10.** *C* = ______
2. *D* = ______	**5.** *E* = ______	**8.** *B* = ______	**11.** *A* = ______
3. *G* = ______	**6.** *I* = ______	**9.** *F* = ______	**12.** *J* = ______

Cartesian Coordinates

How Do You Make a Hot Dog Stand?

The answer to this riddle is written in a special code at the bottom of this page. Each pair of numbers stands for a point on the graph. Write the letter shown at the point near the intersection of each pair of numbers. Read numbers across and then up. The letters will spell out the answer to the riddle.

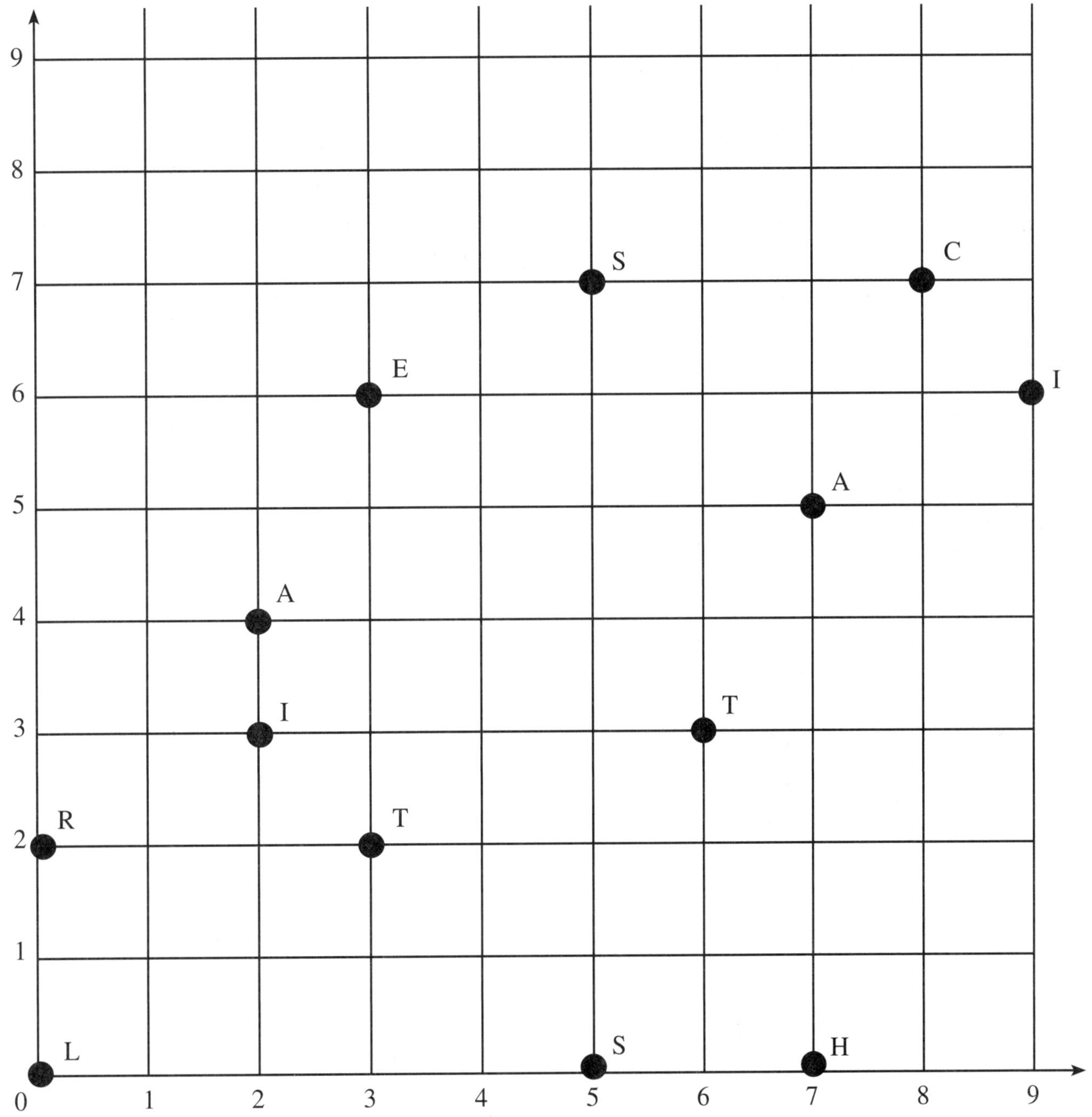

____	____	____	____	____	____	____	____	____	____	____	____	____.
(5, 7)	(6, 3)	(3, 6)	(7, 5)	(0, 0)	(2, 3)	(3, 2)	(5, 0)	(8, 7)	(7, 0)	(2, 4)	(9, 6)	(0, 2)

Working with Four Quadrants

Coordinates must always be plotted using the *x* axis for the first number in a number pair and the *y* axis for the second number of each pair. (*Note:* Always go across before you go up or down.)

Second Quadrant **First Quadrant**

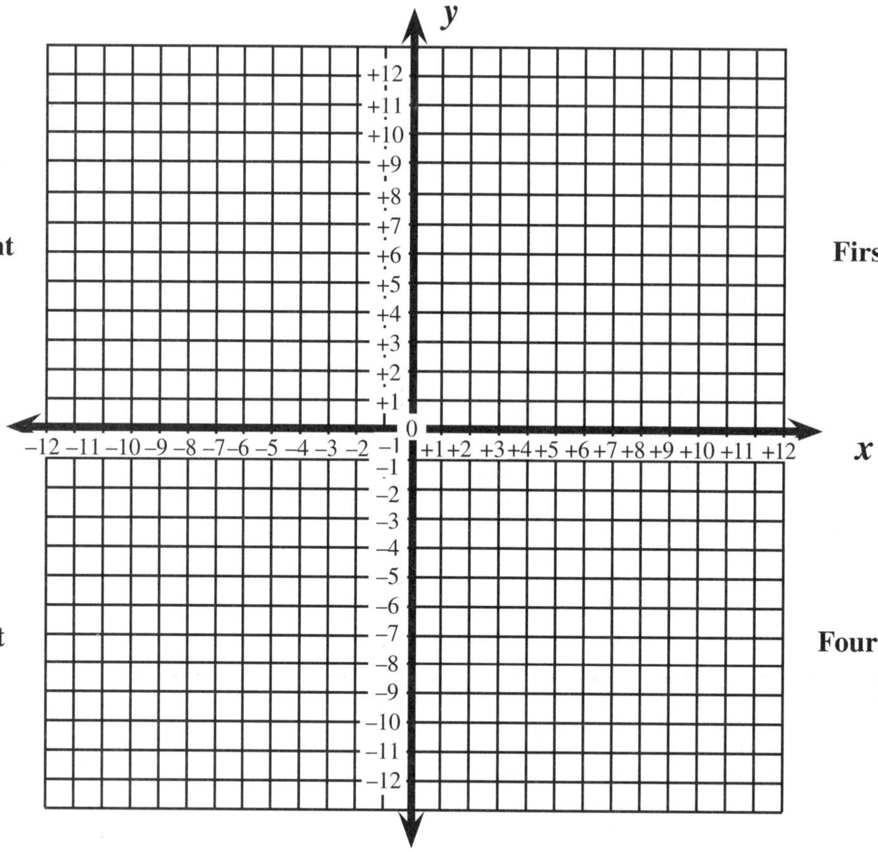

Third Quadrant **Fourth Quadrant**

Directions: Graph these coordinate number pairs in each quadrant. Connect each dot within a quadrant with a ruler as you proceed. (*Note:* You will go over some line segments more than once.)

First Quadrant

A. (+9, +2)	B. (+9, +9)	C. (+2, +9)	D. (+2, +2)	E. (+3, +2)
F. (+8, +2)	G. (+8, +8)	H. (+3, +8)	I. (+3, +2)	J. (+9, +9)
K. (+2, +9)	L. (+8, +2)	M. (+9, +2)		

Second Quadrant

A. (–3, +1)	B. (–5, +4)	C. (–3, +7)	D. (–5, +10)	E. (–8, +10)
F. (–10, +7)	G. (–3, +7)	H. (–10, +7)	I. (–8, +4)	J. (–5, +4)
K. (–8, +4)	L. (–10, +1)	M. (–3, +1)		

Third Quadrant

A. (–4, –2)	B. (–4, –6)	C. (–3, –8)	D. (–3, –10)	E. (–9, –10)
F. (–9, –8)	G. (–8, –6)	H. (–8, –2)	I. (–4, –2)	J. (–2, –10)
K. (–10, –10)	L. (–8, –2)			

Fourth Quadrant

A. (+1, –2)	B. (+9, –2)	C. (+10, –11)	D. (+7, –8)	E. (+5, –11)
F. (+3, –8)	G. (0, –11)	H. (+1, –2)	I. (+5, –8)	J. (+9, –2)
K. (+5, –2)	L. (+1, –8)	M. (+9, –8)	N. (+5, –2)	O. (+3, –5)
P. (+7, –5)				

Coordinate Pairs

Use this grid to help you answer the questions on page 129.

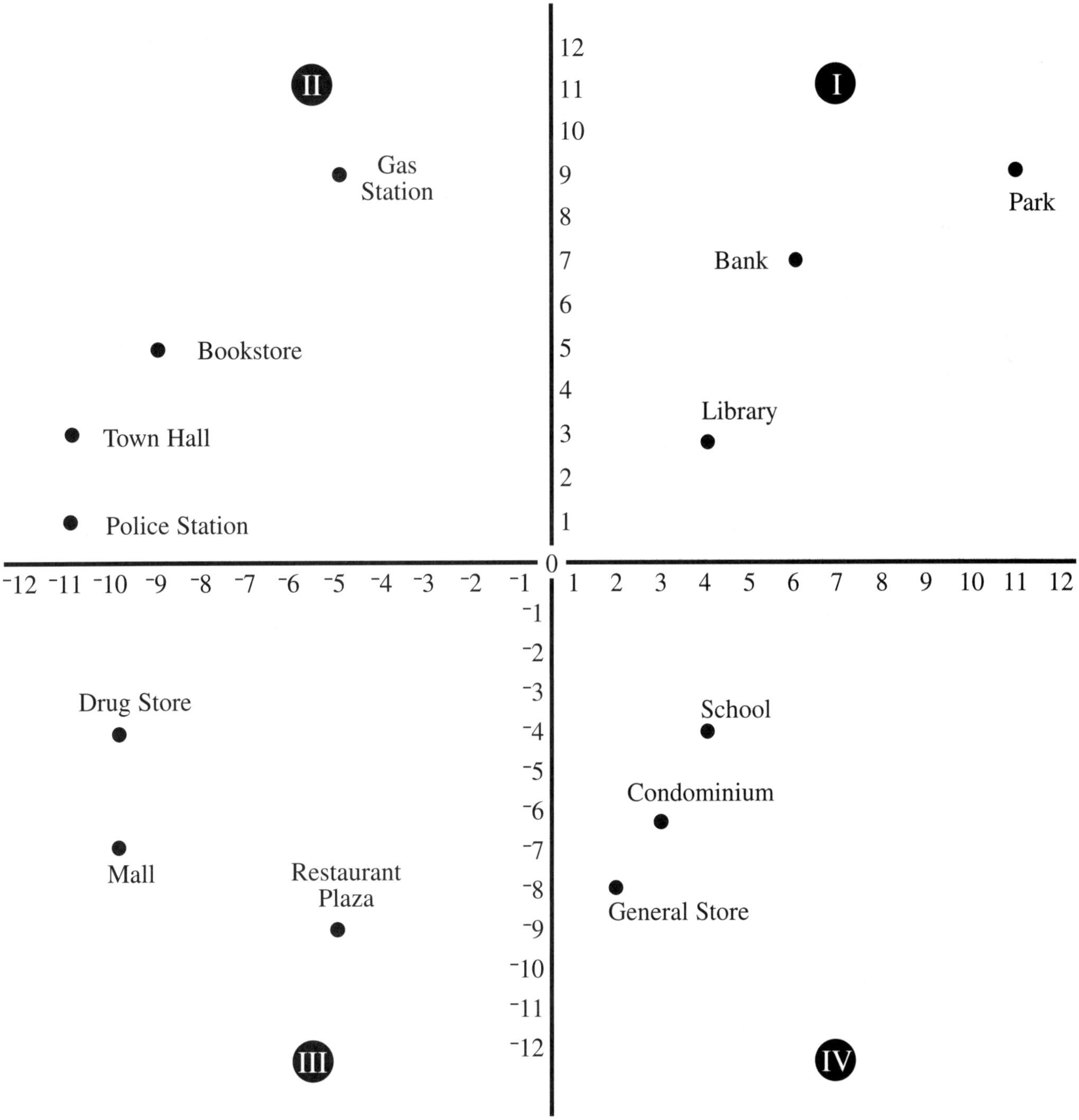

Coordinate Pairs *(cont.)*

Directions

- Study the grid shown on page 123.
- Notice where landmarks such as the school and library are located.
- Notice which numbers are positive and which are negative.
- Note how the four quadrants are labeled: I, II, III, and IV.
- Remember: Always go across before going up or down.
- Use the information to answer these word problems.

1. What building is located at coordinates (4, 3)? ____________________

2. What city building is located at coordinates ($^-11$, 3)? ____________________

3. Which business is located at ($^-5$, 9)? ____________________

4. What are the coordinates of the police station? ____________________

5. What are the coordinates of the school? ____________________

6. What are the coordinates of the restaurant plaza? ____________________

7. What public area is located at coordinates (11, 9)? ____________________

8. What are the coordinates of the mall? ____________________

9. What are the coordinates of the bookstore? ____________________

10. What is located at coordinates (2, $^-8$)? ____________________

11. What is located at coordinates ($^-10$, $^-4$)? ____________________

12. Which quadrant has all negative coordinates? ____________________

13. Which quadrant has only positive coordinates? ____________________

14. Which quadrant always begins with a negative number and concludes with a positive number?

____

Graphing Coordinate Pairs

Directions: Graph each of the points on the graph paper on page 126. Connect the points as you go. You should have a picture when you are finished.

1. (-5.5, 17)
2. (-5, 16)
3. (-4.5, 15.5)
4. (-6, 12)
5. (-9, 9)
6. (-8.5, 8.5)
7. (-8, 8)
8. (-7, 8.5)
9. (-6.5, 8.5)
10. (-7, 8.5)
11. (-8, 8)
12. (-7, 7)
13. (-6, 7.5)
14. (-6, 8)
15. (-5, 8.5)
16. (-4, 9)
17. (-3, 10)
18. (-4, 10)
19. (-4.5, 10.5)
20. (-4, 10)
21. (-3, 10)
22. (-2, 10.5)
23. (-1.5, 12)
24. (-2, 10.5)
25. (-3, 10)
26. (-2, 9)
27. (-2, 8)
28. (-2, 6)
29. (-1.5, 5)
30. (-1, 3.5)
31. (-3, 3)
32. (-7, 3.5)
33. (-11, 0)
34. (-11, -3)
35. (-9, -3)
36. (-9, -2)
37. (-11, -2)
38. (-9, -2)
39. (-9, -1)
40. (-7.5, 0)
41. (-6, 2)
42. (-7.5, 0)
43. (-9, -2)
44. (-8, -5)
45. (-6, -6)
46. (-5.5, -5)
47. (-5.5, -4)
48. (-6.5, -3)
49. (-7, -3)
50. (-4, 0)
51. (2, 0)
52. (0, 0)
53. (0, -1)
54. (5.5, -7.5)
55. (5.5, -4.5)
56. (5.5, -7.5)
57. (6, -10)
58. (7, -12)
59. (1, -16)
60. (0, -18.5)
61. (1, -19)
62. (2, -19)
63. (3, -18.5)
64. (3.5, -17.5)
65. (3, -17)
66. (9, -15)
67. (11, -12)
68. (13.5, -8)
69. (13.5, -10)
70. (13, -11)
71. (12.5, -12)
72. (12, -13)
73. (11.5, -14)
74. (11, -16)
75. (11, -20)
76. (13, -21)
77. (13, -20.5)
78. (15, -21)
79. (15, -20.5)
80. (16, -21)
81. (14.5, -19)
82. (15, -17)
83. (15, -14.5)
84. (15.5, -12)
85. (15.5, -9)
86. (15, -7)
87. (14, -5)
88. (12, -3)
89. (10, 0)
90. (9, 2)
91. (8, 4)
92. (7.5, 6)
93. (7, 8.5)
94. (9.5, 7)
95. (8, 10.5)
96. (9, 10.5)
97. (7, 15)
98. (9, 16)
99. (3, 18)
100. (4, 20)
101. (0, 18)
102. (-4, 16)
103. (-5.5, 17)

Graphing Coordinate Pairs *(cont.)*

Graph Paper

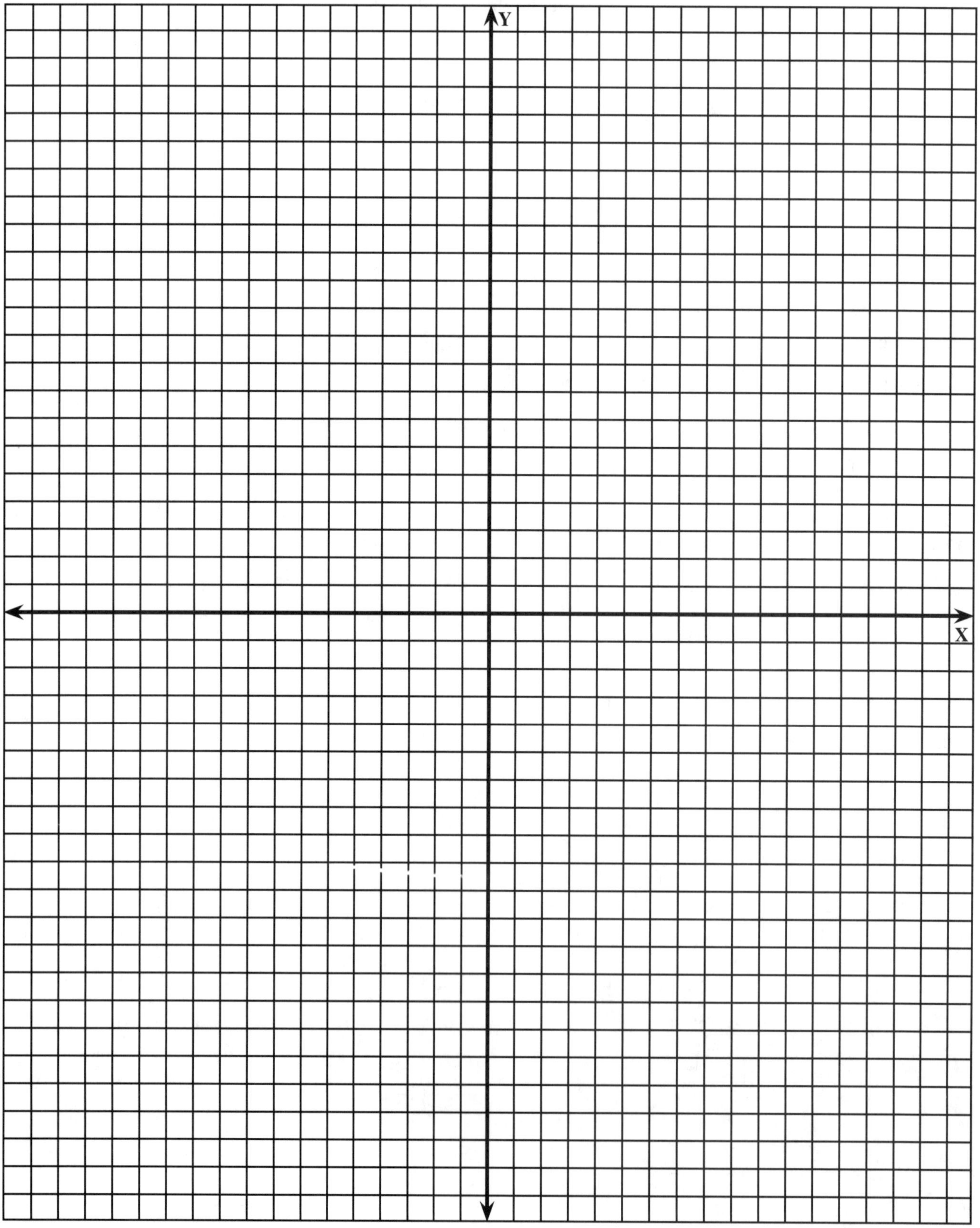

Metric Measurement

Metric Measurement Tips:

- A *meter* (m) is about the length from your fingertips to the end of your opposite shoulder if your arms are extended outward from your shoulder.
- A *centimeter* (cm) is about the distance across the nail of your pinky.
- A *millimeter* (mm) is about the thickness of a dime.
- A *kilometer* (km) is the distance a person can walk in about 10–12 minutes.

Circle the best estimate.

1. length of a workbook	a. 35 m	b. 35 mm	c. 35 cm	d. 2 km
2. length of a bus	a. 2 km	b. 12 m	c. 50 cm	d. 6 ml
3. length of a new pencil	a. 20 kg	b. 20 mm	c. 20 cm	d. 20 m
4. distance on plane Vancouver to Quebec	a. 5,000 km	b. 5,000 kg	c. 5,000 m	d. 5,000 L
5. width of your hand	a. 12 cm	b. 1.2 cm	c. 120 m	d. 12 mm

Choose the most appropriate measurement: mm, cm, m, km

6. height of a tree ________________

7. diameter of Mars ________________

8. length of a small turtle ________________

9. width of a paper clip ________________

10. diameter of a penny ________________

11. height of a vase ________________

12. perimeter of a room ________________

13. Nile River ________________

Match the best estimate for each picture below. Remember that the width of your pinky is 1 cm.

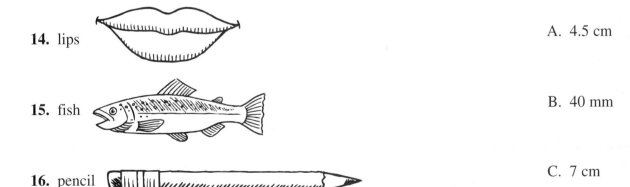

14. lips 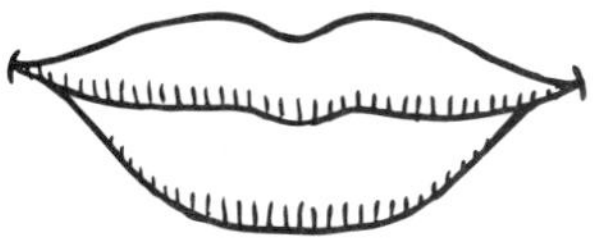

15. fish 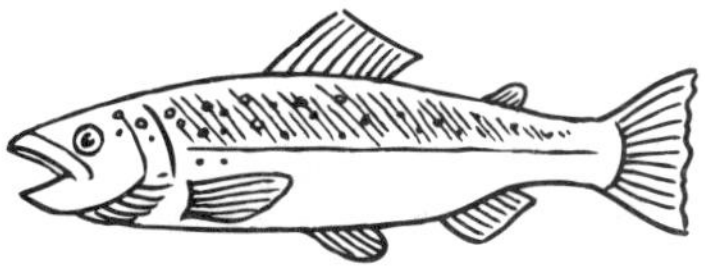

16. pencil 

A. 4.5 cm

B. 40 mm

C. 7 cm

Converting Metric Measurements

10 mm = 1 cm	1 L = 1,000 mL
100 cm = 1 m	1 kg = 1,000 g
1,000 mm = 1 m	1 kL = 1,000 L
1,000 m = 1 km	1 g = 1,000 mg

Complete the conversions.

1. 10 mm = ______ cm

2. 50 cm = ______ mm

3. 30 mm = ______ cm

4. 10 cm = ______ mm

5. 50 mm = ______ cm

6. 90 cm = ______ mm

7. 65 mm = ______ cm

8. 33 cm = ______ mm

9. 100 cm = ______ m

10. 1,000 m = ______ km

11. 600 cm = ______ m

12. 5,000 m = ______ km

13. 800 cm = ______ m

14. 7,000 m = ______ km

15. 753 cm = ______ m

16. 8,350 m = ______ km

17. 4 m = ______ cm

18. 3 km = ______ m

19. 7 m = ______ cm

20. 6 km = ______ m

21. 9 m = ______ cm

22. 10 km = ______ m

23. 6.8 m = ______ cm

24. 15.5 km = ______ m

Complete the equations.

25. 4 mL = ______ L

26. 7 mm = ______ m

27. 650 mm = ______ cm

28. 70 mm = ______ m

29. 650 mm = ______ m

30. 4 mL = ______ L

31. 650 cm = ______ m

32. 4 L = ______ mL

33. 4 g = ______ kg

34. 7.5 L = ______ mL

35. 4 kg = ______ g

36. 6,500 L = ______ kL

37. 225 g = ______ kg

38. 3.5 kL = ______ L

39. 225 kg = ______ g

40. 57 g = ______ kg

Perimeter of Polygons

Reminder

The perimeter of a parallelogram is computed by adding the length plus the width and multiplying the sum times two.

P = 2 x (l + w)

Directions: Compute the perimeter of these shapes

1.

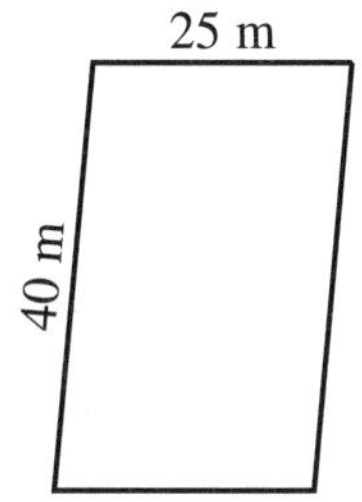

____

2.

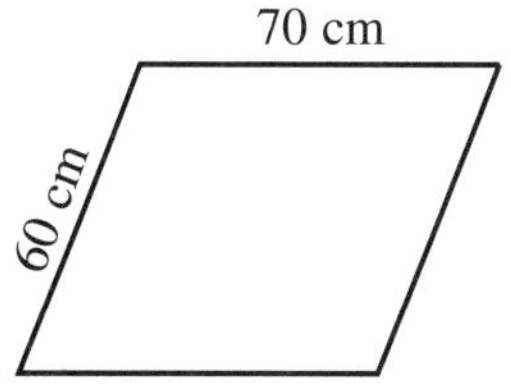

____

3.

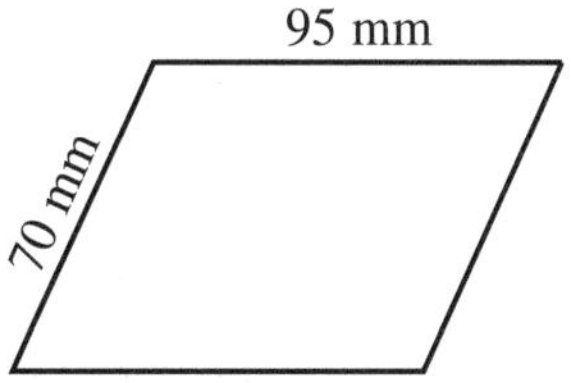

____

4.

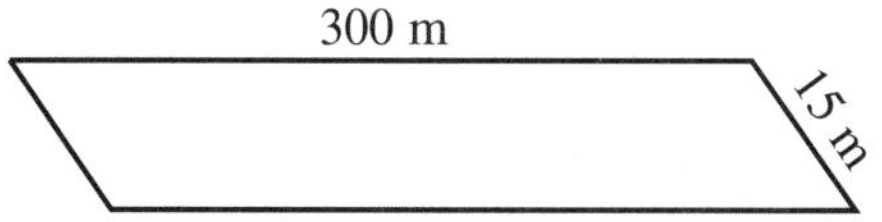

____

5.

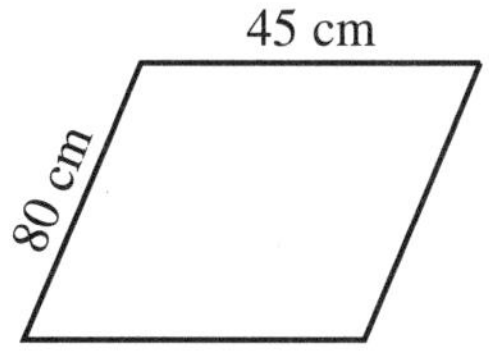

____

6.

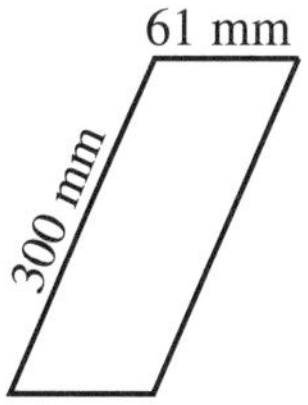

____

7.

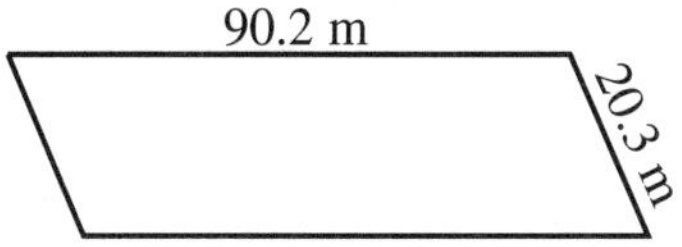

____

8.

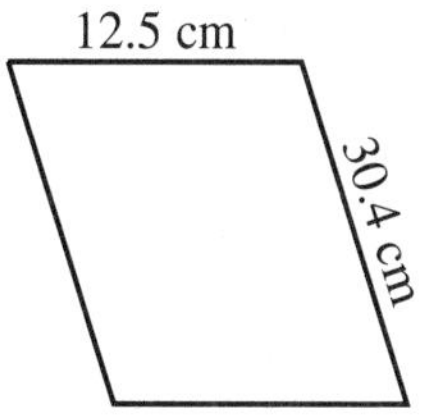

____

Perimeter of Other Polygons

Reminder

- The perimeter of a regular polygon is computed by multiplying the length of one side by the number of sides.
- The perimeter of a polygon with unequal sides is computed by adding the lengths of each side.

Directions: Compute the perimeter of each polygon.

1.

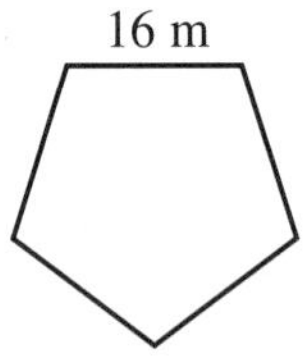

____

2.

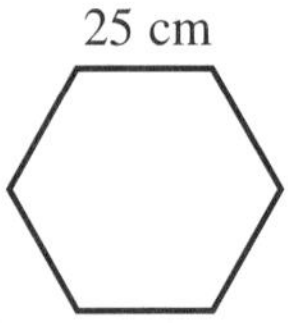

____

3.

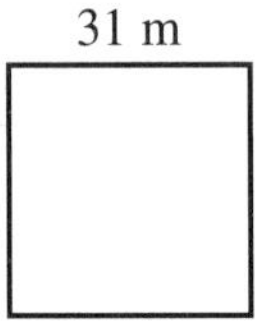

____

4.

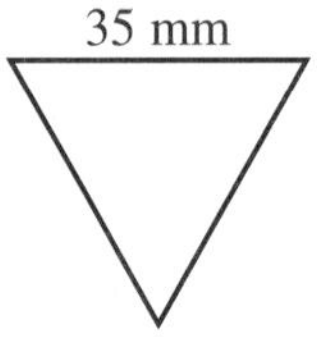

____

5.

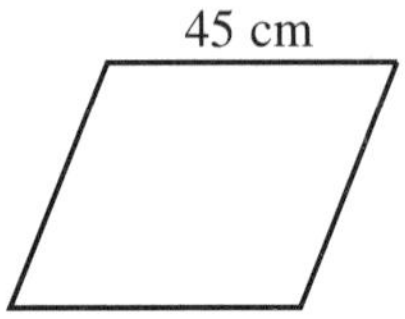

____

6.

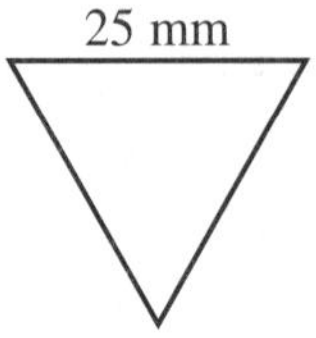

____

7.

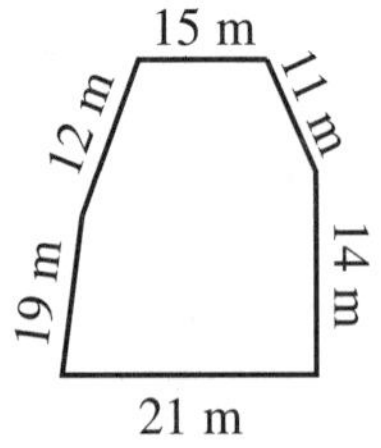

15 ft.

____

8.

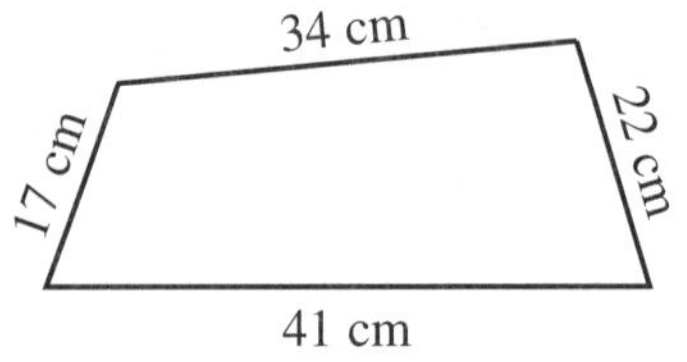

____

9.

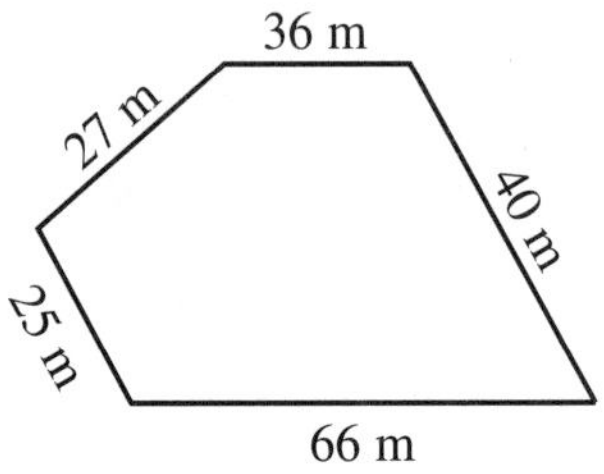

____

10.

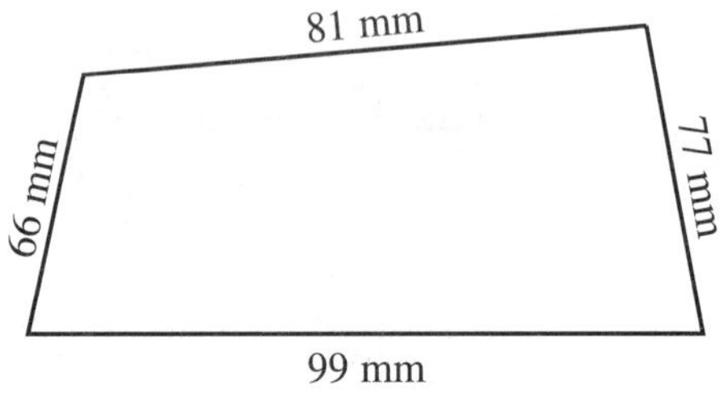

____

Computing Circumference

Reminder

- The circumference is the distance around a circle.
- pi = 3.14
- The circumference is computed by multiplying 3.14 times the diameter.
  C = πd (pi times the diameter)

Directions: Compute the circumference of each circle.

1.

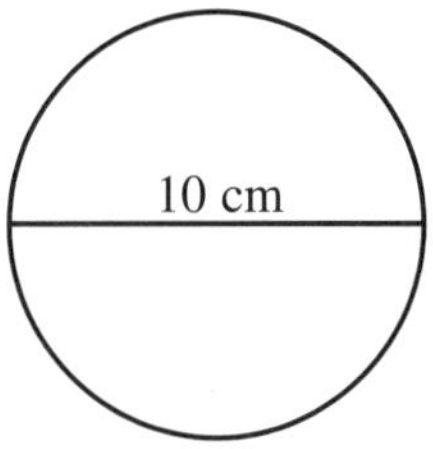

C = ________________

2.

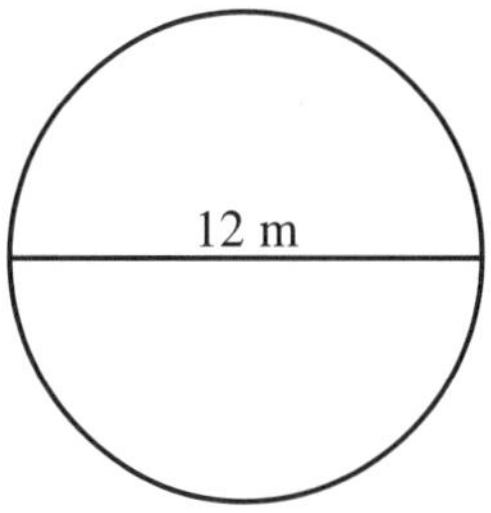

C = ________________

3.

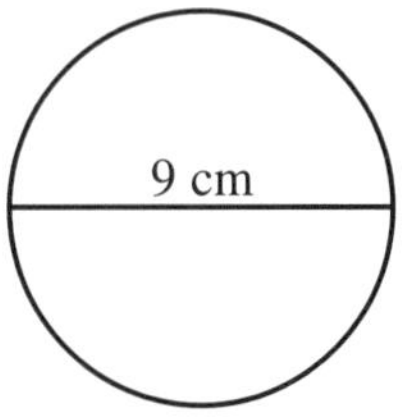

C = ________________

4.

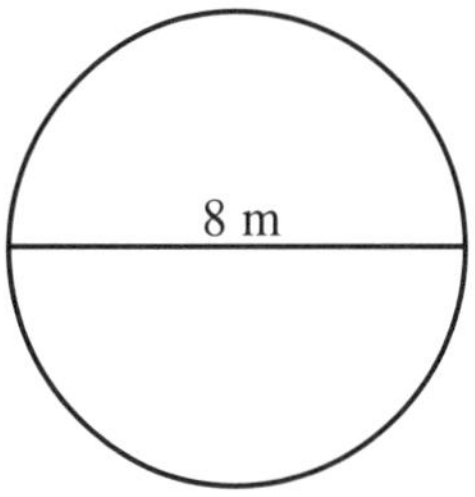

C = ________________

5.

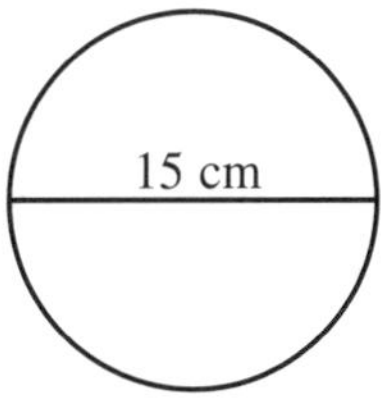

C = ________________

6.

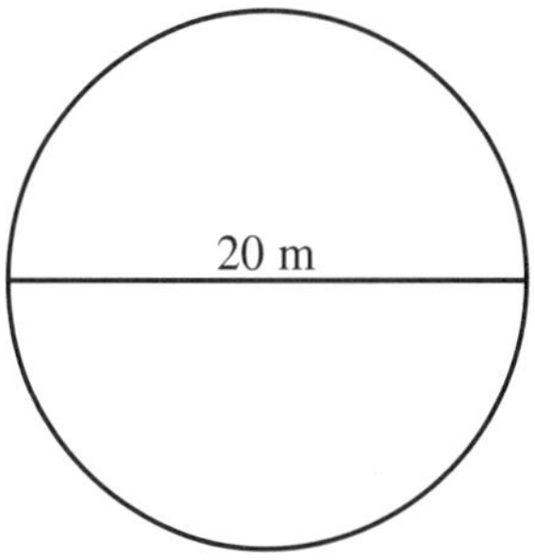

C = ________________

7.

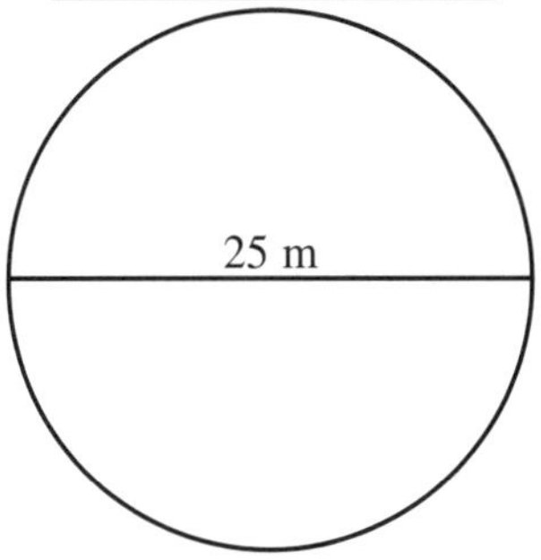

C = ________________

8.

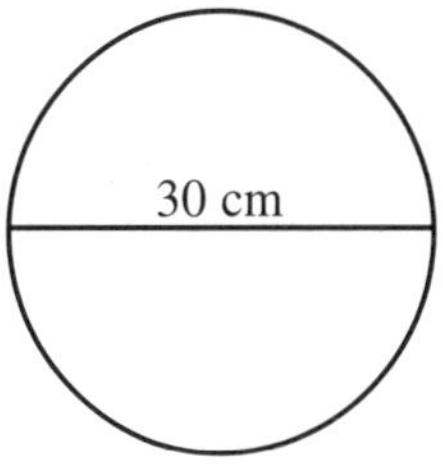

C = ________________

Area of Rectangles and Squares

This rectangular figure is 8 meters long and 3 meters wide.

Area = length x width

A = 8 m x 3 m = 24 m^2

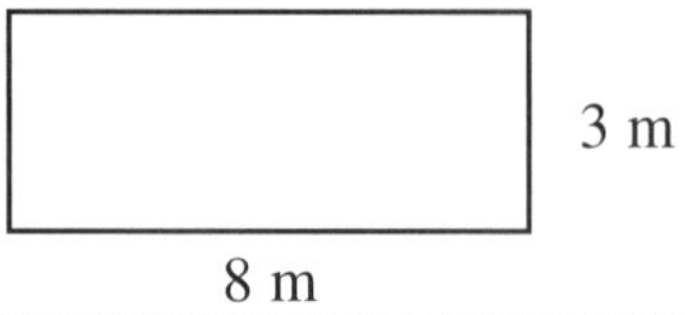

Directions: Use the information in the example above to compute the area for the problems below. Remember, answers must be expressed in square units.

1. l = 60 meters A = __________
w = 40 meters

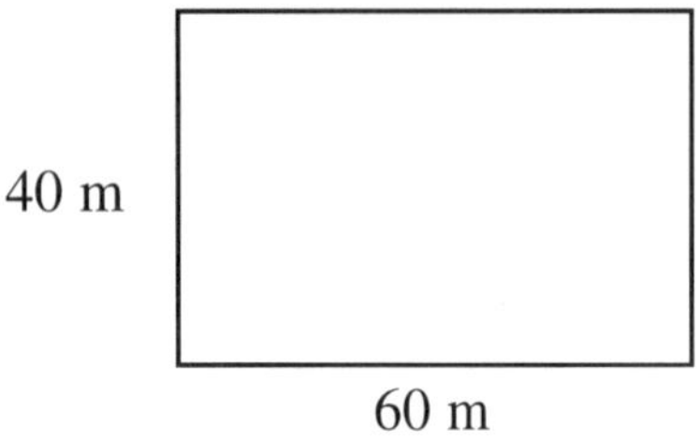

2. l = 60 m A = __________
w = 50 m

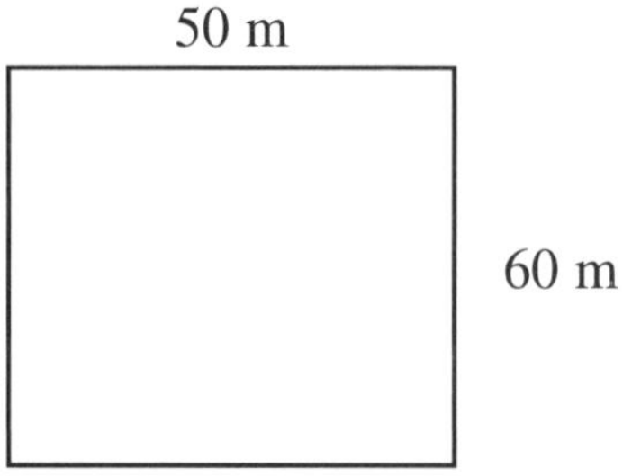

3. s = 40 cm A = __________

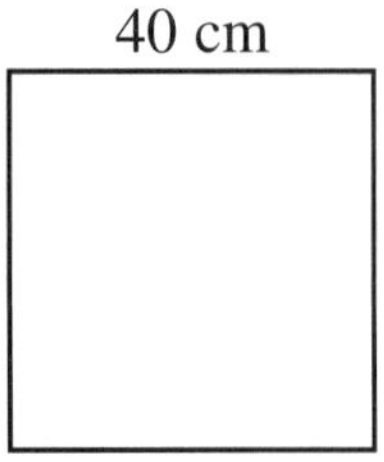

4. l = 70 centimeters A = __________
w = 40 centimeters

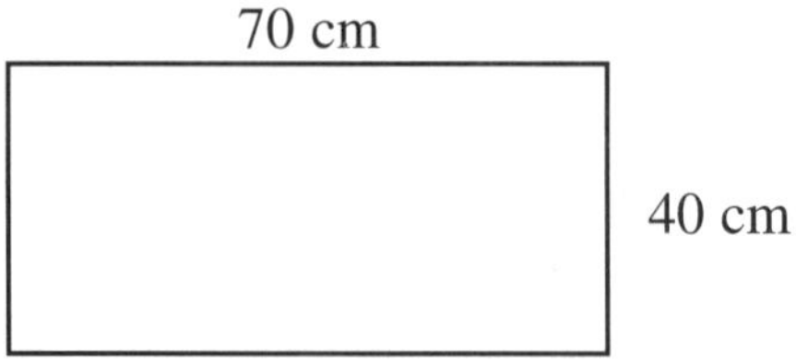

5. l = 60 millimeters A = __________
w = 30 millimeters

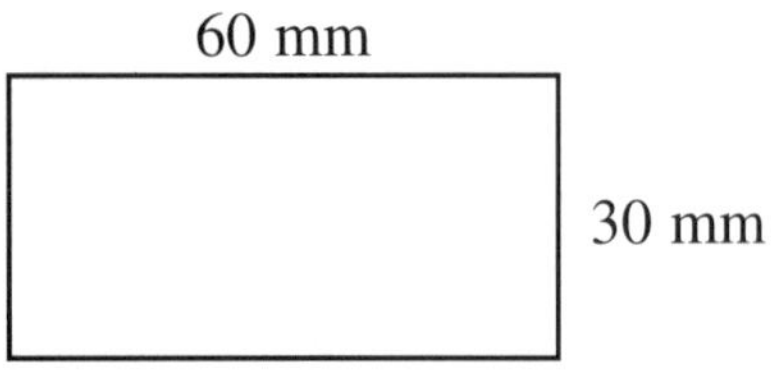

6. l = 90 millimeters A = __________
w = 70 millimeters

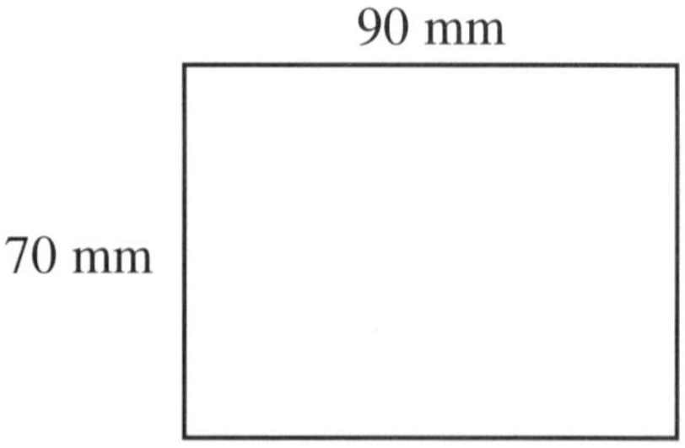

7. A classroom is 7 meters long and 6 meters wide. What is the area? ____________

8. A square plot of land is 70 m long on each side. What is the area of the house? ____________

9. A warehouse is 92 m long and 65 m wide. What is the area? ____________

10. A model of a city is 47 cm long and 32 cm wide. What is the area of the model? _______

Area of Parallelograms

Reminder

The area of a parallelogram is computed by multiplying the base times the height, or A = b x h, and then writing the total in square units.

Directions: Compute the area of each rectangle.

1.

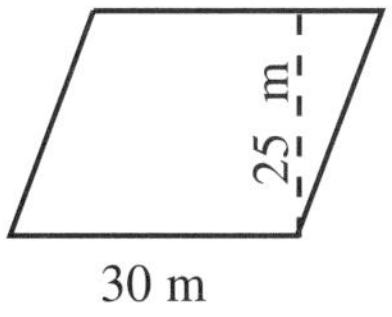

__________________ m^2

2.

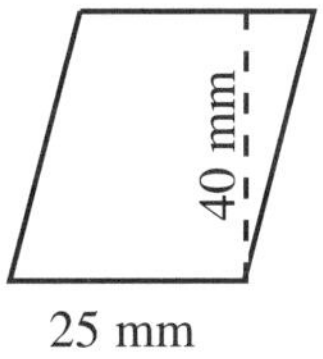

__________________ mm^2

3.

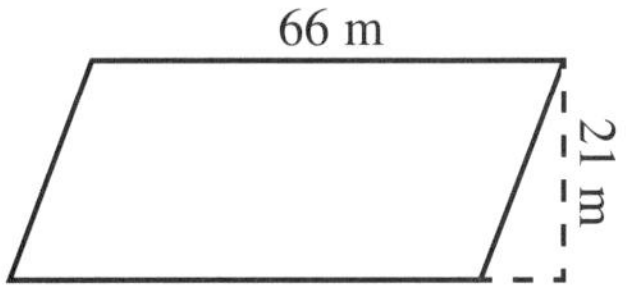

__________________ m^2

4.

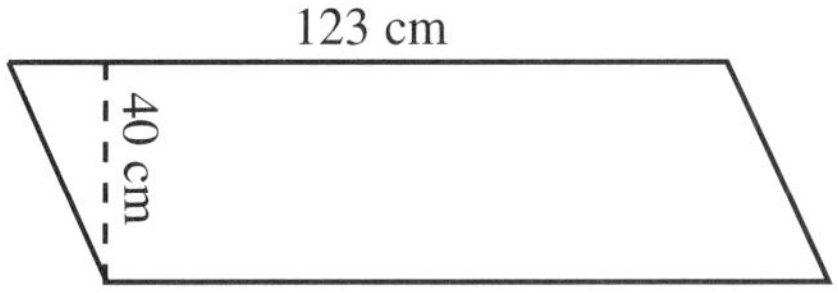

__________________ cm^2

5.

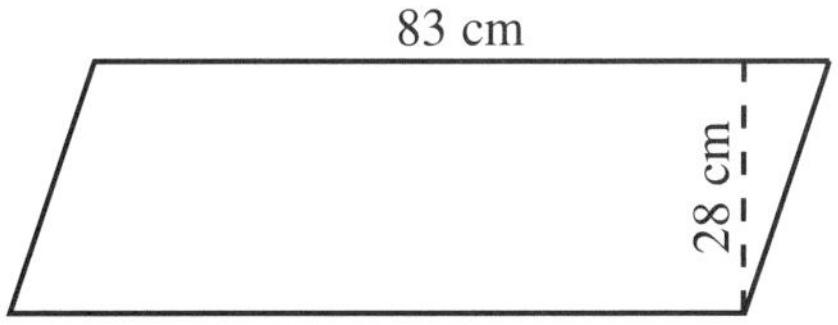

__________________ cm^2

6.

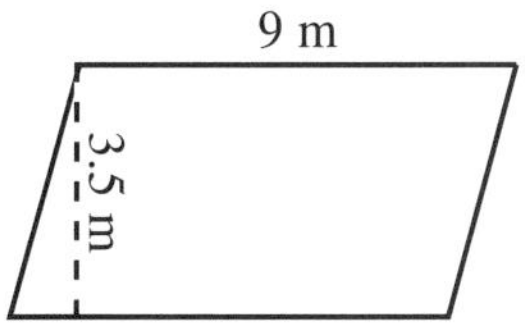

__________________ m^2

7. b = 56 mm
h = 41 mm
A = ______________

8. b = 3.1 m
h = 8 m
A = ______________

9. b = 300 cm
h = 48 cm
A = ______________

10. b = 1.9 m
h = 20 m
A = ______________

11. b = 121 mm
h = 40 mm
A = ______________

12. b = 7.5 cm
h = 3.1 cm
A = ______________

13. b = 6.2 m
h = 3.2 m
A = ______________

14. b = 900 cm
h = 68 cm
A = ______________

Area of Triangles

Reminder

- The area of a triangle is one-half the area of a parallelogram or a rectangle.
- To compute the area of a triangle, multiply the base times the height and divide by 2, or multiply 1/2 the base times the height, or **A = 1/2 (b x h)** or **A = (b x h) ÷ 2**

Directions: Compute the area of each triangle.

1.

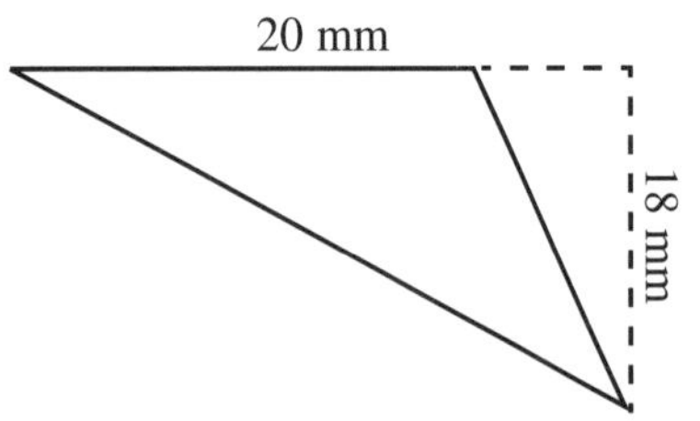

______________ mm^2

2.

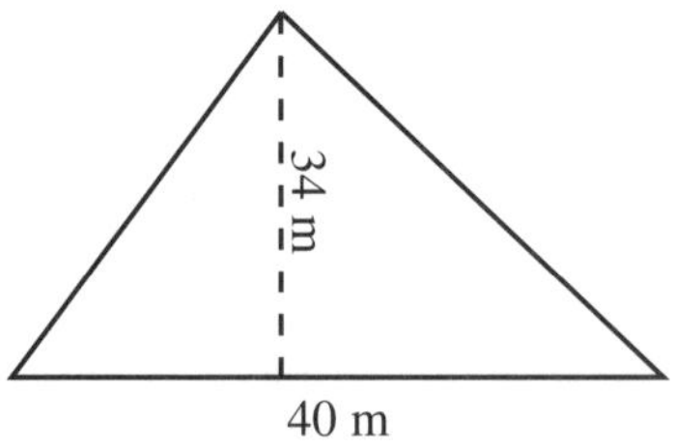

______________ m^2

3.

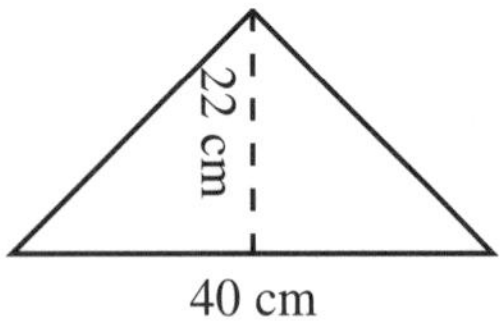

______________ cm^2

4.

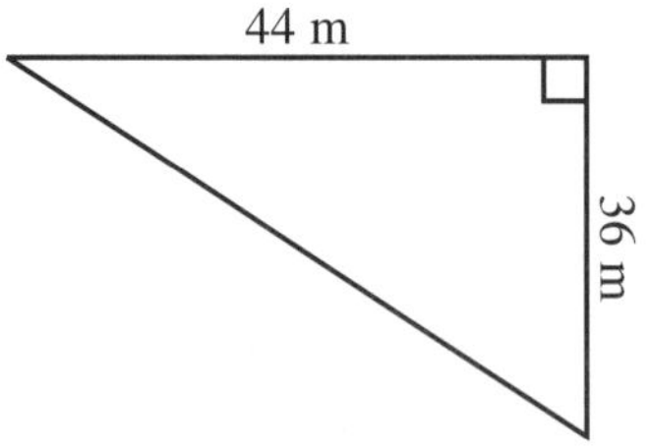

______________ m^2

5.

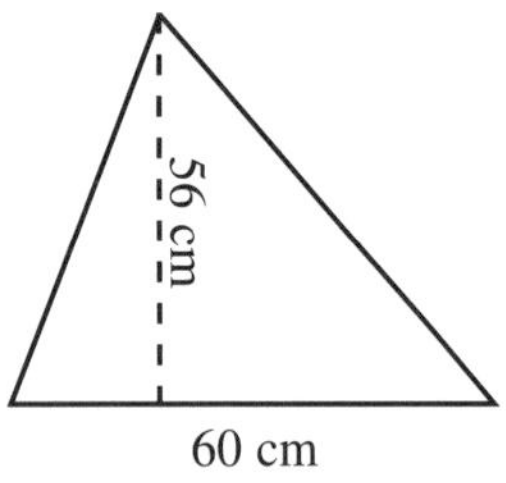

______________ cm^2

6.

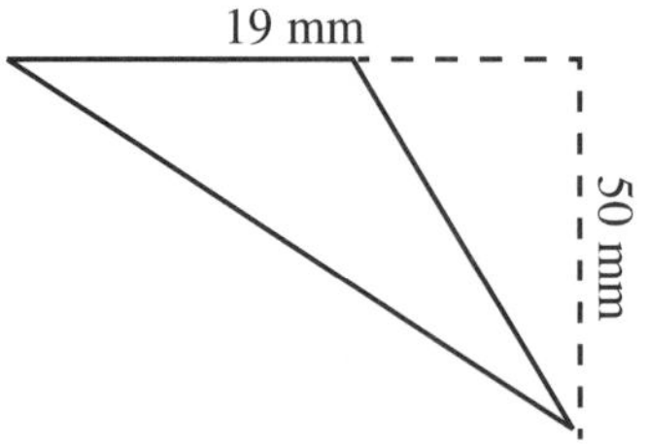

______________ mm^2

7.

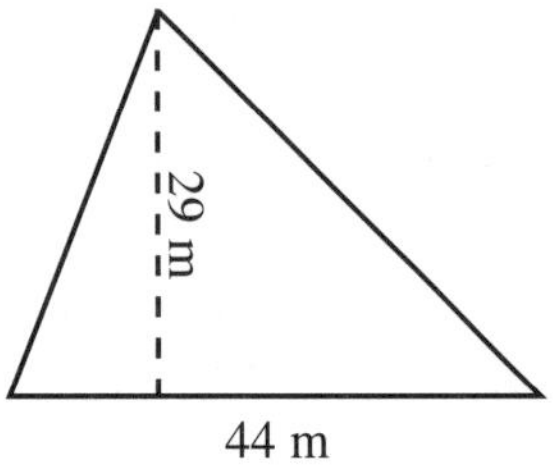

______________ m^2

8.

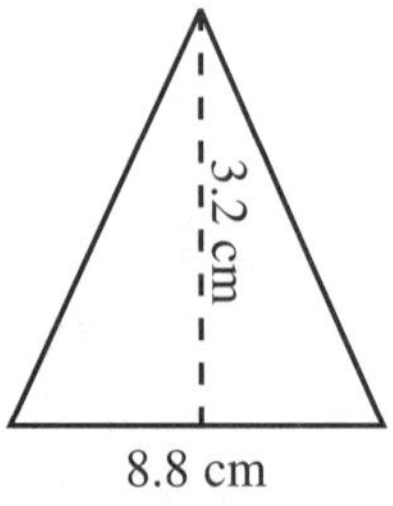

______________ cm^2

Area of a Circle

Reminder

- The area of a circle is computed by multiplying the radius times itself and that answer by 3.14.
- **A = πr^2** (pi times the radius squared) (**Remember**, pi = 3.14)

Directions: Compute the area of each circle.

1.

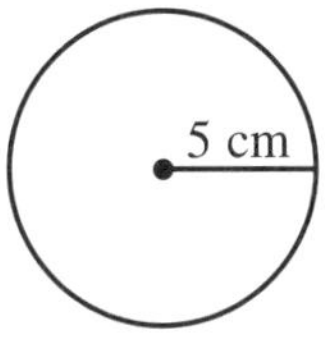

A = ________ cm^2

2.

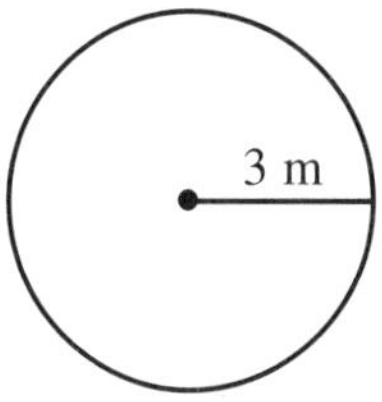

A = ________ m^2

3.

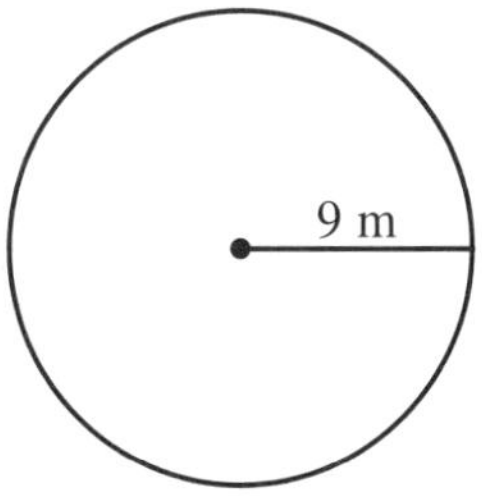

A = ________ m

4.

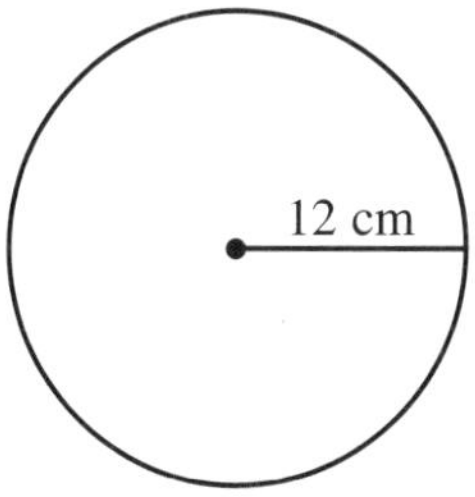

A = ________ cm^2

5.

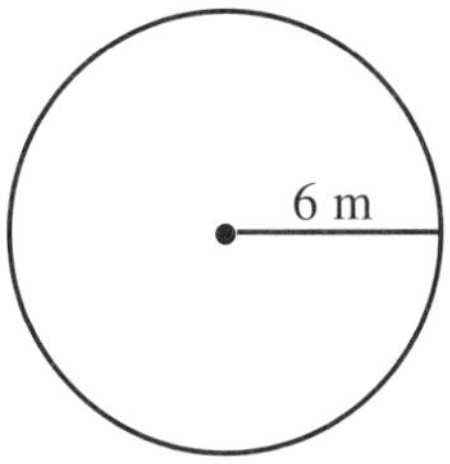

A = ________ m^2

6.

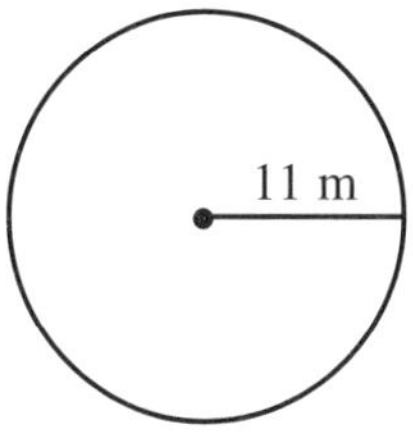

A = ________ m^2

7.

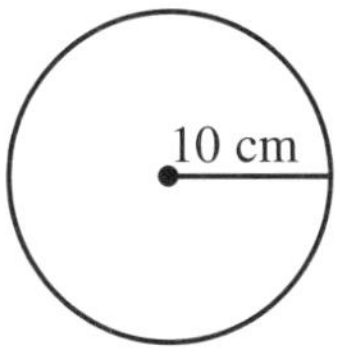

A = ________ cm^2

8.

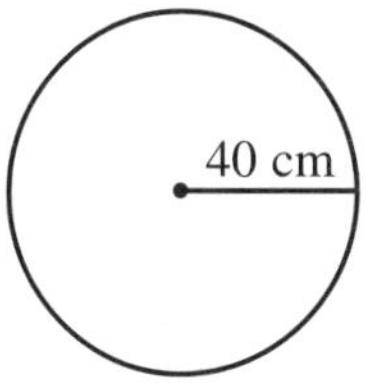

A = ________ cm^2

Volume of a Rectangular Prism

Reminder

The volume of a rectangular prism is computed by multiplying the length times the width times the height of the prism, or **V = l x w x h,** or **V = lwh.**

Directions: Compute the volume of each rectangular prism

1.

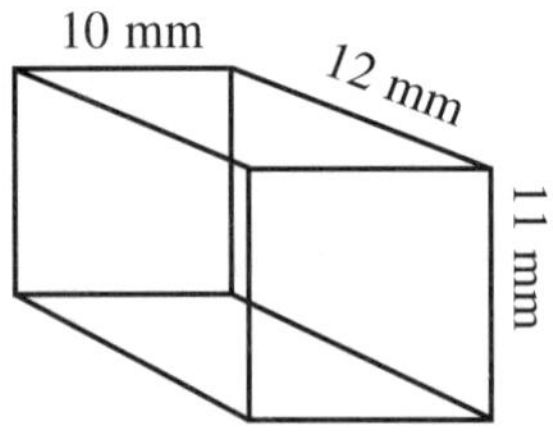

V = ________ mm^3

2.

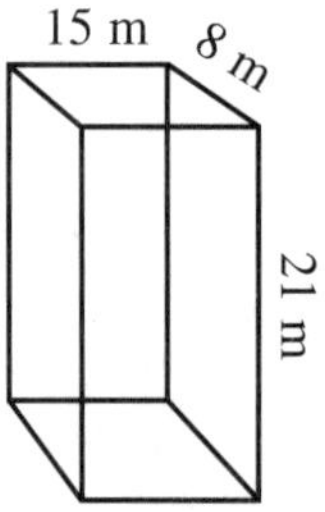

V = ________ m^3

3.

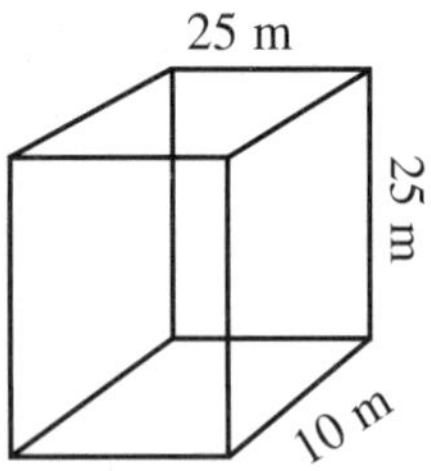

V = ________ m^3

4.

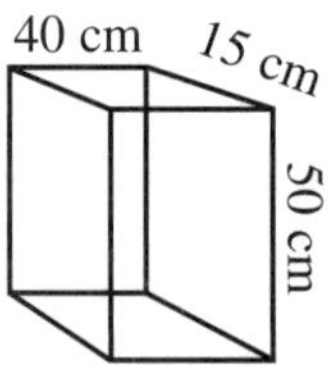

V = ________ cm^3

5.

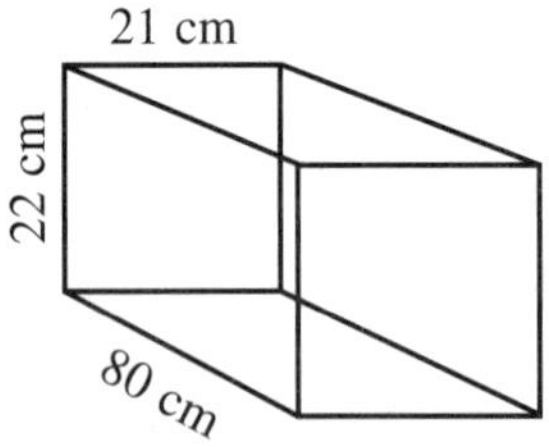

V = ________ cm^3

6.

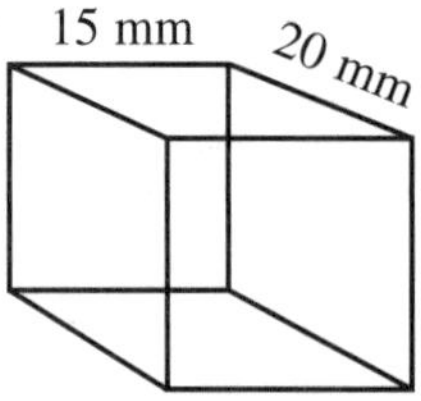

V = ________ mm^3

7.

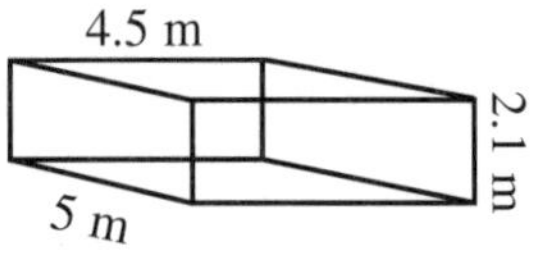

V = ________ m^3

8.

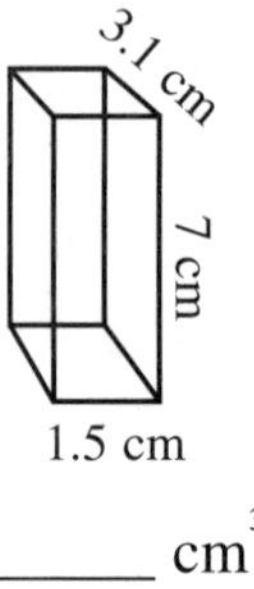

V = ________ cm^3

Volume of Cylinder

Reminder

The volume of a cylinder is computed by multiplying the height times the area of the base.

$$V = h \times \pi r^2$$

Directions: Compute the volume of each cylinder.

1.

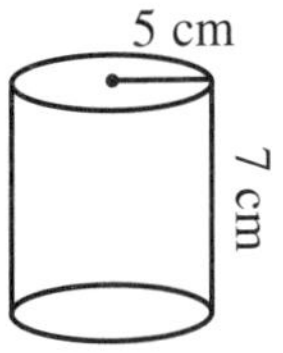

V = ________ cm^3

2.

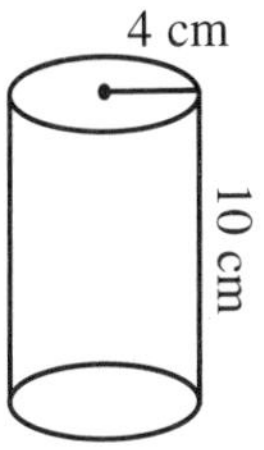

V = ________ cm^3

3.

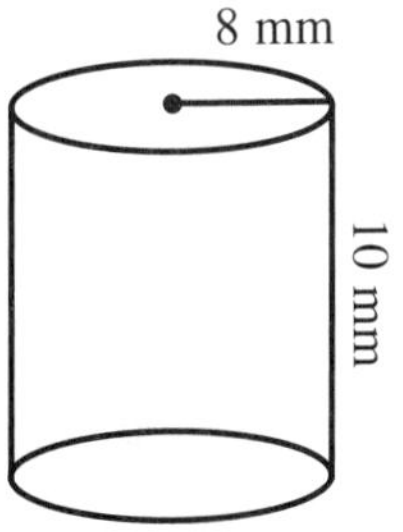

V = ________ mm^3

4.

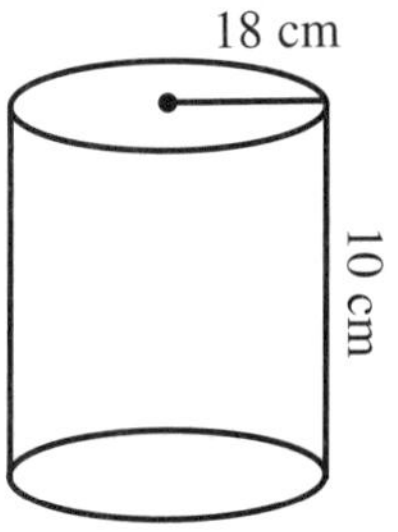

V = ________ cm^3

5.

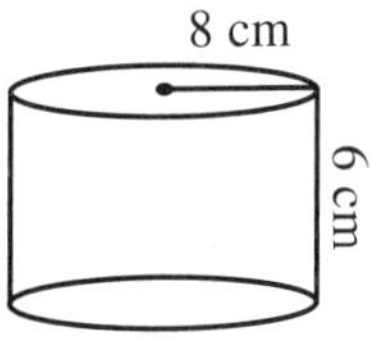

V = ________ cm^3

6.

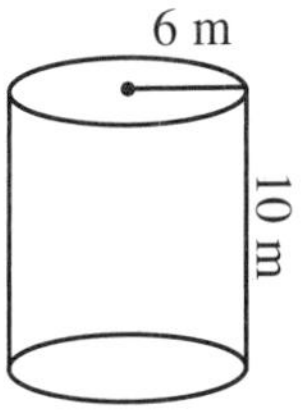

V = ________ m^3

7.

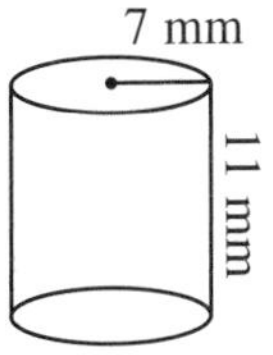

V = ________ mm^3

8.

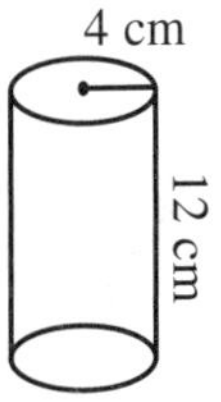

V = ________ cm^3

Volume of a Pyramid

Reminder

- The volume of a pyramid is 1/3 the volume of a prism with the same base.
- The volume of a pyramid is computed by multiplying 1/3 times the length times the width of the base times the height of the pyramid.

V = 1/3 x l x w x h or V = 1/3 (lwh)

Directions: Compute the volume of each pyramid.

1.

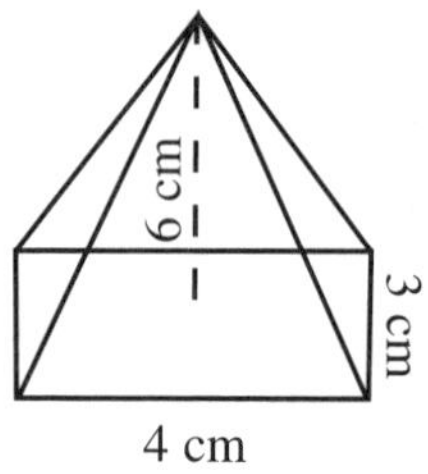

V = ________ cm^3

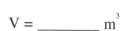

2.

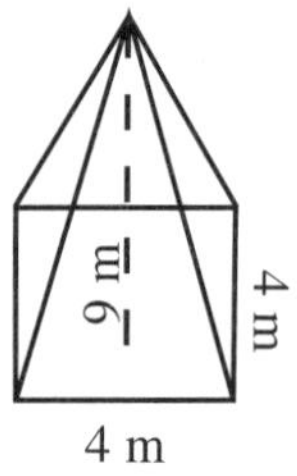

V = ________ m^3

3.

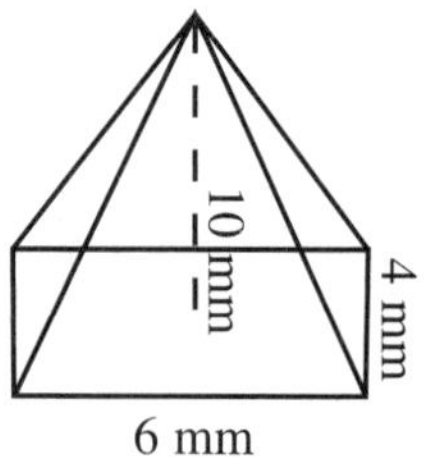

V = ________ mm^3

4.

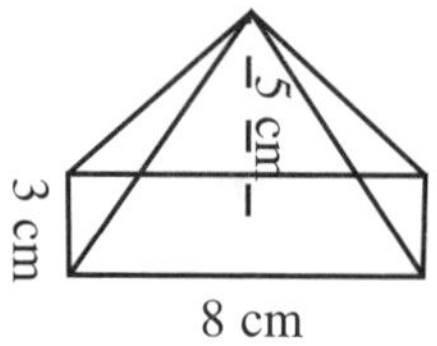

V = ________ cm^3

5.

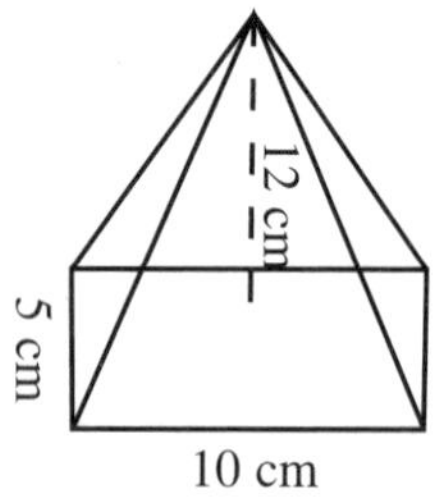

V = ________ cm^3

6.

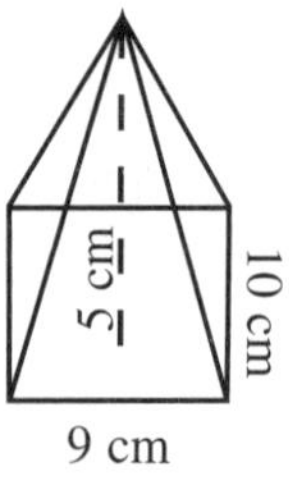

V = ________ cm^3

7.

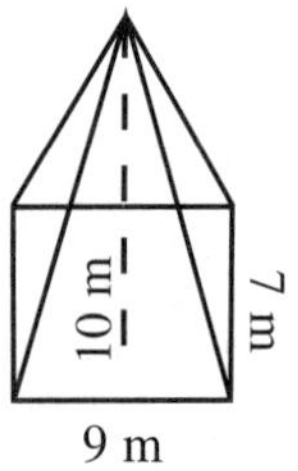

V = ________ m^3

8.

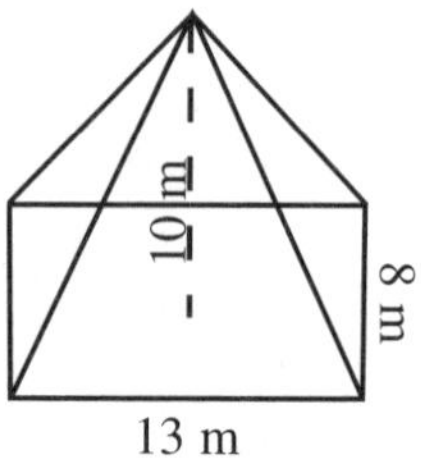

V = ________ m^3

Surface Area

Reminder

To compute the surface area of a rectangular prism, calculate the area of each face then add the six areas.

Directions: Compute the surface area of each rectangular prism.

1.

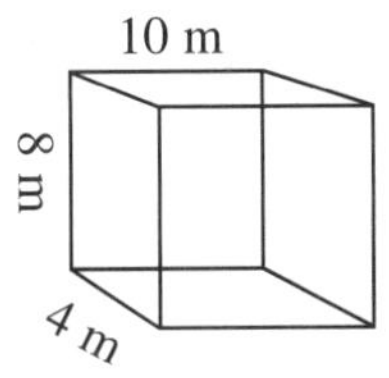

face 1 ____________
face 2 ____________
face 3 ____________
face 4 ____________
face 5 ____________
face 6 ____________
Total __________ m^2

2.

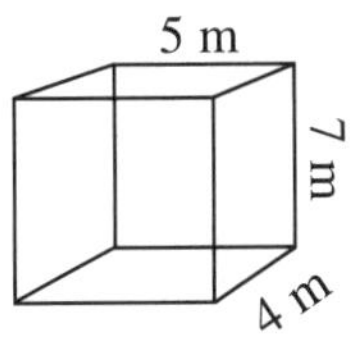

face 1 ____________
face 2 ____________
face 3 ____________
face 4 ____________
face 5 ____________
face 6 ____________
Total __________ m^2

3.

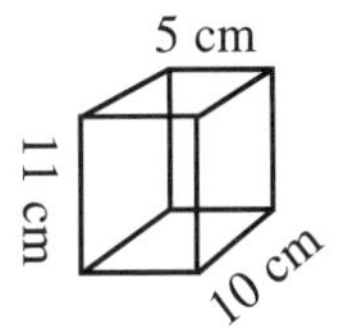

face 1 ____________
face 2 ____________
face 3 ____________
face 4 ____________
face 5 ____________
face 6 ____________
Total __________ cm^2

4.

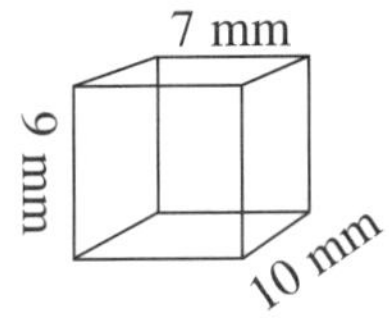

face 1 ____________
face 2 ____________
face 3 ____________
face 4 ____________
face 5 ____________
face 6 ____________
Total __________ mm^2

5.

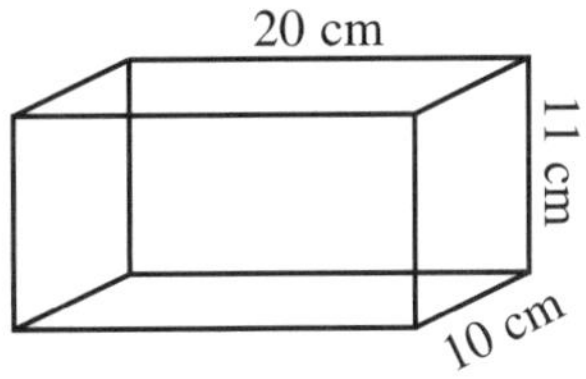

face 1 ____________
face 2 ____________
face 3 ____________
face 4 ____________
face 5 ____________
face 6 ____________
Total __________ cm^2

6.

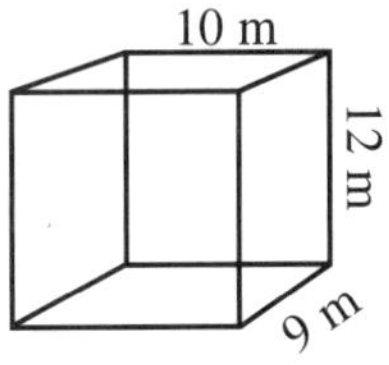

face 1 ____________
face 2 ____________
face 3 ____________
face 4 ____________
face 5 ____________
face 6 ____________
Total __________ m^2

Probability

What is the probability of two heads landing when you flip two coins, a penny and a nickel, at one time?

Possible outcomes:
- penny (heads); nickel (heads)
- penny (tails); nickel (tails)
- penny (heads); nickel (tails)
- penny (tails); nickel (heads)

Probability of two heads: 1 in 4 or 1/4

Directions: List the possible outcomes for each problem. The first one is done for you.

1. What is the probability of a penny landing heads when you flip it?

Possible outcomes: head or tail

Probability of heads: 1 in 2 or 1/2

2. What is the probability of rolling a 4 with one die?

Possible outcomes:____________________

Probability of rolling a 4: ______________

3. What is the probability of rolling a 6 with one die?

Possible outcomes:____________________

Probability of rolling a 6: ______________

4. What is the probability of rolling a 4 or a 6 with one die?

Possible outcomes:____________________

Probability of rolling a 4 or 6:____________

5. A black cloth bag holds one red marble, one green marble, one blue marble, and one black marble. All are the same size. Without looking into the bag, what is the probability of drawing a black marble from the bag?

Possible outcomes:____________________

Probability of drawing the black marble:

____

6. What is the probability of drawing either the black or the blue marble from the bag?

Possible outcomes:____________________

Probability of drawing the black or blue marble: ______________________________

7. What is the probability of drawing a white marble?

Possible outcomes:____________________

Probability of drawing a white marble:

____

8. What is the probability of drawing either the black, the green, or the blue marble from the bag?

Possible outcomes:____________________

Probability of drawing the black, green, or blue marble: _________________________

9. What is the probability of one head and one tail landing when you flip two coins, a penny and a nickel, at the same time?

Possible outcomes:____________________

Probability of one head and one tail:

____

Area and Probability

Look at the spinner below, next to the first set of questions. There are eight spaces. Each is the same size. Four spaces are dark. Four spaces are light.

What is the probability of landing on a dark space? The probability is 4/8 or 1/2 because half of the spaces on the spinner are dark.

Directions: Use the spinner on the left to answer these questions.

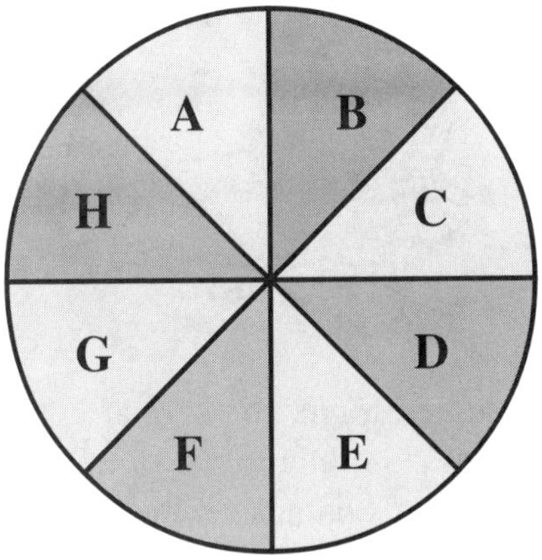

1. What is the probability of landing on space A? ____________________
2. What is the probability of landing on a light space? ____________________
3. What is the probability of landing on either space A or B? ____________________
4. What is the probability of landing on either space G or H? ____________________
5. What is the probability of landing on either a dark or light space? ____________________
6. What is the probability of landing on any space? ____________________

Directions: Use the dartboard on the right to answer these questions. Use fractions or percentages to express probability.

7. What is the probability of hitting space A on this dartboard? ____________________
8. What is the probability of hitting space C on this dartboard? ____________________
9. What is the probability of hitting space A or D on this dartboard? ____________________
10. What is the probability of hitting space B or C on this dartboard? ____________________
11. What is the probability of hitting space A, B, or C on this dartboard? ____________________

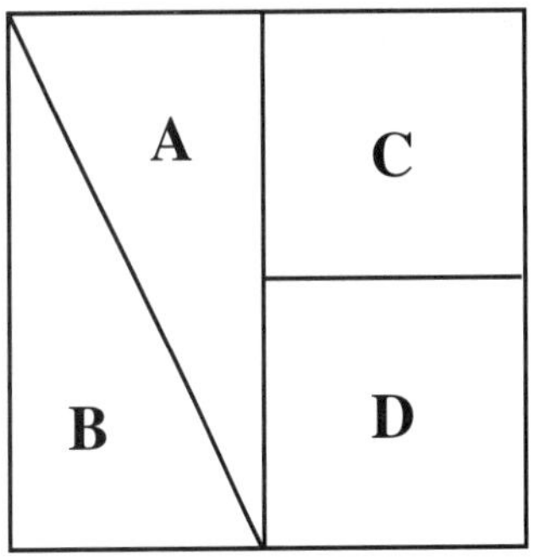

Directions: Use the dartboard on the left to answer these questions. Use fractions or percentages to express probability.

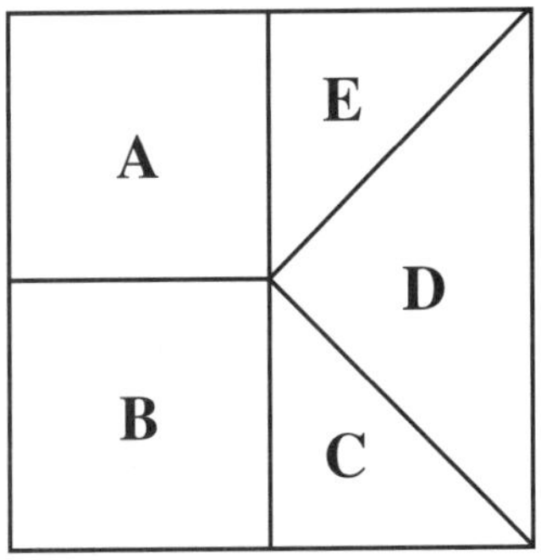

12. What is the probability of hitting space A on this dartboard? ____________________
13. What is the probability of hitting space D on this dartboard? ____________________
14. What is the probability of hitting space A or D on this dartboard? ____________________
15. What is the probability of hitting space C or E on this dartboard? ____________________
16. What is the probability of hitting space D, C, or E on this dartboard? ____________________

Showing Probability with Fractions

Directions: Read each situation. Think about the occurrence of each event. Then, write the probability of each occurrence as a fraction.

A bag has two green marbles, two blue marbles, and one yellow marble. If you were to reach into the bag, write as a fraction what the probability would be that you would randomly select a:

1. blue marble ________

2. green marble ________

3. yellow marble ________

4. red marble ________

Six children entered a drawing to win a bike. John's name is in the box three times. Karen's name is in the box two times. Roger's name is in the box once. Sarah's name is in the box twice. Joe's name is in the box once. Linda's name is in the box once. Write the children's names on the cards below as described and determine the probability that . . .

5. John's name will be randomly picked. _______

6. Sarah's name will be randomly picked. _______

7. Joe's name will be randomly picked. _______

8. a boy's name will be randomly picked. _______

9. a girl's name will be randomly picked. _______

10. Whose name is most likely to be randomly picked?________________________

11. Should Linda expect to be the winner of the bike? Explain your answer.________________

____

____

____

Alphabet tiles are placed in a bag during a kindergarten lesson. Each student is asked to pull a tile at random to identify the letter, then put it back. What is the probability that . . .

12. a vowel will be selected? _______

13. a consonant will be selected? _______

14. the letter "Y" will be selected? _______

15. the Greek letter "Σ" will be selected? _______

16. a letter before "J" will be selected? _______

17. a letter in the word "pig" will be selected? _______

Showing Probability with Decimals and Percents

You can show the numerical probability of an event occurring as a **decimal** or **percent**. To find the **decimal**, first find the fractional probability, then divide the numerator by the denominator.

Example: fractional probability = $\frac{2}{5} \longrightarrow 2 \div 5 = .40$

To find the **percent**, multiply the decimal by 100 and add a percent sign.

Example: decimal probability = .40 $\longrightarrow$ .40 x 100 = 40%

Directions: Look at each situation below. Calculate the probability of each event as a decimal and percent.

Jake decided to color his picture by selecting crayons from the box at random. There were 10 crayons in the box: blue, red, yellow, orange, green, purple, white, brown, black, and gray. Write the probability for each event.

	Decimal	**Percent**
1. Jake will color the duck blue.	________	________
2. Jake will color the sky orange.	________	________
3. Jake will color the tree a primary color.	________	________
4. Jake will color the cloud a color that starts with the letter "b".	________	________

Gina went to the pet store to get a new puppy. When she got there, she couldn't decide which one to get. So she asked the storeowner to select one for her at random. Use the list of different kinds of puppies available to determine the probability of each event. (*Hint:* Drawing a picture might help. Draw one on the back.)

Puppies
2 puppies with black stripes, both male
3 tan puppies with white spots, 1 male, 2 female
2 white puppies with black spots, both female
1 black puppy, male
1 white puppy, male
1 tan puppy, female

	Decimal	Percent
5. Gina receives an all-white puppy.	________	________
6. Gina receives a male puppy.	________	________
7. Gina receives a female spotted puppy.	________	________
8. Gina receives a female striped puppy.	________	________
9. Gina receives a white female puppy with black spots.	________	________
10. Gina receives a puppy without any black.	________	________

Algebra: Solving Equations

An *equation* is a brief way of saying that two expressions are equal in value. Below are some examples of equations.

$x + 3 = 7$ $n - 5 = 15$ $2a = 20$

You can use the axioms of equality to find the value of the unknown (represented by a letter such as x, n, or a) in an equation. The number added, subtracted, multiplied, or divided will leave the unknown on one side of the equation and the numerical value on the other side of the equation.

Steps

1. Decide which number to add or subtract from each side of the equation.
2. Find the numerical value of each unknown.
3. Check your answer by using it instead of the unknown in the equation.

$n - 5 = 15$
$+5 \quad +5$
$n = 20$

n (unknown) = 20 (numeral value)

$20 - 5 = 15$

Directions: Solve these equations. The first one is done for you.

1. $n + 9 = 20$
$-9 \quad -9$
$n = 11$
Check: $11 + 9 = 20$

2. $n + 16 = 19$

3. $a + 12 = 16$

4. $n + 15 = 40$

5. $a + 10 = 25$

6. $n + 13 = 39$

7. $x - 17 = 10$

8. $n - 6 = 4$

9. $a - 5 = 15$

10. $n - 11 = 20$

11. $x - 10 = 15$

12. $a - 4 = 10$

13. $n + 6 = 30$

14. $a - 11 = 80$

15. $n + 14 = 41$

16. $a - 15 = 50$

17. $x + 22 = 60$

18. $n - 13 = 53$

Algebra: Working with Equations

You can find the value of the unknown quantity in an equation by using the axioms of equality. The number added, subtracted, multiplied, or divided will leave the unknown on one side of the equation and the numerical value on the other side of the equation.

Remember the following steps:

1. Decide the number by which to multiply or divide each side of the equation.
2. Find the numerical value of each unknown.
3. Check your answer by using it instead of the unknown in the equation.

Sample

Divide both sides of the equation by 3.
When $3a$ is divided by 3, the answer is a.
When 30 is divided by 3, the answer is 10.
So, $a = 10$.
Check your answer.

$$3a = 30$$
$$\frac{3a}{3} = \frac{30}{3}$$
$$a = 10$$
$$3 \times 10 = 30$$

Directions: Solve these equations. The first one is done for you.

1. $4n = 20$
$\frac{4n}{4} = \frac{20}{4}$
$n = 5$

2. $6n = 66$

3. $7n = 2$

4. $8a = 32$

5. $5n = 35$

6. $12n = 120$

7. $10n = 50$

8. $12a = 72$

9. $6a = 90$

10. $\frac{n}{2} = 10$

11. $\frac{n}{2} = 30$

12. $\frac{a}{5} = 12$

13. $\frac{n}{4} = 4$

14. $\frac{n}{4} = 15$

15. $\frac{a}{8} = 8$

16. $\frac{n}{4} = 40$

17. $7a = 490$

18. $12n = 480$

Roman Numerals

The Seven Basic Roman Numerals	Value
I	1
V	5
X	10
L	50
C	100
D	500
M	1000

Roman Numerals 1–20			
I	1	XI	11
II	2	XII	12
III	3	XIII	13
IV	4	XIV	14
V	5	XV	15
VI	6	XVI	16
VII	7	XVII	17
VIII	8	XVIII	18
IX	9	XIX	19
X	10	XX	20

Directions: Study the tables above. Write the present-day number equivalent to each Roman numeral.

1. I = ____________ **2.** IV = ____________ **3.** VI = ____________

4. X = ____________ **5.** III = ____________ **6.** V = ____________

7. VIII = ____________ **8.** XII = ____________ **9.** VII = ____________

10. IX = ____________ **11.** XV = ____________ **12.** XIII = ____________

Directions: Using the chart above, write these numbers as Roman numerals.

13. 21 = ____________ **14.** 22 = ____________ **15.** 23 = ____________

16. 24 = ____________ **17.** 25 = ____________ **18.** 26 = ____________

19. 27 = ____________ **20.** 28 = ____________ **21.** 29 = ____________

Directions: Write the value for each of these Roman numerals.

22. XXX = ____________ **23.** XXVI = ____________ **24.** XXXIII = ____________

25. XXXV = ____________ **26.** XXIX = ____________ **27.** XXXVIII = ____________

28. XXXIX = ____________ **29.** XXXIV = ____________ **30.** XXXVII = ____________

Directions: Write these values as Roman numerals.

31. 45 = ____________ **32.** 49 = ____________ **33.** 48 = ____________

34. 47 = ____________ **35.** 16 = ____________ **36.** 46 = ____________

37. 27 = ____________ **38.** 37 = ____________ **39.** 29 = ____________

40. Write your age in Roman numerals: ____________

41. Write a friend's age in Roman numerals: ____________

42. Write an older relative's age in Roman numerals: ____________

Using Roman Numerals

Directions: Study the tables on page 146. Convert these Roman numeral dates to present-day numerals.

1. MM = ______________

2. MMI = ______________

3. MMV = ______________

4. MCM = ______________

5. MDCCC = ______________

6. MDCCCIII = ______________

7. MCMXII = ______________

8. MCML = ______________

9. MCMLXXXIII = ______________

10. MDC = ______________

11. MDCCXVIII = ______________

12. MCMXCVIII = ______________

Directions: Convert these dates to Roman numerals.

13. 2000 = ______________

14. 2001 = ______________

15. 2010 = ______________

16. 1900 = ______________

17. 1960 = ______________

18. 1800 = ______________

19. 1910 = ______________

20. 1940 = ______________

21. 1881 = ______________

22. 1654 = ______________

23. 1492 = ______________

24. 1588 = ______________

Directions: Determine the value of each of these Roman numerals.

25. V = ______________

26. X = ______________

27. L = ______________

28. C = ______________

29. D = ______________

30. M = ______________

31. MM = ______________

32. CCC = ______________

33. MD = ______________

34. MDCC = ______________

35. MMMDCL = ______________

36. MDCLXVI = ______________

Directions: Write these answers in Roman numerals.

37. What is the sum of XXXVIII and XXV? ______________

38. What is the sum of LXXXVI and XI? ______________

39. What is the sum of XC and CX? ______________

40. What is the sum of XXIII and XXVII? ______________

Base Two (The Binary System)

Using Base Two

Sticks	Eights	Fours	Twos	Ones
	0	0	1	0
	0	0	1	1
	0	1	0	0
	0	1	0	1

Base two has only two counting numbers or digits. They are 0 and 1.

The two sticks shown above would be represented this way in base two: 10_{two}. It is read as **1** two and **0** ones—base two.

The three sticks shown above would be represented this way in base two: 11_{two}. It is read as **1** two and **1** one—base two.

The four sticks shown above would be represented this way in base two: 100_{two}. It is read as **1** four with **0** twos and **0** ones—base two.

These five sticks shown above would be represented this way in base two: 101_{two}. It is read as **1** four, **0** twos, and **1** one—base two.

(Note: Notice how the base-two groupings increase: ones, twos, fours, eights, sixteens, etc.)

Directions: Study the information above. Express the number of sticks indicated in each problem below in base two.

1. /

__________ two

2. //

__________ two

3. // /

__________ two

4. ////

__________ two

5. //// /

__________ two

6. //// //

__________ two

7. //// // /

__________ two

8. ////////

__________ two

9. //////// /

__________ two

Directions: Express the number of stars indicated in each problem below in base two.

10. ** *

__________ two

11. **** *

__________ two

12. **

__________ two

13. ******** *

__________ two

14. ****

__________ two

15. **** **

__________ two

16. **** ** *

__________ two

17. *

__________ two

18. ********

__________ two

Charting Base Two

This chart illustrates the number of sticks shown here expressed in base two.

Sticks	Eights	Fours	Twos	Ones
//////// // /	1	0	1	1

Directions: Use the chart shown below to indicate the number of sticks shown expressed in base two.

Sticks	Eights	Fours	Twos	Ones
1. // /				
2. //// /				
3. //// //				
4. //// // /				
5. //				
6. ////				
7. /				
8. ////////				
9. //////// /				
10. //////// // /				

Directions: Draw sticks to represent these base-ten numbers. Then express the numbers in base two on the chart. The first one is done for you.

Base Ten Number	Sticks	Eights	Fours	Twos	Ones
11. 5	//// /	0	1	0	1
12. 3					
13. 4					
14. 7					
15. 8					
16. 2					
17. 6					
18. 9					
19. 11					
20. 10					
21. 12					
22. 15					
23. 14					
24. 13					

Geology Facts

Directions: Discover some interesting facts about geology. Solve each problem below. Then write the answer in the blank.

1. 52×25	2. $4\overline{)680}$	3. 10 x 16 =
4. $1345 + 438$	5. 81 ÷ 9 =	6. 32.40×0.25
7. 2.5×100	8. $49 + 46$	9. $33 - 28$

1. Worldwide, more than _______ volcanoes have erupted at least once during the past 10,000 years.
2. A tsunami *(tsoo-NA-me)* is an extremely destructive sea wave, usually triggered by large earthquakes or eruptions, and can reach heights of _______ feet.
3. Yakima, located about _______ kilometers downwind of a volcano, received more than two centimeters of ash.
4. After observing the weird weather patterns that followed the eruption at Laki Volcano in Iceland in _______ , Benjamin Franklin became the first person to figure out that volcanic eruptions could affect climate.
5. The strength of earthquakes is measured on the Richter scale, which is numbered from 1 to _____. Most earthquakes are caused by land shifting along faults.
6. In 1949, an earthquake with a magnitude of _______ occured near Queen Charlotte Islands.
7. In 1929, a 7.2 magnitude earthquake occured _______ km south of Newfoundland, resulting in a tsunami.
8. In the top 16 kilometers of the Earth's crust, _______ % of the rocks are either igneous (formed from molten magma) or metamorphic (changed by heat, pressure, or chemical action).
9. Geologists think that the age of the Earth is about _______ billion years.

Rock and Mineral Facts

Directions: Learn some facts about rocks and minerals as you find the missing words in the sentences. Use the number pairs listed in each sentence to determine the missing letters on the grid. Then, write the correct letter on the proper line in the sentence. (*Reminder:* Use the numbers at the bottom of the grid to find the first number of the pair.)

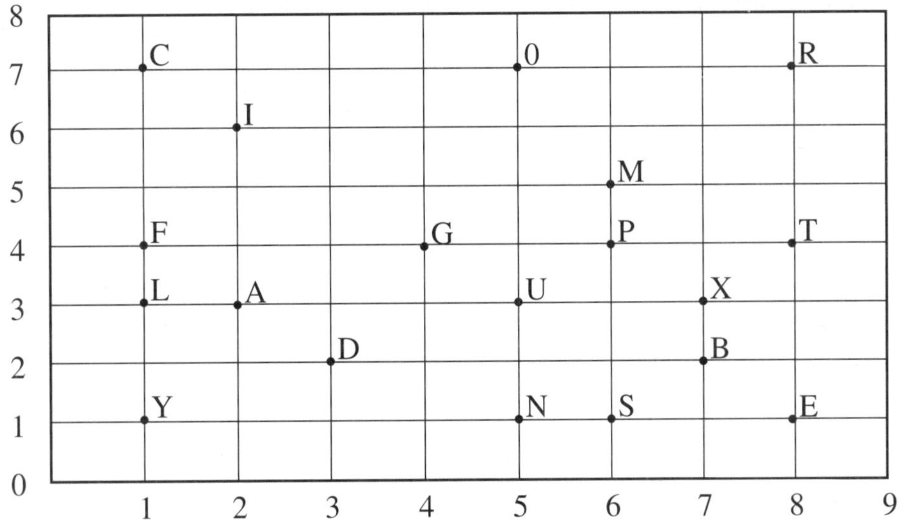

1. Sulfides are ___ ___ ___ ___ ___ ___ ___ ___ ___ that have atoms of sulfur and
   1,7 5,7 6,5 6,4 5,7 5,3 5,1 3,2 6,1
   atoms of a metal.

2. The sulfides are important because they provide important metals. Minerals that are mined for their metals are called ___ ___ ___ ___ .
   5,7 8,7 8,1 6,1

3. Pyrite is the most common sulfide mineral on Earth and is found just about everywhere. Sometimes it looks like gold. Pieces in streams have fooled miners, so it was nicknamed
   ___ ___ ___ ___ ' ___ ___ ___ ___ ___ .
   1,4 5,7 5,7 1,3 6,1 4,4 5,7 1,3 3,2

4. Sulfosalts are minerals that have sulfur, a metal (either silver, copper, or lead), and a semimetal. The semimetals are bismuth, antimony, and ___ ___ ___ ___ ___ ___ ___ .
   2,3 8,7 6,1 8,1 5,1 2,6 1,7

5. The ___ ___ ___ ___ ___ ___ are very important minerals. Oxygen is a part of the air
   5,7 7,3 2,6 3,2 8,1 6,1
   we breathe. It is also in water and magmas.

6. The ___ ___ ___ ___ ___ ___ ___ ___ ___ ___ are a group of beautiful and very
   1,7 2,3 8,7 7,2 5,7 5,1 2,3 8,4 8,1 6,1
   common minerals.

7. ___ ___ ___ ___ ___ ___ ___ ___ have a nitrogen atom surrounded by three oxygen
   5,1 2,6 8,4 8,7 2,3 8,4 8,1 6,1
   atoms. Sodium is a nitrate found in dry, desert areas.

8. ___ ___ ___ ___ ___ ___ is probably the most common sulfate. It has a Mohs
   4,4 1,1 6,4 6,1 5,3 6,5
   hardness of two and can be scratched with your fingernail.

Meteors and Comets

During Columbus's first voyage to the Indies he reported seeing "...a marvelous bolt of fire fall from the heavens into the sea..." This phenomenon was actually a meteor. Learn about meteors. Read the paragraph below and then answer the questions below it.

Meteors are sometimes called "shooting stars," but they are not stars at all. They are chunks of iron and stone that have broken off from asteroids. Meteors fall to Earth very quickly and, unlike comets, they only appear to last for a few seconds. As meteors make their descent, they become hot and begin to glow brightly. Meteors can burn up before they reach the Earth, but occasionally a meteor will hit the ground hard enough to form a crater. When a meteor makes it all the way to Earth, it is then called a meteorite. One famous meteorite crater is in Arizona. The Barringer Meteor Crater is almost 300 meters deep and was made by a giant meteorite weighing more than 450 tons (or 500,000 kilograms)!

Other bright objects which can be seen traveling through space are comets. A comet is a ball of dust, ice, and gases that travels in an orbit around the sun. As it speeds along in space, the sun's energy causes the comet to lose some of its dust and gas. This dust and gas streams out from behind the comet forming a tail millions of kilometers long. Probably the most famous comet is Halley's Comet, named after English astronomer Edmund Halley. He observed and studied the comet in 1682; he predicted that it would reappear in 1759. Halley's comet has been seen every 76 years since the year 240 BCE. It was last seen in 1986. In what year will the next sighting take place?

Read each statement below. Write a **T** if the sentence is true; write an **F** if the sentence is false.

1. _________All meteors burn up before they reach the Earth.

2. _________A comet orbits the Earth.

3. _________Meteors are composed of iron and stone.

4. _________As meteors fall to the ground they cool off.

5. _________The Barringer Meteor Crater can be found in Arizona.

6. _________Comets are the same as meteors.

7. _________Meteors are stars.

8. _________Another name for meteor is "shooting star."

9. _________Halley's Comet was seen in 1999.

10. _________Some meteorites hit the ground hard enough to form craters.

11. _________A comet has a tail millions of kilometers long.

12. _________Meteors glow brightly as they make their descent.

13. Complete the Venn diagram on the next page comparing meteors and comets.

Meteors and Comets *(cont.)*

Complete the comet and meteor Venn diagram by writing each statement below in the correct section of the intersecting circles.

- are members of the solar system
- tails are millions of kilometers long
- appear in the night sky for many days
- are made of iron, stone, and other metals
- have a tail
- fall quickly to Earth
- are called "shooting stars"
- orbit around the sun
- hardly made of anything
- some are visible without telescopes

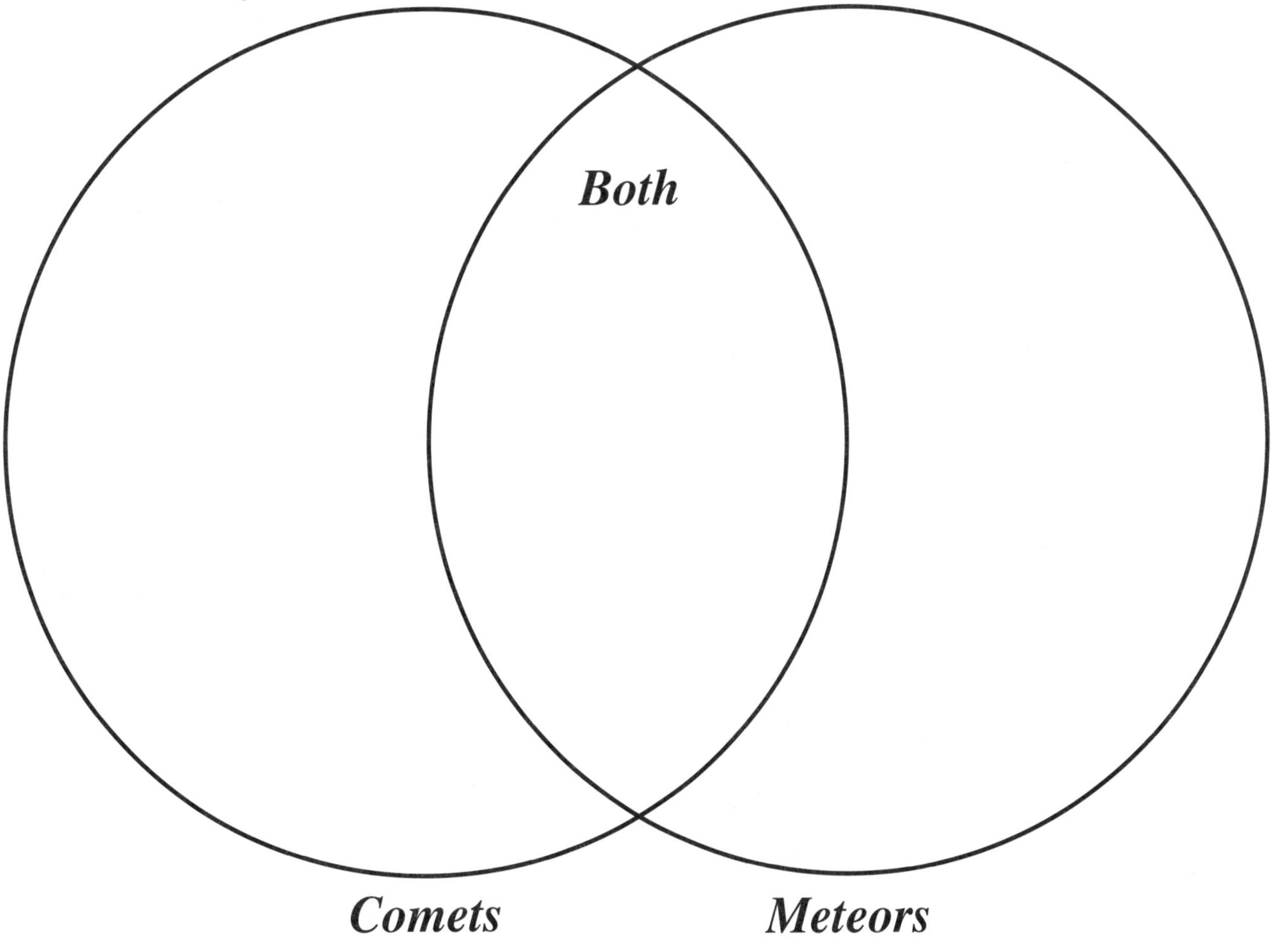

Asteroids

Asteroids, or minor planets, have been described as "mountains in space." They are large rocks typically ranging from a few meters to several hundred kilometers across. Most asteroids move between the orbits of Mars and Jupiter in what is often called the "asteroid belt." They appear star-like in telescopes. Against the background of stars, their motion is usually so slow that several hours may pass before any movement is noticed. Most asteroids within the asteroid belt never come closer than 150 million kilometers from Earth, but there are some which come closer to—and even cross—Earth's orbit. These objects can occasionally pass within a few million kilometers of us, or even within the orbit of the moon. They move so fast in this location that the change is apparent after only a few minutes. Asteroids within the asteroid belt can be observed every year, while ones passing especially close to Earth may be visible for only a few weeks or months.

Astronomers distinguish asteroids and comets on the basis of their telescopic appearance. If the object is star-like in appearance, it is called an *asteroid.* If it has a visible atmosphere or tail, it is a comet. Scientists do not distinguish between asteroids and comets in methods to warn of impacting Earth. Both can collide with our planet.

Earth is located in a swarm of comets and asteroids that can, and do, collide with it periodically. The solar system has a huge population of asteroids and comets, remnants of its origin. From time to time some are bumped into orbits that cross the orbits of Earth and other planets. Spacecraft exploration of **terrestrial** (solid, of Earth) planets and most of the moons of planets shows cratered surfaces made by continuous impacts from projectiles.

Additional evidence about asteroids near Earth has been collected since the first asteroid was discovered decades ago. Improvements in telescopic search techniques have resulted in the discovery of dozens of near-Earth asteroids and short-period comets each year. The role of impacts in Earth's geological history, its ecosphere, and the evolution of life itself, has become a major topic of discussion among scientists.

The possible dangers of such impacts was focused when, in 1989, father-and-son geologist team Luis and Walter Alvarez, found evidence indicating that an asteroid estimated at 10–16 kilometers long impacted Earth 65 million years ago, resulting in extinction of many life forms and ending the age of dinosaurs. The greatest risk is from the impact of the largest objects—those with diameters greater than 1 kilometer. Such impacts may occur once to several times per million years and would affect the entire planet.

Asteroids *(cont.)*

Comprehension Questions

1. Asteroids have been described as . . .

a. asteroid belts.
b. mountains in space.
c. comets.
d. meteors.

2. Astronomers distinguish asteroids and comets on the basis of . . .

a. their telescopic appearance.
b. their weight in relation to Earth.
c. how many times they orbit Mars and Jupiter.
d. how close they come to Earth.

3. If an object has a visible "tail," it is a(n) . . .

a. asteroid.
b. meteor.
c. comet.
d. star.

4. The word *terrestrial* means . . .

a. outer space.
b. alien.
c. star.
d. solid.

5. When was the first asteroid discovered?

a. 60 years ago
b. 50 years ago
c. 20 years ago
d. 75 years ago

6. Describe the evidence and possible results found by the Alvarez team.

____

____

____

____

____

The Moon

Many of the planets in our solar systems have satellites. Satellites are objects that orbit around a planet. These can be manmade or they can be natural satellites. Did you know the moon is a natural satellite of the Earth? There are moons in this solar system that are larger, but it is still very big. On the other hand, the moon is less massive than the Earth. That is why objects weigh less on the moon than they do on Earth. When the astronauts traveled to the moon, they could float and bounce around because they weighed less on the moon.

The moon does not have any liquid water on it. However, it does have craters, mountain ranges, and lava plains as well as other special features. The inside of the moon is made up of layers. Some of these layers are rock solid while others are molten like lava.

One thing that scientists have learned is that there is no wind on the moon. That is because there is no atmosphere on the moon. Because there is no atmosphere, there is no protection from the sun. The moon can get very hot during the day and very cold at night.

Humans have been able to see the moon since the beginning, but Galileo was the first person to look at the moon close up. He used a telescope to let him see things more closely. Galileo learned a lot of amazing things about the moon.

Directions: Circle the correct answer.

1. **Which paragraph explains the physical features of the moon?**
   a. first paragraph
   b. second paragraph
   c. third paragraph
   d. fourth paragraph

2. **What inferences can you make about the moon after reading this passage?**
   a. Unaided, humans cannot live on the moon.
   b. The moon used to be considered one of the planets.
   c. The moon has living organisms on it.
   d. The moon rotates around the sun more quickly than the Earth.

3. **Which statement shows the author's opinion about the moon?**
   a. Galileo learned a lot of amazing things about the moon.
   b. Scientists have been studying the moon and its surface for years.
   c. On the other hand, the moon is smaller than the Earth.
   d. He used a telescope to let him see things more closely.

Sun Storms

You know that the sun **sustains** life here on Earth. You know that you should never look directly at the sun because it could blind you. But did you know that the sun has weather? Of course it's nothing like the weather on Earth. In comparison, our most powerful storm seems like a mild breeze. And believe it or not, what it's doing up there on the sun affects us down here!

Our sun is a huge ball of burning plasma—a state of matter where gas is superheated. Most of this plasma is hydrogen gas. The sun has an 11-year cycle. Throughout the cycle, the sun has periods of major storm activity and minor storm activity. During the major storm part of the cycle, the sun has lots of solar flares. Solar flares are plasma eruptions that shoot off the sun's surface, causing solar wind. Just one average-sized solar flare releases enough energy to meet all the current power needs of Canada for over 10,000 years! The biggest solar flares extend out into space like gigantic clouds. These clouds move over a million and a half kilometers per hour toward Earth as solar wind. When strong solar winds hit Earth's atmosphere, the night sky glows with colored lights reflecting off the ice at the Earth's North Pole. People call them the Northern Lights.

Unfortunately, solar winds don't just provide interesting sky effects. They can cause harmful magnetic storms. These storms can disrupt phone, TV, and radio signals, the Internet, and e-mail. They can make radar systems crash. They can destroy satellites and kill astronauts working outside the space shuttle. The biggest threat comes from the magnetic storm's ability to knock out electrical power. This happened in 1989 when Quebec, lost its entire electrical power grid in less than 90 seconds. The problem took so long to fix that many people had to go without heat or electricity for a month.

Sun Storms *(cont.)*

Comprehension Questions

1. The Northern Lights are caused by . . .

a. magnetic storms.
b. solar wind.
c. plasma.
d. hydrogen gas.

2. What happened *second* in 1989?

a. The sun had one or more major plasma eruptions.
b. People went without electricity for a month.
c. Solar wind created a magnetic storm.
d. Quebec's power grid was heavily damaged.

3. Even small solar flares cause some . . .

a. solar wind.
b. plasma.
c. Northern Lights.
d. hydrogen gas.

4. An antonym for *sustains* is . . .

a. burns.
b. chills.
c. maintains.
d. destroys.

5. What usually protects us from the harmful effects of solar wind?

a. the Northern Lights
b. power grids
c. Earth's atmosphere
d. plasma eruptions

6. Picture a team of scientists discovering a way to collect and use solar-flare energy. What is the expression on their faces?

a. excited
b. upset
c. annoyed
d. bored

7. Do you think it's important for scientists to continue studying solar weather? Explain.

____

____

____

Genetics

It is hard to imagine that an Augustinian monk of the 19th century would provide the basis for modern genetics. However, that is precisely what happened.

Born in 1822 in Heinzendorf near Austria, Gregor Mendel learned his love of gardening from his father who was a farmer. Gregor attended high school in a nearby town.

Since his family was poor and could not afford to pay the full tuition, Gregor received only half the amount of food as the other boys. He nearly starved, and the experience remained in his memory forever.

On the advice of a professor he greatly admired, Gregor entered the monastery where he could continue his studies. There he became the caretaker of the gardens and a substitute teacher for an elementary school.

From 1856 until 1864, Mendel worked with 10,000 specimen pea plants. He cross-fertilized 22 kinds of peas and studied seven characteristics of the plants. After eight years of accurate record-keeping, he formulated three laws that became the basis of the science of heredity. He proudly wrote a paper to describe his findings. No one seemed to recognize the genius of his work, though, and Gregor was crushed. In 1883, he died of a heart attack, embittered that no one recognized or appreciated his scientific revelations.

Then, in 1990, three botanists from three different countries completed papers on the heredity of plants. Each of them had come across Mendel's paper when they made a routine check of the scientific literature before they published their own findings.

In each case, Mendel's forgotten paper reached the same conclusions that they had reached. Gregor Mendel's time had finally come.

Genetics *(cont.)*

You inherit many traits from your parents, such as eye color, hair color, and blood type. One gene comes from each parent. Many times, the gene from one parent is stronger than the corresponding gene from the other. This is called the dominant gene. The weaker gene is called recessive. Two features whose traits are controlled by gene inheritance are the fingers and the ear lobes. Discover which traits you and your family share by determining the recessive and dominant genes you inherited.

Directions: Categorize the ear lobes and fingers of members of your family by checking with grandparents, parents, uncles/aunts, brothers/sisters, or even cousins. Record your findings in the charts. Then, answer the questions at the bottom of the page.

Lobes

Joined **Free**

(Check the appropriate box.)

Relation to you	Free	Joined

Fingers

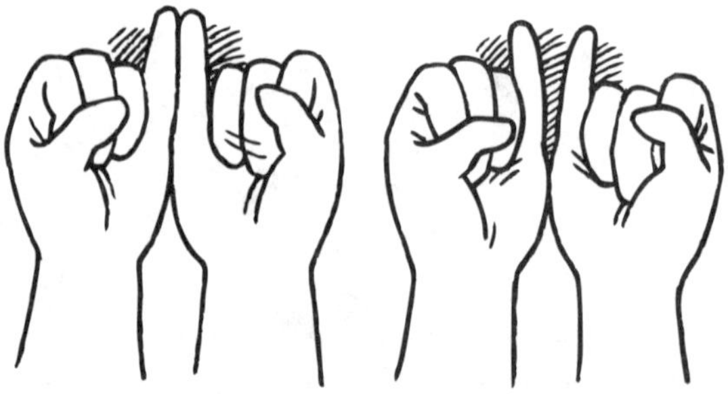

Straight **Bent**

(Check the appropriate box.)

Relation to you	Straight	Bent

Which seems to be dominant, free or joined lobes? ________________________________

Which seems to be dominant, bent or straight fingers? ________________________________

Cells

The cell is the smallest unit of living matter. Many living things are made up of millions and millions of cells. Cells come in all different sizes, shapes, and forms. They each have different jobs to perform as well. There are three main parts to a cell. Each cell has a cell membrane, a nucleus, and cytoplasm.

The cell membrane is found along the outer edge of the cell. It works like a filter or a sieve, letting different things in and out of the cell. It serves as a protection to the cell.

The nucleus of a cell is like the brain of the cell. It is dark and is usually located in the center of the cell. It controls all the actions of the cell. The nucleus also contains the DNA. The DNA is like a blueprint or a plan that the cell will use to reproduce.

The cytoplasm is located inside the cell membrane and around the nucleus. It is a jelly-like substance. The cytoplasm responds to the nucleus. This is where the cell uses the nutrients. It is made of water and other chemicals. Cells can live for different amounts of time. Cells are constantly reproducing.

Directions: Circle the correct answer.

1. **What are the three parts of a cell?**
   a. cell membrane, shell, cytoplasm
   b. cell membrane, brain, cytoplasm
   c. cell membrane, nutrients, cytoplasm
   d. cell membrane, nucleus, cytoplasm

2. **What does the word *sieve* mean as used in the passage?**
   a. strainer
   b. proof
   c. instruction
   d. plan

3. **What role does DNA play in the cell?**
   a. It depends on the amount of cytoplasm in the cell.
   b. It carries the information to the brain.
   c. It carries the overall plan or blueprint of the cell's reproduction.
   d. It depends on how many years it has been a cell.

4. **Which paragraph helps answer the previous question?**
   a. first paragraph
   b. fifth paragraph
   c. third paragraph
   d. fourth paragraph

Atomic Numbers

All of the objects around you are composed of molecules. These molecules, in turn, are made up of atoms. Within each atom is a nucleus or center. Electrons revolve around the nucleus, and are arranged in orbits. For example, an atom of lithium can be illustrated like this:

Since there are three electrons, its atomic number is 3. Use the chart below to identify the elements pictured. Write the name of the element on the space provided.

Element	Symbol	Atomic #
Helium	He	2
Nitrogen	N	7
Oxygen	O	8
Sodium	Na	11
Aluminum	Al	13
Sulfur	S	16
Argon	Ar	18
Calcium	Ca	20

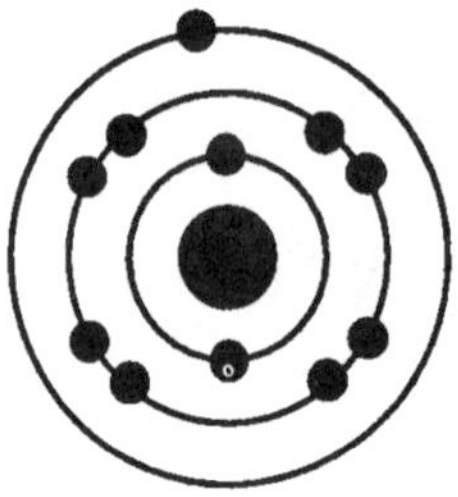

1. ____________________

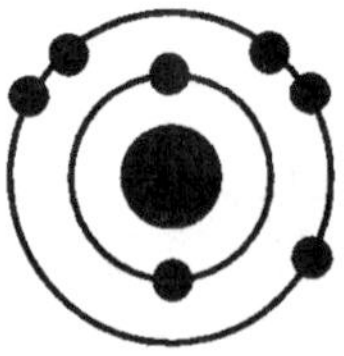

2. ____________________

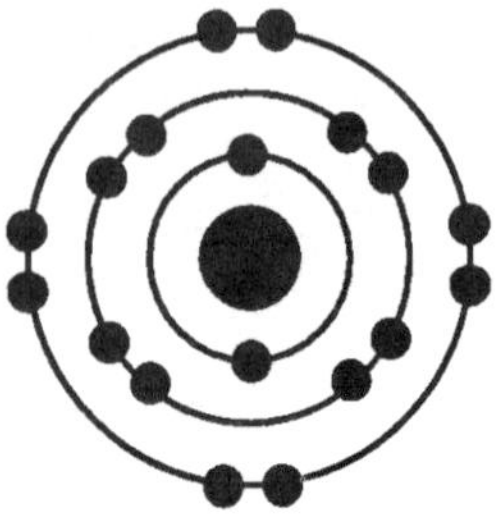

3. ____________________

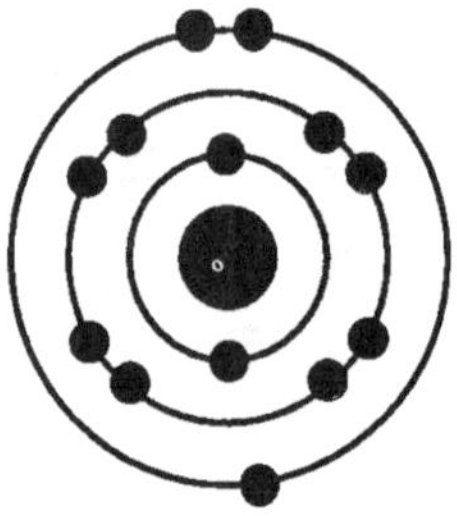

4. ____________________

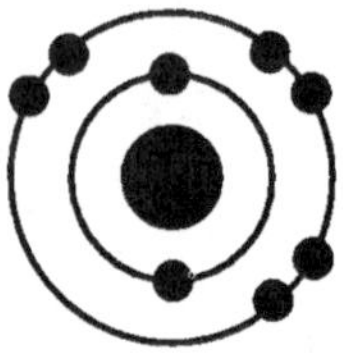

5. ____________________

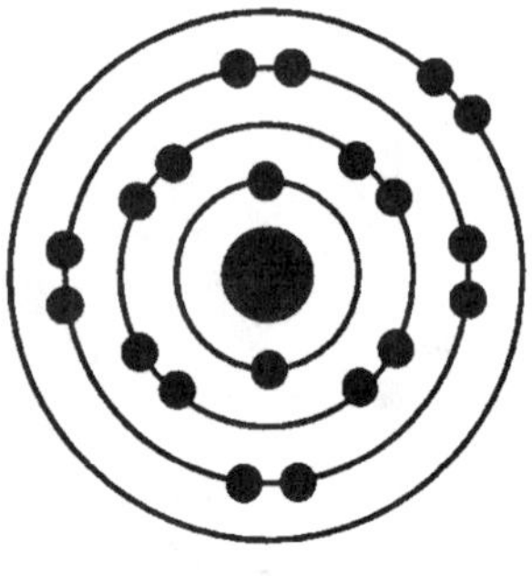

6. ____________________

7. ____________________

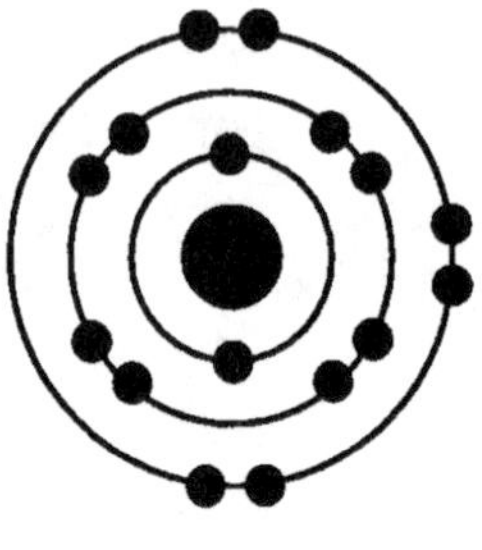

8. ____________________

Matter

What is matter? Everything is made up of matter. Matter is ordinarily found in three states. These states are liquid, gas, or solid. There are two forces at work regardless of the state of matter. These two forces are energy and attraction. Attraction pulls and keeps the particles together.

Solids are packed together. Examples of solids are wood, plastic, stone, and iron. You can hold solids in your hand. Liquids are a state between gases and solids. Liquids flow and change shape. The best example of a liquid is water. Gases are floating around you and inside bubbles. Gases don't have any particular shape, but they are fluid. They can also be compressed. "Vapor" and "gas" mean the same thing.

Matter can change from one state to another. For example, a liquid can change to a solid or gas. Solids can change to a liquid. Temperature influences the changes in matter from one state to another. For example, heating a liquid can turn it into a gas. Cooling or freezing a liquid can turn it into a solid. Scientists continue to study matter, molecules, and ions to better understand our world.

Directions: Circle the correct answer.

1. **After reading the passage, what do you think would happen if a liquid was boiled?**
   a. It would immediately double in size.
   b. It would turn into a gas.
   c. It would turn into a solid.
   d. Scientists have not yet determined what happens in this case.

2. **The main idea of this passage is . . .**
   a. to inform the reader about what happens when it is raining.
   b. to inform the reader about matter.
   c. to inform the reader about how important it is to see ice, rain, and condensation.
   d. to share general information about the universe and how it is organized.

3. **Where can you find information about the three types of matter?**
   a. second paragraph
   b. all three paragraphs
   c. third paragraph
   d. first paragraph

Fixed by Bacteria

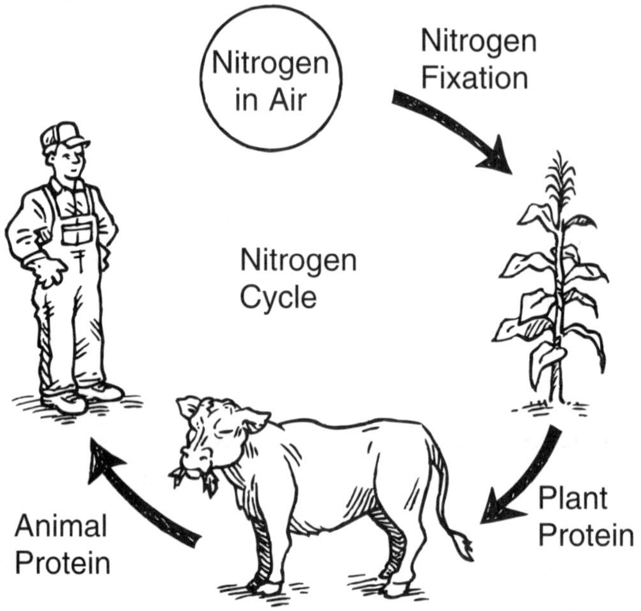

We need nitrogen. Nitrogen is a chemical element. Nitrogen is essential for all forms of life. When something is essential, it is needed. It is necessary. All proteins contain nitrogen. Proteins perform essential tasks, or jobs, in living things. They provide structure. They control the rates of chemical reactions. Nucleic acids contain nitrogen, too. DNA is a nucleic acid. So is RNA. DNA contains genetic information. RNA translates the genetic information. It translates the information into protein production.

Nitrogen is a gas that has no color. It has no taste. It has no odor. The air we breathe is made up mostly of nitrogen. In fact, around four-fifths of the air we breathe is nitrogen. But we cannot use the nitrogen in the air. We cannot use the nitrogen when it is in the form of a gas. Most living things can't. So how do we get our necessary nitrogen?

The answer lies with bacteria. Some bacteria can use nitrogen in the air. They convert it. They change it. They convert it to a compound we can use. A compound is a substance. It is formed from two or more chemical elements. The bacteria "fix" the nitrogen. They "fix" it into a compound we can use. This process is called nitrogen fixation.

The bacteria live on plants. They live off of the plants, too. They get their food from the plants. But the plants get something from the bacteria. They get fixed nitrogen. They get essential nitrogen in a form they can use. They get nitrogen compounds. What does the plant do with the nitrogen? The plant uses it to make proteins.

The bacteria help the plants. Plants help the bacteria. The bacteria and plants have a symbiotic relationship. A symbiotic relationship is a relationship that benefits both organisms. Both the bacteria and plants are helped. They both benefit. So how do people get their nitrogen? People eat plants. They eat plant seeds like corn, rice, and beans. They eat animals that eat plants and seeds. They get essential nitrogen and proteins from what they eat.

Fixed by Bacteria *(cont.)*

**After reading the passage, answer the questions.
Circle the correct answer.**

1. **This story is mainly about . . .**
   a. nitrogen in the air.
   b. how we get and use nitrogen.
   c. bacteria that make nitrogen.
   d. nitrogen and chemical elements.

2. **About how much of the air we breathe is made up of nitrogen?**
   a. one-fifth
   b. one-fourth
   c. four-fifths
   d. five-fourths

3. **Think about how the word *convert* relates to *change*. Which words relate in the same way?**

   convert : change

   a. bacteria : fix
   b. benefit : help
   c. use : nitrogen
   d. symbiotic : relationship

4. **What translates genetic information?**
   a. RNA
   b. DNA
   c. proteins
   d. nucleic acids

5. **Which answer lists how useable nitrogen gets to people in the right order?**
   a. bacteria, plants, animals, air, people
   b. plants, animals, air, bacteria, people
   c. air, plants, bacteria, animals, people
   d. air, bacteria, plants, animals, people

Fire Fuels the Cycle of Life

True or false: forest fires can be good for an ecosystem. Think it's false? No, it's true! Forests actually need fires to release the minerals stored within dead and living plants and trees. Fires keep the forest from taking over the meadows that border it. After a large fire, these fields grow rapidly because of the nutrients set free by the blaze. Forest fires make new habitats, encouraging greater plant and animal variety. The greatest number of different species is found about 25 years after a major blaze.

In 1972, when scientists found out that fires were helpful, national parks adopted a new policy: no one would fight any fire started by a lightning strike. Most fires caused by lightning would go out by themselves in a few hours. This would result in **minimal** damage while allowing natural and necessary blazes.

However, during the summer of 1988, Yellowstone National Park in Wyoming (U.S.) had a serious drought. No rain fell. Old, dead pine trees lay stacked on the forest floor like logs in a fireplace. On June 14 lightning started a fire. Due to the policy, it was left to burn. When it still hadn't gone out on its own after five weeks, things looked grim. Finally, people started fighting the fire. By then the situation was completely out of control. The fire raged all summer, stopping only when snow fell in September. The gigantic blaze had destroyed almost half of the Park, burning about 4,000 kilometers. It seemed like a big disaster.

Yet, in a forest, the cycle of life is based on fire. Just one year after Yellowstone's huge fire, its forest showed new growth. Its most plentiful trees, lodgepole pines, have cones that actually need the high temperatures of a fire to open and drop their seeds. Their tiny saplings poked up through the charred soil. A flowering plant called fireweed blanketed the area. Scientists figured that Yellowstone's cycle of life includes a major fire every 200 years.

After another 200 years, Yellowstone will burn again, and the cycle will start over.

Fire Fuels the Cycle of Life *(cont.)*

Comprehension Questions

1. **How is a forest fire beneficial?**
   a. It gives firefighters jobs.
   b. It releases trapped nutrients from plants and trees.
   c. It gives scientists a chance to study forest fires.
   d. It attracts lightning strikes away from people's homes.

2. **What happened second during the summer of 1988?**
   a. People did not respond immediately.
   b. Lightning caused a forest fire in Yellowstone National Park.
   c. The fire was stopped by snowfall.
   d. New habitats formed.

3. **The 1988 drought caused Yellowstone National Park to. . .**
   a. be cooler than normal.
   b. support greater plant and animal variety.
   c. have very dry conditions.
   d. attract more lightning strikes than usual.

4. **An antonym for minimal is. . .**
   a. costly. b. much. c. little. d. limited.

5. **Based on Yellowstone's forest-fire cycle prior to 1988, when had its last major blaze occurred?**
   a. around 1588
   b. around 1688
   c. around 1788
   d. around 1888

6. **Picture Yellowstone in October of 1988. What do you see?**
   a. Firefighters are spraying water on a huge forest fire.
   b. Most of the trees have colored leaves, and colored leaves blanket the ground.
   c. Tiny pine trees and flowering fireweed are everywhere you look.
   d. There's snow on the ground, and the few standing trees are black and bare.

7. **Do you agree with the policy of allowing fires started by lightning to burn themselves out? Explain.**

____

____

____

Answer Key

Page 4

1. B
2. A
3. B
4. A
5. B
6. A
7. B
8. A
9. B
10. B
11. A
12. B
13. A
14. B
15. A

Page 5

1. The sun set on the horizon. Wasn't the sight astonishing?
2. When the snowflakes stop falling, we will go to the store.
3. Where did you get that beautiful, blue ribbon?
4. Hurrah! We can finally go swimming in the ocean since the storm has abated.
5. When will the sound of cracking thunder stop frightening me?
6. The daffodils are blooming all over the hillside, creating a waving carpet of yellow.
7. The gazelles ran smoothly and silently in the distance.
8. When will the moon escape from behind the clouds?
9. Wow! I am impressed with the colorful vibrancy of fall.
10. How often will you be able to come over to my house this summer?
11. Although I like the refreshing coolness of snow cones, I usually don't like ice cream.
12. Why is the wind picking up speed? Will there be a hurricane?
13. The puppy quickly scurried under the bushes, hoping that nobody had noticed him.
14. I will be glad when this project is over and I feel a sense of accomplishment.

Page 6

1. Michael shouted, "Let's get busy with the paint!"
2. "Those who deny freedom to others deserve it not for themselves," stated Abraham Lincoln.
3. "Has anyone in this group ever climbed Mount Everest?" asked the mountain guide.
4. Mr. Cummings said, "Please watch your step through the pond."
5. Donna and Chandra complained, "We don't want to do the dishes."
6. "Help!" cried the frightened girl as she grasped the end of the rope.
7. "What is the time difference between Winnipeg and Toronto?" he asked the flight attendant.

Page 7

Tuesday, March 16, 1999
Dear Aunt Judy,
I want to thank you for the lovely new dress you sent me for my birthday. I'm sorry you were unable to attend my party on Saturday, March 13. We had lots of fun. I plan to come visit you in Victoria, B.C., this summer. Mother wants you to check your calendar for July. She has booked me on a flight to arrive Wednesday, July 27, in the evening. Please write or call to let us know if that is all right. I can't wait to see you!
Yours truly,
Kara

Kara James
7008 Milton Road
Calgary, A.B. T2A 807
Mrs. Judy Kimball
1454 Dresser Road
Victoria, B.C. VOY 8M2

Page 8

2. women's careers
3. my friend's comments
4. my baby's toys
5. its horn
6. the passengers' tickets
7. the children's clothes
8. Chris' store or Chris's store
9. an artist's paintbrush
10. the hostess's invitations

Page 9

Exercise 1

1. teachers'
2. country's
3. children's
4. Ross' or Ross's
5. men's
6. cities'
7. dogs'
8. Argus' or Argus's
9. Karla's
10. girls'

Exercise 2

1. A
2. B
3. B
4. A
5. B
6. A
7. A
8. B
9. A
10. A

Page 10

Answers will vary

Page 11

1. On our first trip to California, I wanted to visit the San Diego Zoo; my little sister wanted to go to Disneyland.
2. Our parents settled the dispute for us; they decided we could go to both places.
3. At the zoo we saw a zebra, elephant, and lion; the tigers were not in their display area.
4. Three days later we went to Disneyland; it has imaginative rides.
5. We can't wait to vacation in California again; there are so many sights to see.

Page 12

Answers will vary

Page 13

Part I

Answers will vary.

Part II

1. family
2. sister-in-law
3. trolley car
4. herd
5. class
6. editor-in-chief
7. pile
8. passers-by
9. flock
10. group

Page 14

1. a. churches
   b. trees
   c. bushes
   d. boxes
   e. peaches
   f. buses/busses
2. a. geese
   b. men
   c. feet
   d. lice
   e. teeth
   f. women
   g. children
   h. mice
3. a. potatoes
   b. photos
   c. volcanoes
   d. hippos
   e. heroes
   f. tomatoes

Page 15

1. big truck, little car
2. good book
3. cute kitty, sweet face
4. nice (Ms. Bronowski)
5. delicious cake
6. silly thing
7. chocolate ice cream
8. red car, blue one
9. old (book)
10. shiny, new penny

Answer Key *(cont.)*

Page 16
Exercise 1: Accept appropriate responses.
Exercise 2: Accept appropriate responses.

Page 17
Exercise 1

1. talks	6. think
2. is	7. hope, get
3. ran	8. like
4. read	9. had
5. enjoyed	10. was

Exercise 2
1. plays (A)
2. watches (A)
3. likes (A)
4. looks (L)
5. spit (A)
6. is (L)
7. seems (L)
8. looked (A)
9. saw (A)
10. is (L)
11. asked (A)
12. heard (A)
13. sounded (L)
14. is (L)
15. like (A)

Page 18
1. known, frozen
2. chosen, began
3. worn, stolen
4. chosen, torn
5. rung, have
6. stolen, known
7. have, sung
8. driven, begun
9. began, chosen
10. fell, frozen
11. worn, rung
12. fallen, broken
13. sang, chosen
14. brought, stolen
15. rang, began

Page 19
Exercise 1

1. I	8. her, us
2. me	9. us
3. We	10. me
4. she	
5. he	
6. them	
7. they	

Exercise 2

1. We	11. her
2. us	12. He, I
3. I	13. her, him
4. him, her	14. He
5. we	15. They
6. me	16. I
7. him, me	17. we, they
8. us	18. him, her
9. me	19. her
10. him, her	20. them, us

Page 20
Accept appropriate responses.

Page 21
Exercise 1
1. <u>at</u> the (South Pole)
2. <u>during</u> the (speech)
3. <u>with</u> the (bathwater)
4. <u>in</u> the (pan)
5. <u>on</u> (TV)
6. <u>under</u> the (table)
7. <u>to</u> the (movies)
8. <u>across</u> the (road)
9. <u>on</u> the (table)
10. <u>to</u> the (top)

Exercise 2: Accept appropriate responses.

Page 22
Exercise 1

1. but	6. after
2. or	7. and
3. so	8. since
4. if	9. although
5. until	

Exercise 2: Accept appropriate responses.

Page 31
1. familiar
2. accommodate, appropriate
3. vacuum
4. separate
5. irrelevant
6. guarantee
7. calendar
8. foreign
9. embarrass
10. privilege
11. weird
12. rhythm
13. a lot

Page 32
1. rhythm
2. guarantee
3. appropriate
4. calendar
5. vacuum
6. weird
7. irrelevant
8. embarrass
9. a lot
10. accommodate
11. privilege
12. familiar
13. foreign
14. separate

Page 33 and 34

1. c	10. b
2. b	11. c
3. c	12. c
4. c	13. a
5. a	14. b
6. b	15. c
7. b	16. c
8. a	17. a
9. c	

Page 35 and 36

1. b	8. b
2. a	9. c
3. c	10. b
4. a	11. b
5. b	12. a
6. b	13. c
7. c	14. a

Page 37
1. assent, ascent
2. course, strait
3. coarse
4. compliment
5. cite
6. taut
7. there, their
8. lesson, lessen
9. presence, presents
10. passed, past

Page 38 and 39

1. c	6. c	11. b
2. a	7. c	12. c
3. b	8. a	13. a
4. a	9. b	14. b
5. b	10. c	15. b
		16. b
		17. a

Page 40
A.

1. G	6. D
2. F	7. A
3. E	8. I
4. H	9. C
5. B	

B.
1. ophthalmologist
2. neonatologist
3. criminologist
4. ornithologist
5. mineralogist
6. psychologist
7. etymologist
8. histologist
9. radiologist

Page 45
1. Wayne did not go to school.
2. He missed so much school.
3. He decided to start working on his attendance.
4. He did not think that his brother and mom cared about his decision.
5. He felt better.

Page 47

1. b	4. c
2. a	5. d
3. b	6. c

Page 49

1. b	4. c
2. a	5. a
3. c	6. d

Page 51

1. a	5. d
2. b	6. b
3. c	7. Accept well-supported answers.
4. c	

Page 53

1. c	4. c
2. b	5. d
3. b	6. c

Answer Key *(cont.)*

Page 55

1. d
2. d
3. b
4. c
5. a
6. c

Page 57

1. a
2. d
3. d
4. b
5. b
6. d

Page 59

1. c
2. d
3. b
4. b
5. b
6. b

Page 61

1. b
2. d
3. a
4. a
5. d
6. c

Page 78

1. -10
2. -8
3. +7
4. -16
5. -21
6. -24
7. -13
8. +10
9. +2
10. -13
11. -6
12. -2
13. +7
14. -24
15. -4
16. -23
17. +25
18. -3
19. -25
20. -15
21. -21

Page 79

1. +6
2. -4
3. +16
4. -59
5. +11
6. -13
7. -22
8. +31
9. -23
10. -22
11. -21
12. -34
13. -110
14. -32
15. -56
16. -40
17. +450
18. -579
19. +176
20. -1
21. -198

Page 80

H. 2
Q. 4
D. -2
B. -18
F. 0
G. -11
O. -3
W. -15
K. -6
Q. -4
X. -21
S. -1
A. -9
Y. 6
U. 11
E. -16
Y. 5
J. -21
Z. 8
N. 1
M. 12
I. -5
P. 22
T. 3
R. -20
L. -41
C. 13

Riddle: He thought he would be a good drill sergeant.

Page 81

1. 36
2. 9
3. 25
4. 4
5. 100
6. 121
7. 125
8. 216
9. 81
10. 512
11. 49
12. 1,000
13. 343
14. 169
15. 8
16. 81
17. 16
18. 729
19. 125
20. 32
21. 196
22. 1
23. 225
24. 400
25. 900
26. 1,600
27. 2,500

Page 82

1. 3 x 3 = 9
2. 7 x 7 = 49
3. 4 x 4 = 16
4. 9 x 9 = 81
5. 2 x 2 = 4
6. 8 x 8 = 64
7. 10 x 10 = 100
8. 6 x 6 = 36
9. 11 x 11 = 121
10. 12 x 12 = 144
11. 2 x 2 = 4
    4 x 2 = 8
    $2^3 = 8$
12. 3 x 3 = 9
    9 x 3 = 27
    $3^3 = 27$
13. 5 x 5 = 25
    25 x 5 = 125
    $5^3 = 125$
14. 7 x 7 = 49
    49 x 7 = 343
    $7^3 = 343$
15. 4 x 4 = 16
    16 x 4 = 64
    $4^3 = 64$
16. 6 x 6 = 36
    36 x 6 = 216
    $6^3 = 216$
17. 10 x 10 = 100
    100 x 10 = 1,000
    $10^3 = 1,000$
18. 9 x 9 = 81
    81 x 9 = 729
    $9^3 = 729$
19. 11 x 11 = 121
    121 x 11 = 1,331
    $11^3 = 1,331$
20. 12 x 12 = 144
    144 x 12 = 1,728
    $12^3 = 1,728$

Page 83

1. $12
2. $20
3. +42
4. $7
5. -9
6. +10
7. $270
8. 156
9. -64
10. +5
11. $5
12. +20

Page 84

1. 72
2. 72
3. 42
4. 42
5. 80
6. 80
7. 170
8. 170
9. 190
10. 190
11. 600
12. 600
13. 2,000
14. 2,000
15. 4,800
16. 4,800
17. 2,800
18. 2,800
19. 2,700
20. 2,700
21. 4,200
22. 4,200
23. 4,125
24. 4,125
25. 1,125
26. 1,125
27. 1,541
28. 1,541
29. 714
30. 714

Page 85

1. 504
2. 504
3. 300
4. 300
5. 600
6. 600
7. 6,000
8. 6,000
9. 80,000
10. 80,000
11. 180,000
12. 180,000
13. 3,750
14. 3,750
15. 12,300
16. 12,300
17. 379,500
18. 379,500
19. 264,264
20. 264,264

Page 86

1. 18,759
2. 35,322
3. 53,656
4. 2,700
5. 27,315
6. 11,856
7. 10,486
8. 38,684
9. 53,504
10. 69,894
11. 22,275
12. 26,862
13. 18,018
14. 18,785
15. 53,754
16. 25,806

Page 87

1. $93.96
2. $4.47
3. $105.30
4. $69.93
5. $53.38
6. $420.52
7. $585.39
8. $256.50
9. 2.646
10. 1.872
11. 2.6628
12. 0.00228
13. $6.30
14. 4.78
15. 137.74
16. $1.38
17. $8.37
18. 0.1218

Page 88

1. 11r1
2. 16r4
3. 13
4. 11r1
5. 28r2
6. 24r3
7. 9
8. 34
9. 13
10. 10r6
11. 11r1
12. 14r1
13. 16r1
14. 18r2
15. 11r2
16. 16r3
17. 23
18. 6r4
19. 8r4
20. 9r2
21. 10
22 5
23. 12r2
24. 21r3
25. 23r1

Page 89

1. 21r17
2. 31r14
3. 32r12
4. 31r10
5. 15r2
6. 11r2
7. 42r5
8. 21r22
9. 23r13

Answer Key *(cont.)*

10. 13r25
11. 22r6
12. 32r17

Page 90

1. 8,400 ÷ 40 = 210
Check: 210 x 40 = 8,400
2. 41,916 ÷ 28 = 1,497
Check: 1,497 x 28 = 41,916
3. 33,320 ÷ 136 = 245
Check: 245 x 136 = 33,320
4. 3,600 ÷ 90 = 40
Check: 40 x 90 = 3,600
5. 8,928 ÷ 9 = 992
Check: 992 x 9 = 8,928
6. 28,917 ÷ 81 = 357
Check: 357 x 81 = 28,917
7. 35,620 ÷ 260 = 137
Check: 137 x 260 = 35,620
8. 180,930 ÷ 37 = 4,890
Check: 4,890 x 37 = 180,930
9. 8,840 ÷ 65 = 136
Check: 136 x 65 = 8,840

Page 91

1. 0.21 kg
2. 100.2 grams
3. 1.09 grams
4. 10.2 candies
5. 45.1 kg
6. 80.5 ants
7. 969.624 grams
8. $0.23
9. $0.38
10. 157.68 kg

Page 92

1. 5
2. 0.14
3. 10.80
4. 625
5. 0.01
6. 0.04
7. 0.03
8. $750
9. $175
10. $81.25
11. 5.7
12. 0.04
13. 4.9
14. 80
15. 50
16. 7/20
17. 8/125
18. 3 2/5
19. 3 1/8
20. 3 1/8
21. 4 ⅝
22. 21/2500
23. 66 ¾
24. 159/500
25. 1/16
26. 4 ¼
27. 1 1/10
28. 0.8
29. 0.38
30. 0.67
31. 0.78
32. 0.83
33. 0.63
34. 0.33
35. 0.7

Page 93

1. 2
2. 4
3. 7
4. 9
5. 10
6. 8
7. 11
8. 12
9. 13
10. 15
11. 14
12. 20
13. 30
14. 70
15. 80
16. 40
17. 700
18. 800
19. 400
20. 900
21. 500
22. 300
23. 600
24. 100
25. 3,000
26. 9,000
27. 5,000
28. 6,000
29. 7,000
30. 8,000

Page 94

1. 4
2. 6
3. 12
4. 5
5. 8
6. 9
7. 11
8. 1
9. 3
10. 10
11. 7
12. 2
13. 50
14. 60
15. 20
16. 10
17. 80
18. 70
19. 30
20. 130
21. 90
22. 40
23. 120
24. 110
25. Answers may vary.

Page 95

1. 10
2. 30
3. 25
4. 1
5. 63
6. 53
7. 6
8. 18
9. 0
10. 20
11. 86
12. 36
13. 8
14. 5
15. 18

Page 96

1. 53
2. 15
3. 41
4. 10
5. 11
6. 61
7. 38
8. 34
9. 95
10. 22
11. 46
12. 6
13. 138
14. 44
15. 2
16. 21

Page 97

1. 0
2. 18
3. 20
4. 24
5. 27
6. 70
7. 13
8. 2
9. 9
10. 45
11. 29
12. 58
13. 107
14. 117
15. 72
16. 48

Page 98

1. 1/3
2. 6/7
3. ¼
4. ½
5. 17/20
6. 1 11/35
7. 5/18
8. 1/20
9. 1/5
10. 19/24
11. 11/20
12. 11/16
13. 10 7/12
14. 3 3/8
15. 3 2/9

Page 99

1. 13/20
2. ¾
3. 7/8
4. 1/6
5. 4/9
6. 11/12
7. 7/8
8. 9/10
9. 8/9
10. 11/15
11. 3/20
12. 7/24
13. 26/21 = 1 5/21
14. 35/24 = 1 11/24
15. 22/18 = 1 2/9
16. 5/24
17. 13/36
18. 14/72 = 7/36
19. 59/42 = 1 17/42
20. 29/24 = 1 5/24
21. 3/20
22. 23/18 = 1 5/18
23. 55/60 = 11/12
24. 25/30 = 5/6

Page 100

1. 1/12
2. 5/12
3. 2/9
4. 1/9
5. 1/6
6. 11/24
7. 1/9
8. 3/7
9. 1/3
10. 1/6
11. 9/16
12. 3/5
13. 2/5
14. 4/15
15. 4/15
16. 1/6
17. 5/42
18. 3 3/10
19. 3/10
20. 3/64
21. ½

Page 101

1. 3/8
2. 2/21
3. 9/40
4. 6/35
5. 1/6
6. 1/6
7. 2/7
8. 2/9
9. 1/4
10. 3/4
11. 1/4
12. 1/6
13. 3/20
14. 35/72
15. 1/8
16. 1/10
17. 1/5
18. 2/9
19. 3/5
20. 1/2
21. 1/5
22. 2/27
23. 3/7
24. 15/154
25. 11/16
26. 1/8

Answer Key *(cont.)*

27. $\frac{4}{39}$
28. $\frac{2}{7}$
29. $\frac{11}{30}$
30. $\frac{4}{47}$
31. $\frac{17}{611}$
32. $\frac{1}{800}$

Page 102

1. 2
2. 2
3. 2
4. 4
5. 3
6. 4
7. $1\frac{3}{4}$
8. $\frac{5}{6}$
9. $\frac{7}{6} = 1\ 1/6$
10. $\frac{9}{5} = 1\ 4/5$
11. $\frac{7}{2} = 3\frac{1}{2}$
12. 1
13. 3
14. 8
15. $\frac{1}{3}$

Page 103

1. $\frac{11}{14}$
2. $1\frac{13}{18}$
3. $\frac{14}{19}$
4. $\frac{82}{87}$
5. $\frac{18}{29}$
6. $1\frac{1}{4}$
7. $\frac{2}{3}$
8. 5
9. $\frac{3}{4}$
10. $\frac{3}{4}$
11. $2\frac{1}{6}$
12. $\frac{3}{7}$
13. $\frac{5}{12}$
14. $\frac{8}{9}$
15. $1\frac{5}{27}$
16. $\frac{3}{10}$
17. $3\frac{1}{9}$
18. $6\frac{1}{4}$
19. $9\frac{3}{4}$
20. $\frac{1}{4}$
21. $\frac{25}{133}$
22. $\frac{5}{64}$
23. $2\frac{31}{32}$
24. $33\frac{3}{4}$
25. $\frac{18}{175}$
26. $\frac{1}{32}$
27. 150
28. $7\frac{1}{2}$
29. $4\frac{2}{27}$
30. 10

Page 104

1. $4\frac{1}{6}$
2. $3\frac{1}{4}$
3. 8
4. $5\frac{3}{7}$
5. 3
6. $\frac{23}{7}$
7. $\frac{28}{5}$
8. $\frac{65}{9}$
9. $\frac{35}{8}$
10. $\frac{29}{10}$
11. $2\frac{1}{5}$
12. $4\frac{3}{4}$
13. $9\frac{3}{5}$
14. $9\frac{1}{4}$
15. 0.25
16. 0.75
17. 6.20
18. 0.5
19. 0.38
20. 0.6
21. 3.6

Page 105

1. 12
2. 24
3. 40
4. 21
5. 31.5
6. 50.4
7. 43.5
8. 122.4
9. 18.8
10. 9.9
11. 18.2
12. 33.6
13. 40
14. 77
15. 1.75

Page 106

1. 0.7
2. 0.4
3. 0.75
4. 0.15
5. 1.75
6. $\frac{26}{100}$
7. $\frac{3}{100}$
8. $\frac{2}{10}$
9. $\frac{78}{100}$
10. $\frac{825}{1000}$
11. $\frac{1}{20}$
12. $\frac{1}{50}$
13. $\frac{1}{8}$
14. $\frac{1}{25}$
15. $6\frac{9}{10}$
16. 0.06, 6%
17. 0.70, 70%
18. 0.63, 63%
19. 0.03, 3%
20. 0.31, 31%
21. $\frac{25}{100}$, 0.25
22. $\frac{2}{100}$, 0.02
23. $\frac{0.5}{100}$ or $\frac{5}{1000}$, 0.005
24. $\frac{33}{100}$, 0.333
25. $\frac{40}{100}$, .4

Page 107

1. $300; $90; 210
2. $26.45
3. $25 students
4. $150 children
5. $20 homes
6. 225 cards
7. $0.87
8. $1.50
9. 26 minutes
10. 288 boxes
11. 6 kg
12. 6.25%

Page 108

1. a. 12, 25, 25, 35, 73
   b. 73 – 12 = 61
   c. 34
   d. 25
   e. 25
2. a. 23, 23, 30, 49, 51, 88, 100
   b. 100 – 23 = 77
   c. 52
   d. 49
   e. 23

Page 109

3. a. 18, 18, 24, 36
   b. 36 – 18 = 18
   c. 24
   d. 21
   e. 18
4. a. 22, 22, 36, 42, 70, 84
   b. 84 – 22 = 62
   c. 46
   d. 39
   e. 22
5. a. 170, 200, 305
   b. 135
   c. 225
   d. 200
   e. none
6. a. 22, 45, 66, 66, 69, 77, 89
   b. 67
   c. 62
   d. 66
   e. 66

Page 110

1. **Mode:** 13 **Median:** 13
   Mean: 9.6 (10)

Most representative: mode and median
Reason: They reflect the values best and are midway between high and low values.

2. **Mode:** 23 **Median:** 23
   Mean: 23.3 (23)

Most representative: 23
Reason: They are all the same.

3. **Mode:** 8 **Median:** 8
   Mean: 8.3 (8)

Most representative: all
Reason: They all are the same value.

4. **Mode:** 46 **Median:** 49
   Mean: 51.9 (52)

Most representative: mean and median
Reason: They are closer to the center of the numbers in terms of value.

5. **Mode:** 23 **Median:** 29.5
   Mean: 32.3 (32)

Most representative: median and mean
Reason: The mode is too near the first values; the others are representatives of the numbers.

Page 111

1. 65
2. 65
3. 64
4. 31
5. 73
6. 74
7. 74
8. 48

Page 112

1. 37
2. 38.5
3. 60%
4. 20
5. 300
6. 80
7. 100 and 80

Page 113

Check students' stem-and-leaf plots

1. 19

Answer Key *(cont.)*

2. 20
3. 4
4. 848
5. 870
6. Answers will vary.
7. 23
8. 32
9. 134.5
10. 141

Page 114

	Frequency
1. 6	Cat 8
2. 1	Dog 12
3. 4	Snake 2
4. 5	Bird 3
5. 2	Mouse 3
6. 11	Hamster 4
7. 18	Fish 6
8. 2	Other 3
9. 4	

10. dog
11. snake
12. 5
13. 41
14. 27

Page 115
1. 30%
2. 5th/8th
3. 60%
4. no
5. 45%
6. 40%

Page 116
Riddle: Outback
Stems 4, 5, 6, 7, 8, 9, 10
Leaves
7,
7, 8
2, 3, 3, 7
0, 4, 5, 9, 9
0, 1, 3, 7, 8, 8
1, 1, 3, 3, 6, 6, 8
0, 0, 0
Number of leaves
1, 2, 4, 5, 6, 7, 3
Letters
O, U, T, B, A, C, K

Page 117
Answer: The girl necks-door.

Page 118
1. Check student graphs.
2. Check student graphs.
   T-shirts ¼
   Sneakers ½
   Athletic Posters ⅛
   Other ⅛
3. Check student graphs.

Page 119

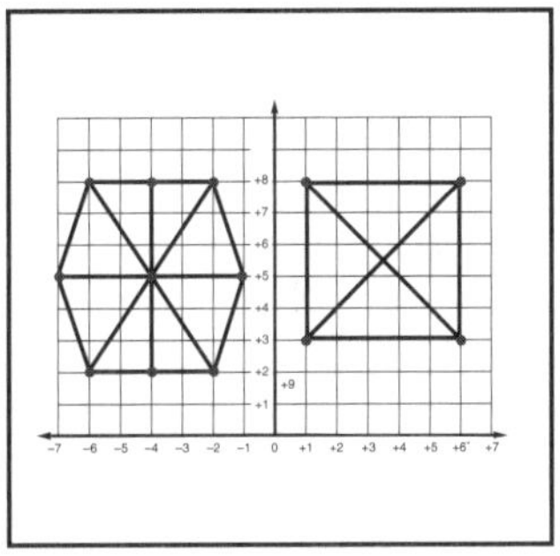

Page 120
1. (11, 5)
2. (3, 0)
3. (6, 1)
4. (12, 12)
5. (4, 4)
6. (10, 8)
7. (8, 6)
8. (2, 11)
9. (6, 10)
10. (3, 7)
11. (1, 3)
12. (10, 2)

Page 121
Answer: Steal its chair.

Page 122

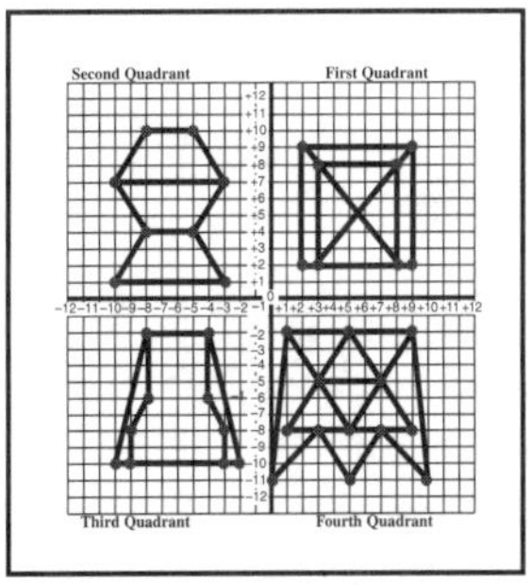

Page 124
1. library
2. town hall
3. gas station
4. (-11, 1)
5. (4, -4)
6. (-5, -9)
7. park
8. (-10, -7)
9. (-9, 5)
10. general store
11. drug store
12. III
13. I
14. II

Page 126

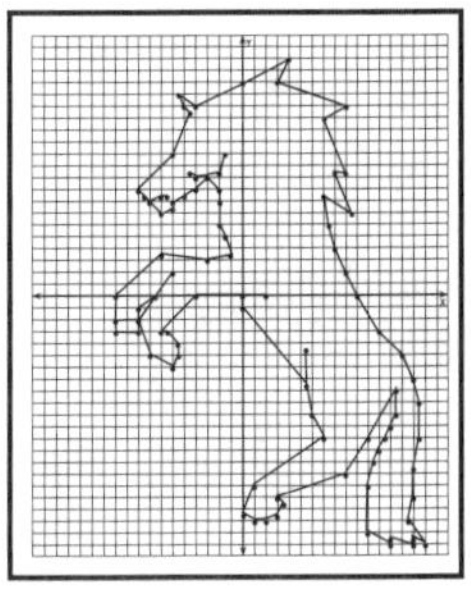

Page 127
1. C
2. B
3. C
4. A
5. A
6. m
7. km
8. cm
9. cm or mm
10. mm
11. cm
12. m
13. km
14. B
15. A
16. C

Page 128
1. 1
2. 500
3. 3
4. 100
5. 5
6. 900
7. 6.5
8. 330
9. 1
10. 1
11. 6
12. 5
13. 8
14. 7
15. 7.53
16. 8.35
17. 400
18. 3,000
19. 700
20. 6,000
21. 900
22. 10,000
23. 680
24. 15,500
25. 0.004
26. 0.007
27. 65
28. 0.07
29. 0.65
30. 0.004
31. 6.5
32. 4,00
33. 0.004
34. 7,500
35. 4,00
36. 6.5
37. 0.225
38. 3,500
39. 225,000
40. 0.057

Page 129
1. 130 m
2. 260 cm
3. 330 mm
4. 630 m
5. 250 cm
6. 722 mm
7. 221 mm
8. 85.8 cm

Page 130
1. 80 m
2. 150 cm
3. 124 mm
4. 105 mm
5. 180 cm
6. 75 mm
7. 92 m
8. 114 cm
9. 194 m
10. 323 mm

Page 131
1. 31.4 cm
2. 37.68 m
3. 28.26 cm
4. 25.12 m
5. 47.1 cm
6. 62.8 m

Answer Key *(cont.)*

7. 78.5 m
8. 94.2 cm

Page 132

1. 2,400 m^2
2. 3,000 m^2
3. 1,600 cm^2
4. 2,800 cm^2
5. 1,800 mm^2
6. 6,300 mm^2
7. 42 m^2
8. 4,900 m^2
9. 5,980 m^2
10. 1,504 cm^2

Page 133

1. 750 m^2
2. 1,000 mm^2
3. 1,386 m^2
4. 4,920 cm^2
5. 2,324 cm^2
6. 31.5 m^2
7. 2,296 mm^2
8. 24.8 m^2
9. 14,400 cm^2
10. 38 m^2
11. 4,840 mm^2
12. 23.25 cm^2
13. 19.84 m^2
14. 61,200 cm^2

Page 134

1. 180 mm^2
2. 680 m^2
3. 440 cm^2
4. 792 m^2
5. 1,680 cm^2
6. 475 mm^2
7. 638 m^2
8. 14.08 cm^2

Page 135

1. 78.5 cm^2
2. 28.26 m^2
3. 254.34 m^2
4. 452.16 cm^2
5. 113.04 m^2
6. 379.94 m^2
7. 314 cm^2
8. 5,024 cm^2

Page 136

1. 1,320 mm^3
2. 2,520 m^3
3. 6,250 m^3
4. 30,000 cm^3
5. 36,960 cm^3
6. 5,400 mm^3
7. 47.25 m^3
8. 32.55 cm^3

Page 137

1. 549.5 cm^3
2. 502.4 cm^3
3. 2,009. mm^3
4. 10,173.6 cm^3
5. 1,205.76 cm^3
6. 1,130.4 m^3
7. 1,692.46 mm^3
8. 602.88 cm^3

Page 138

1. 24 cm^3
2. 48 m^3
3. 80 mm^3
4. 40 cm^3
5. 200 cm^3
6. 150 cm^3
7. 210 m^3
8. 346.7 m^3

Page 139

1.
   face 1: 32 m^2
   face 2: 32 m^2
   face 3: 40 m^2
   face 4: 40 m^2
   face 5: 80 m^2
   face 6: 80 m^2
   Total 304 m^2
2.
   face 1: 35 m^2
   face 2: 35 m^2
   face 3: 20 m^2
   face 4: 20 m^2
   face 5: 28 m^2
   face 6: 28 m^2
   Total 166 m^2
3.
   face 1: 110 cm^2
   face 2: 110 cm^2
   face 3: 55cm^2
   face 4: 55 cm^2
   face 5: 50 cm^2
   face 6: 50 cm^2
   Total 430 cm^2
4.
   face 1: 63 mm^2
   face 2: 63 mm^2
   face 3: 70 mm^2
   face 4: 70 mm^2
   face 5: 90 mm^2
   face 6: 90 mm^2
   Total 446 mm^2
5.
   face 1: 200 cm^2
   face 2: 200 cm^2
   face 3: 220 cm^2
   face 4: 220 cm^2
   face 5: 110 cm^2
   face 6: 110 cm^2
   Total 1,060 cm^2
6.
   face 1: 120 m^2
   face 2: 120 m^2
   face 3: 108 m^2
   face 4: 108 m^2
   face 5: 90 m^2
   face 6: 90 m^2
   Total 636 m^2

Page 140

1. H – T; ½
2. 1 – 2 – 3 – 4 – 5 – 6; ⅙
3. 1 – 2 – 3 – 4 – 5 – 6; ⅙
4. 1 – 2 – 3 – 4 – 5 – 6; 2⁄6 = ⅓
5. Red – Green – Blue – Black; ¼
6. Red – Green – Blue – Black; 2⁄4 = ½
7. Red – Green – Blue – Black; 0
8. Red – Green – Blue – Black; ¾
9. HH – TT – HT – TH; 2⁄4= ½

Page 141

1. ⅛ or 12.5%
2. ½ or 50%
3. 2⁄8 or ¼ or 25%
4. 2⁄8 or ¼ or 25%
5. 100%
6. 100%
7. ¼ or 25%
8. ¼ or 25%
9. 2⁄4 or ½ or 50%
10. 2⁄4 or ½ or 50%
11. ¾ or 75%
12. ½ or 25%
13. ¼ or 25%
14. 2⁄4 or ½ or 50%
15. 2⁄8 or ¼ or 25%
16. ½ or 50%

Page 142

1. ⅖
2. ⅖
3. ⅕
4. 0⁄5
5. 3⁄10
6. 2⁄10 or ⅕
7. ⅒
8. 5⁄10 or ½
9. 5⁄10 or ½
10. John's
11. No. She only has a ⅒ chance.
12. 5⁄26
13. 21⁄26
14. 1⁄26
15. 0
16. 9⁄26
17. 3⁄26

Page 143

1. 0.1 or 0.10; 10%
2. 0.1 or 0.10; 10%
3. 0.3 or 0.30; 30%
4. 0.3 or 0.30; 30%
5. 0.1 or 0.10; 10%
6. 0.5 or 0.50; 50%
7. 0.4 or 0.40; 40%
8. 0.0 or 0.00; 0%
9. 0.2 or 0.20; 20%
10. 0.5 or 0.50; 50%

Page 144

1. n = 11
2. n = 3
3. a = 4
4. n = 25
5. a = 15
6. n = 26
7. x = 27
8. n = 10
9. a = 20
10. n = 31
11. x = 25
12. a = 14
13. n = 24
14. a = 91
15. n = 27
16. a = 65
17. x = 38
18. n = 66

Page 145

1. n = 5
2. n = 11
3. n = 3
4. a = 4
5. n = 7
6. n = 10
7. n = 5
8. a = 6
9. a = 15
10. n = 20

Answer Key *(cont.)*

11. n = 60
12. a = 60
13. n = 16
14. n = 60
15. a = 64
16. n = 160
17. a = 70
18. n = 40

Page 146

1. 1
2. 4
3. 6
4. 10
5. 3
6. 5
7. 8
8. 12
9. 7
10. 9
11. 15
12. 13
13. XXI
14. XXII
15. XXIII
16. XXIV
17. XXV
18. XXVI
19. XXVII
20. XXVIII
21. XXIX
22. 30
23. 26
24. 33
25. 35
26. 29
27. 38
28. 39
29. 34
30. 37
31. XLV
32. XLIX
33. XLVIII
34. XLVII
35. XVI
36. XLVI
37. XXVII
38. XXXVII
39. XXIX
40. Answers will vary.
41. Answers will vary.
42. Answers will vary.

Page 147

1. 2000
2. 2001
3. 2005
4. 1900
5. 1800
6. 1803
7. 1912
8. 1950
9. 1983
10. 1600
11. 1718
12. 1998
13. MM
14. MMI
15. MMX
16. MCM
17. MCMLX
18. MDCCC
19. MCMX
20. MCMXL
21. MDCCCLXXXI
22. MDCLIV
23. MCDXCII
24. MDLXXXVIII
25. 5
26. 10
27. 50
28. 100
29. 500
30. 1,000
31. 2,000
32. 300
33. 1,500
34. 1,700
35. 3,650
36. 1,666
37. LXIII
38. XCVII
39. CC
40. L

Page 148

1. 1 two
2. 10 two
3. 11 two
4. 100 two
5. 101 two
6. 110 two
7. 111 two
8. 1000 two
9. 1001 two
10. 11 two
11. 101 two
12. 10 two
13. 1001 two
14. 100 two
15. 110 two
16. 111 two
17. 1 two
18. 1000 two

Page 149

1. 0011
2. 0101
3. 0110
4. 0111
5. 0010
6. 0100
7. 0001
8. 1000
9. 1001
10. 1011
11. //// /, 0101
12. // /, 0011
13. ///, 0100
14. //// // /, 0111
15. ///////, 1000
16. //, 0010
17. //// //, 0110
18. /////// /, 1001
19. //////// // /, 1011
20. //////// //, 1010
21. //////// ////, 1100
22. //////// //// // /, 1111
23. //////// //// //, 1110
24. //////// //// /, 1101

Page 150

1. 1300
2. 170
3. 160
4. 1783
5. 9
6. 8.1
7. 250
8. 95
9. 5

Page 151

1. compounds
2. ores
3. fool's gold
4. arsenic
5. oxides
6. carbonates
7. Nitrates
8. Gypsum

Page 152

1. F
2. F
3. T
4. F
5. T
6. F
7. F
8. T
9. F
10. T
11. T
12. T

Page 153

Comets

- tails are millions of kilometers long
- appear in the night sky for many days
- have a tail
- orbit around the sun
- hardly made of anything

Both

- are members of the solar system
- some are visible without telescopes

Meteors

- are made of iron, stones, and other minerals
- fall quickly to earth
- are called "shooting stars"

Page 155

1. b
2. a
3. c
4. d
5. a
6. Luis and Walter Alvarez found evidence that a huge asteroid hit Earth 65 million years ago, resulting in many life forms becoming extinct, including the dinosaurs.

Page 156

1. b
2. a
3. a

Page 158

1. b
2. c
3. a
4. d
5. c
6. a
7. Accept well-supported answers.

Page 161

1. d
2. a
3. c
4. c

Answer Key *(cont.)*

Page 162

1. sodium
2. nitrogen
3. argon
3. aluminum
5. oxygen
6. calcium
7. helium
8. sulfur

Page 163

1. b
2. b
3. b

Page 165

1. b
2. c
3. b
4. a
5. d

Page 167

1. b
2. a
3. c
4. b
5. c
6. d
7. Accept well-supported answers.